THE B-29

Deluxe Full Color Reprint of the 1945

AIRPLANE COMMANDER TRAINING MANUAL FOR THE SUPERFORTRESS
BY U.S. ARMY AIR FORCE

This document reproduces the text of a manual first published by the Department of the Army, Washington DC. All source material contained in the reproduced document has been approved for public release and unlimited distribution by an agency of the U.S. Government. Any U.S. Government markings in this reproduction that indicate limited distribution or classified material have been superseded by downgrading instructions that were promulgated by an agency of the U.S. government after the original publication of the document. No U.S. government agency is associated with the publishing of this reproduction.

This book has been digitally watermarked to prevent illegal duplication.

©2014 Periscope Film LLC
All Rights Reserved
ISBN #978-1-940453-33-0
www.PeriscopeFilm.com

This is an exact reprint of the 1 February, 1945 edition except for the following changes:

1. Revision of the Ditching, Bailout, and Crash Landing section (pages 153 through 159).

2. Addition of the Personal Equipment Supplement (pages 177 to 220).

3. Addition of the Index (pages 221 to 224).

Pilots having the (Brown-covered) edition dated 1 February 1945, which does not have this note can correct their manuals to correspond to this one by obtaining from their Director of Training supplementary pages mentioned in 1, 2, and 3 above.

THE B-29

AIRPLANE COMMANDER TRAINING MANUAL FOR THE SUPERFORTRESS

REVISED 1 FEBRUARY, 1945

PREPARED FOR HEADQUARTERS, AAF

OFFICE OF ASSISTANT CHIEF OF AIR STAFF TRAINING

BY HEADQUARTERS AAF, OFFICE OF FLYING SAFETY

MARSHALL-WHITE, CHICAGO
MARCH, 1945— 13,000

AAF Manual No. 50-9

Foreword

THIS MANUAL is the text for your training as a B-29 pilot and airplane commander.

The Air Forces' most experienced training and supervisory personnel have collaborated to make it a complete exposition of what your pilot duties are, how each duty will be performed, and why it must be performed in the manner prescribed.

The techniques and procedures described in this book are standard and mandatory. In this respect the manual serves the dual purpose of a training checklist and a working handbook. Use it to make sure that you learn everything described herein. Use it to study and review the essential facts concerning everything taught. Such additional self-study and review will not only advance your training, but will alleviate the burden of your already overburdened instructors.

This training manual does not replace the Technical Orders for the airplane, which will always be your primary source of information concerning the B-29 so long as you fly it. This is essentially the textbook of the B-29. Used properly, it will enable you to utilize the pertinent Technical Orders to even greater advantage.

GENERAL, U. S. ARMY,
COMMANDING GENERAL,
ARMY AIR FORCES

RESTRICTED

Additional copies of this manual should be requested from:
HEADQUARTERS AAF, OFFICE OF FLYING SAFETY, SAFETY EDUCATION DIVISION, Winston-Salem 1, North Carolina.

RESTRICTED

MEET THE *Superfortress*

The B-29 is just what the name implies...
a Superfortress... a bigger and better B-17.

Early in 1939, when studies were started to determine just how to produce a bomber bigger and better than the B-17, the XB-29 came into being. Its basic design was determined in 1940. Three airplanes were built as prototypes for the actual production of the B-29, the first of these taking to the air in the fall of 1942.

Many qualities of the B-17 have been built into the B-29. The B-17 tail was one step in the development. In the early experimental stages, a B-17 was flown with dual turbos, the B-29 fin and rudder, the B-29 stabilizer and elevator, and even with the B-29 ailerons.

The B-29 is the first of the "very heavy bombers." Actually, in physical size it is not much larger than a B-17 or a B-24, but its weight and power are twice theirs and its speed is considerably greater. Loaded down with gas and oil for a long ferrying trip, it holds almost as much fuel as a railroad tank car. Under normal loads, it weighs 1/7 as much as a railroad locomotive and has four times the power. It is designed to carry heavy loads for long distances at high speeds and high altitudes.

THE **B-29** IS A YOUNG AIRPLANE, BUT IT IS FAST PROVING ITS CAPABILITIES...
AND YOU AS AN AIRPLANE COMMANDER WILL HAVE A HAND IN ITS FUTURE.

TRAINING ACCOMPLISHED

WEEKS	NUMBER OF EACH MISSION FLOWN	TOTAL NUMBER OF MISSIONS FLOWN	TOTAL NUMBER OF HOURS FLOWN
1st			
2nd			
3rd			
4th			
5th			
6th			
7th			
8th			
9th			
10th			
11th			
12th			

The B-29 is a teamwork airplane, and you are the captain of that team. Your success in combat, and the safety of your crew and airplane, depend on how well you organize your team and how well you lead it.

You are no longer just a pilot—you hold a command post and all the responsibilities that go with it. You are flying an 11-man weapon. It is your airplane and your crew, not only when you are fighting and flying, but for the full 24 hours in every day.

Your crew is made up of specialists, every one an expert in his line. Each one contributes his important part to the whole. Know their capabilities as well as their shortcomings. Know them as men as well as specialists. Know their background, their personalities, their individual problems, their needs for specific training.

You can't fly the B-29 by yourself. You need the full cooperation of your crew and you can get that cooperation only if the morale of your crew is good. You can help build that morale by taking the trouble to know just a little more than usual about your crew members. Find out who they were, where they lived, what they did before the war, and what their favorite hobbies, sports, and women are—it gives a man a considerable lift to have his commanding officer say something casually now and then about the town where he lived, his family, or the work that he once did. Make a point of showing genuine interest in your men; it will pay big dividends. Fill out the accompanying chart; it will help you to keep track of your crew's training progress.

Make your crew members feel that they are an important part of their airplane. Make a point of letting each man take a short turn at the controls during practice missions while you or the copilot stand by on dual. Make a tour of all stations at least once during every practice flight. Talk to the men, ask them questions about their duties, try to clear up any questions they may have. Make them want to have the best team in their squadron.

TRAINING STANDARDS

	COMBAT CREW REQUIREMENTS	DATE COMPLETED
1	The aircraft commander will complete a minimum of 20 hours formation above 25,000 feet mean sea level.	
2	The aircraft commander will accomplish the instrument check prescribed by AAF Regulation 50-3.	
3	The copilot will make a minimum of five landings from his own position.	
4	The copilot will accomplish at least four hours instrument flying under the hood to include at least two instrument let-downs on radio range.	
5	The combat crew will complete a navigational mission for a minimum of approximately 3000 miles. Cruise control will be emphasized.	
6	The combat crew will complete a navigational mission by the use of radar alone, over a Triangular course, for a minimum distance of 900 miles.	
7	The bombardier will drop a minimum of 20 individual bomb releases from above 25,000 feet mean sea level.	
8	The aircraft commander, navigator, and bombardier will combine their efforts in performing a minimum of 12 camera bombing attacks on industrial targets, four of which will be above 25,000 mean sea level.	
9	The combat crew members, except the aircraft commander, copilot, engineer, and radio operator, will accomplish a minimum of four gun camera missions (exposing approximately 50 feet of film on each and aimed at an attacking aircraft). The errors in aiming will be discussed between the instructor and gunner prior to the next gunnery mission.	
10	The combat crew members, with the exception of the aircraft commander, copilot, engineer, and radio operator, will fire 200 rounds above 25,000 feet mean sea level, divided between their primary and secondary gun position.	

As airplane commander, you are responsible for the daily welfare of your crew. See that they are properly quartered, clothed, and fed. See that they are paid when they should be paid. Away from your home station, carry your interest to the point of financing them yourself, if necessary. You are the commander of a combat force all your own—a small but specialized army —and morale is one of the biggest problems in any army, large or small.

During Training

Train your crew as a team. Make teamwork their byword. Keep abreast of their training. It won't be possible for you to attend the courses of instruction with the members of your crew, but you should check their progress and their records constantly. Get to know each man's duties and help him to devise means for performing them quickly and efficiently. If knowledge is lacking on some specific point, supply it. Check your crew frequently.

Pair off your crew members and have them check and train each other. Simulate combat conditions and emergency situations and have each crew member describe his duties. Ask them what they would do under the following and similar conditions:

1. A designated crew member seriously wounded.
2. A designated turret out of commission.
3. Gasoline or oil spurting from a designated part of the airplane.
4. Abandoning the airplane.
5. Bombs failing to drop.
6. Bomb bay doors failing to open.
7. Landing gear failure.
8. Forced landing in enemy territory.
9. Forced landing on water.
10. Fire.

A B-29 crew consists of airplane commander, copilot, bombardier-DR navigator, navigator-radar specialist, flight engineer, radio operator, radar gunner, electrical specialist gunner, air mechanic gunner, a central fire control specialist gunner, and a tail gunner.

As airplane commander you should:

1. Know your airplane and how it operates.
2. Be able to take off and land in the minimum distance.
3. Be able to take off and land under zero-zero conditions.
4. Be able to fly under instrument conditions either with or without radio aids.
5. Be able to use blind-landing systems.
6. Be able to navigate and locate your positions with the various radio and radar aids available.
7. Be proficient at formation flying, including the proper performance of evasive tactics at various speeds and altitudes.
8. Be able to get the most out of your airplane under all conditions.
9. Know your crew.
10. Know yourself.

COPILOT

Your copilot is your assistant—the executive officer of your command post. He should be able to do everything that you can do so that he can assume full command should the occasion arise. You and he should be virtually interchangeable. Let him handle the controls at least 30% of the time. He should be a potential airplane commander.

BOMBARDIER-DR NAVIGATOR

Your bombardier-DR navigator must:

1. Understand the bombsight, radar equipment, and automatic pilot in so far as they pertain to bombing.

2. Understand the normal and emergency operation of bombs, bomb racks, switches, controls, releases, doors, etc.

3. Understand and be able to operate the computing CFC sight.

4. Be proficient at pilotage and dead reckoning.

5. Be proficient at target identification.

NAVIGATOR-RADAR

Your navigator-radar specialist must:

1. Be proficient at pilotage, dead reckoning, and celestial navigation.

2. Understand the operation of, and be able to use, all available radio and radar equipment for navigation and bombing.

3. Be able to perform minor maintenance on all radar equipment.

4. Be proficient at target identification.

FLIGHT ENGINEER

Your flight engineer is an important member of your B-29 combat team. He runs your airplane while you and your copilot fly it. In actual flight, he relieves you and your copilot of duties and responsibilities. On the ground, he supervises maintenance and keeps your airplane flyable. Check your flight engineer with questions frequently to make sure he is on the job. He should:

1. Understand the operation and maintenance of all mechanical equipment.

2. Be thoroughly familiar with the engines and fuel, electrical, and oil systems.

3. Be thoroughly familiar with the cruise control charts, weights and balance, and all operating procedures.

4. Be thoroughly familiar with the pressurized cabin system.

5. Be thoroughly familiar with the putt-putt and auxiliary electrical system.

6. Be thoroughly familiar with the oxygen system.

7. Be thoroughly familiar with all fire-fighting equipment.

RADIO OPERATOR

Your radio operator should:

1. Be thoroughly familiar with the operation and maintenance of all radio equipment aboard the airplane.

2. Be thoroughly familiar with the use of all radio navigational aids.

3. Be proficient in transmitting and receiving.

4. Be thoroughly familiar with IFF procedures and equipment.

5. Understand the operation and care of the radio compass.

6. Be thoroughly familiar with AAF instrument approach procedures and the signal operation instructions (radio authentication, special codes for the day, weather codes, blinker codes, radio call signs).

CENTRAL FIRE CONTROL SPECIALIST GUNNER

Your central fire control specialist gunner should:

1. Be thoroughly familiar with the care, maintenance, and operation of the entire central fire control system.

2. Be thoroughly familiar with the loading and servicing of the turrets.

SPECIALIST GUNNERS

Your specialist gunners should:

1. Know how to operate the computing sight.
2. Be thoroughly familiar with the central fire control system.
3. Know how to load and repair turrets.
4. Know their specialty.

Crew Discipline

Your success as the airplane commander will depend in a large measure on the respect, confidence, and trust which the crew feels for you. It will depend also on how well you maintain crew discipline.

Your position commands obedience and respect. This does not mean that you have to be stiff-necked, overbearing, or aloof. Such characteristics certainly will defeat your purpose.

Be friendly, understanding, but firm. Know your job, and, by the way you perform your duties daily, impress upon the crew that you do know your job. Make fair decisions, after due consideration of all the facts involved; but make them in such a way as to impress upon your crew that your decisions are made to stick.

Crew discipline is vitally important, but it need not be as difficult a problem as it sounds. Good discipline in an air crew breeds comradeship and high morale. And the combination is unbeatable.

You can be a good CO and still be a regular guy. You can command respect from your men, and still be one of them.

"To associate discipline with informality, comradeship, a leveling of rank, and at times a shift in actual command away from the leader, may seem paradoxical," says a former combat group commander. "Certainly, it isn't down the military groove. But it is discipline just the same—and the kind of discipline that brings success in the air."

No crew is ever any more on the ball than its airplane commander. Are your guns working? The only way you can be sure is to know how competent and reliable your gunners are. It is uncomfortable to get caught by a swarm of enemy fighters and find that your guns won't function.

What about your navigator? You can't do his job for him throughout training in the states and expect him to guide you safely over a thousand miles of water to a speck on the map. Remember that there aren't any check points in the ocean and you have to rely on your navigator.

Your bombs miss the target. Long hours of flying wasted . . . why? It may be because the bombsight gyro was not turned on long enough in advance or because the bombsight was not kept warm by means of the heater so that when the bombardier put his warm face to the eyepiece, it fogged up and was unusable. Who is at fault? The bombardier is, of course, primarily to blame, but in the background there is usually lack of leadership, guidance and inspiration.

Enforce these RULES *on every flight*

1. SMOKING

a. No smoking in airplane at an altitude of less than 1,000 feet.

b. No smoking during fuel transfer.

c. Never attempt to throw a lighted cigarette from the airplane. Put it out first.

2. PARACHUTES

a. All persons aboard will wear parachute harness at all times from takeoff to landing.

b. Each person aboard will have a parachute on every flight.

3. PROPELLERS

a. No person will walk near propellers at any time whether they are turning or not.

b. No person will leave the airplane when propellers are turning unless personally ordered to do so by the airplane commander.

4. OXYGEN MASKS

a. Oxygen masks will be carried on all day flights where altitude **may exceed 8000 feet for more than 4 hours**, and on **all night flights.** (Except in Transition training.)

5. TRAINING

a. Tell your crew the purpose of each mission and what you expect each to accomplish.

b. Keep the crew busy throughout the flight. Get position reports from the navigator; send them out through the radio operator. Put the engineer to work on the cruise control and maximum range charts and require him to keep a record of engine performance. Give them a workout. Encourage them to use their skill. Let them sleep in their own bunks—not in a B-29. A team is an active outfit. Make the most of every practice mission.

c. Practice all emergency procedures at least once a week; bailout, ditching and fire drill.

6. INSPECTIONS

a. Check your airplane with reference to the particular mission you are undertaking. **Check everything.**

b. Check your crew for equipment, preparedness and understanding.

7. INTERPHONE

a. Keep the interphone chattering. Ask for immediate reports of aircraft, trains, and ships just as you would expect them in combat—with proper identification.

b. Require interphone reports every 15 minutes from all crew men when on oxygen.

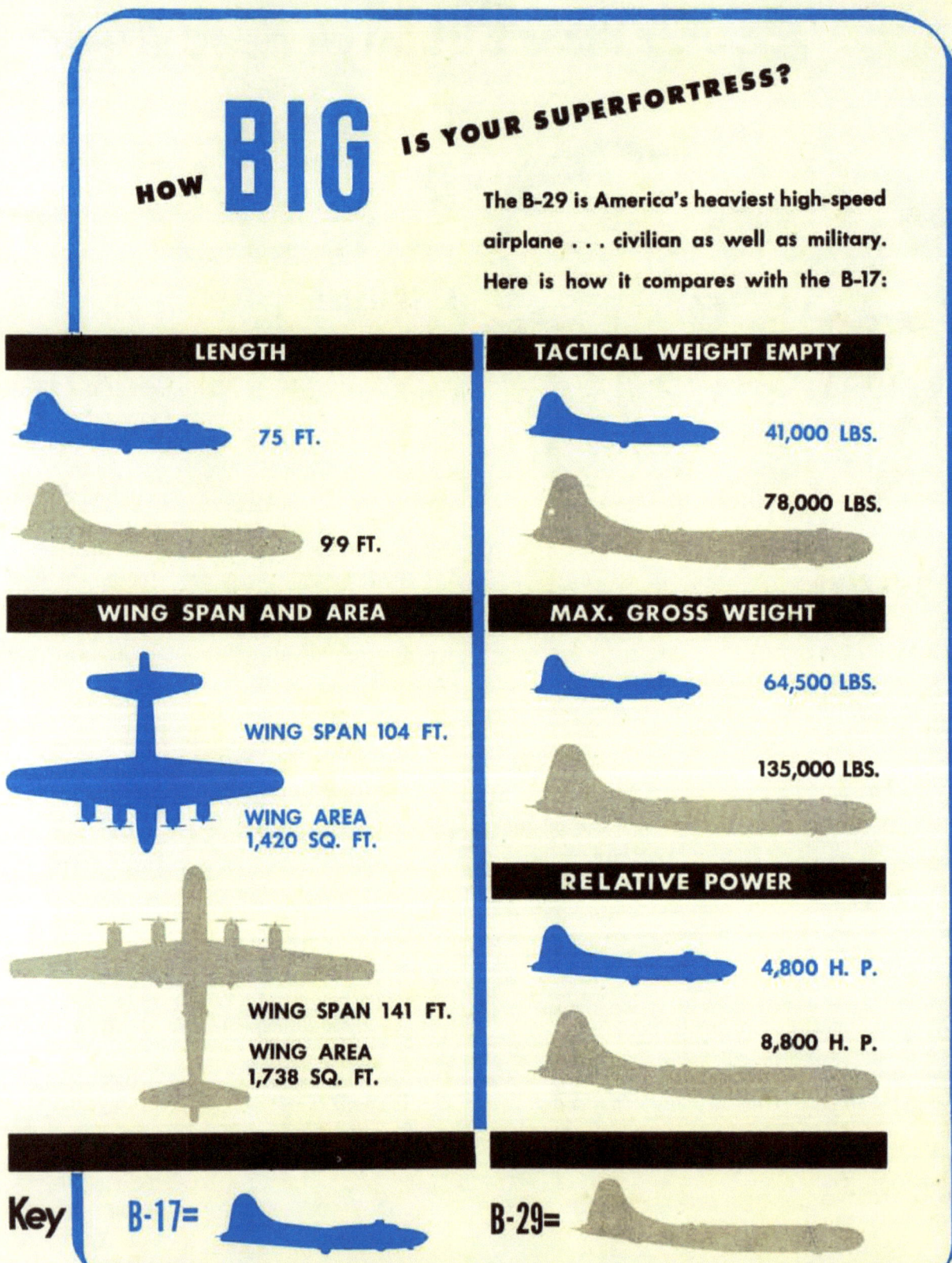

POWER PLANTS

Your B-29 Superfortress has four 18-cylinder, twin-bank R-3350 Wright radial engines capable of delivering more than 2200 Hp each. The 4-bladed propellers, reduction geared (.35) to the crankshaft and rotating clockwise when viewed from the rear, are Hamilton Standard constant-speed, full-feathering, hydromatic. Constant-speed control is maintained by governors which are operated electrically by four momentary-contact toggle switches located on the airplane commander's aisle stand.

Each engine has two exhaust-driven turbo-superchargers mounted vertically on each side of the engine nacelle. The turbo boost on all four engines is controlled simultaneously by a Minneapolis-Honeywell electronic turbo-supercharger control system operated by a single manual rheostat control knob on the copilot's aisle stand. Carburetors are Chandler-Evans automatic. Some late airplanes will have direct fuel injection systems of the Bosch or Bendix type. Vacuum pumps, one on each engine, provide vacuum for the cameras, de-icer boots, and instruments, and pressure for inflating the de-icer boots. Either inboard vacuum pump may be used for vacuum; the other three pumps provide pressure for the de-icer boots.

CONTROLS

FLIGHT ENGINEER'S STAND ▶

From the airplane commander's and copilot's point of view the controls on the B-29 have been simplified—the majority of the power plant controls and most of the basic electrical and mechanical system controls are on the flight engineer's stand directly in back of the copilot.

From his station he can visually check all engines and be in close communication at all times with the airplane commander and copilot.

RESTRICTED

14

RESTRICTED

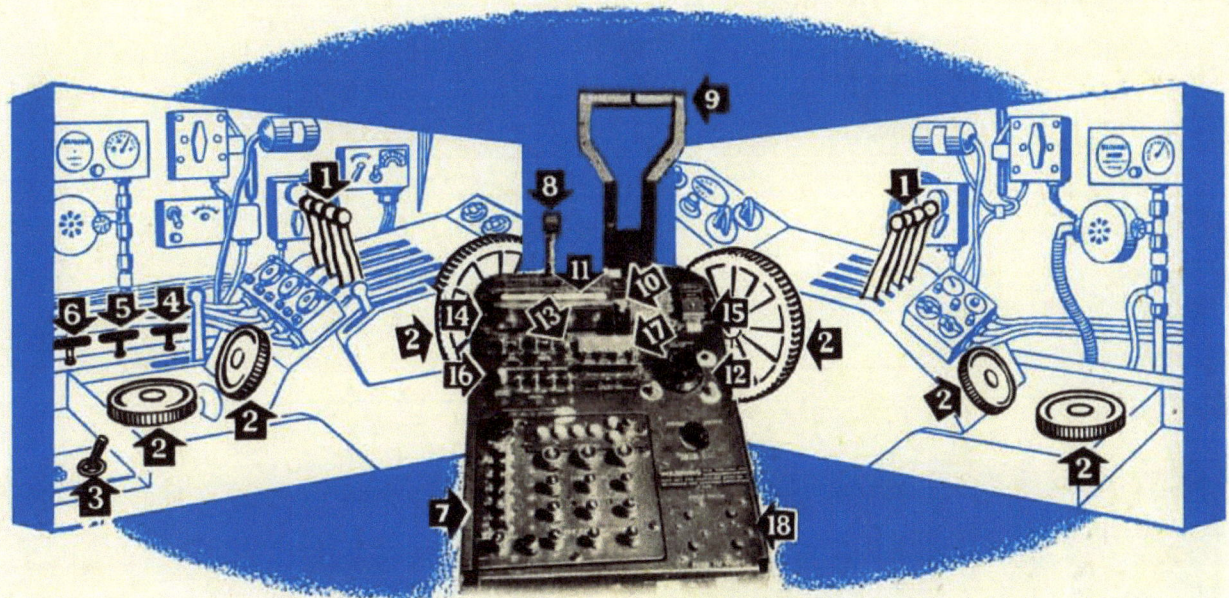

Both airplane commander and copilot have control stands on which throttles (1) and trim tab controls (2) are mounted. The landing gear transfer switch (3) and emergency cabin pressure (4) emergency bomb (5), and emergency landing gear door releases (6) are at the rear of the airplane commander's control stand.

The controls for the C-1 automatic pilot (7), the control surface lock (8), emergency brake levers (9), wing flap control switch (10), propeller feathering switches (11), turbo boost selector (12), phone-call signal light switch (13), alarm bell switch (14), landing gear switch (15), light switches (16), propeller increase and decrease rpm switches (17), and propeller pitch circuit breaker re-sets (18) are on the aisle stand to the right of the airplane commander's seat and within easy reach of the copilot.

Besides throttles, mixture controls, and fuel-tank selectors, the flight engineer's stand mounts the following engine controls and gages:
1. Cowl flap switches and indicators
2. Intercooler flap switches and indicators
3. Oil dilution switches
4. Starter switches
5. Oil cooler shutter switches
6. Pitot and prop anti-icer switches
7. Engine prime switches
8. Fuel shut-off valve switches
9. Fuel boost rheostats
10. Generator switches
11. Fuel transfer switches
12. Inverter switch
13. Hydraulic pump switch
14. Engine fire extinguisher controls and selector valve
15. Ignition switches
16. All engine, fuel, and oil gages
17. Two altimeters (outside and cabin)
18. Two rate-of-climb indicators (outside and cabin)
19. Airspeed indicator
20. Clock
21. Hydraulic pressure gages
22. Propeller anti-icer rheostats and switch
23. Suction gage
24. Emergency system filler valve
25. Landing gear spotlight switch
26. Cabin pressure warning horn switch
27. Cabin differential pressure gage
28. Cabin air rate-of-flow gages (2)
29. Battery switch
30. Fluorescent light rheostats
31. Cabin air conditioner switches
32. Free air temperature gage
33. Cabin air temperature gage
34. Vacuum selector lever

RESTRICTED

EXCEPT FOR MANIFOLD PRESSURE GAGES AND TACHOMETERS, THE INSTRUMENTS ON THE AIRPLANE COMMANDER'S PANEL ARE ALL FLIGHT INSTRUMENTS:

1. Airspeed indicator
2. Altimeter
3. Bank-and-turn indicator
4. Rate-of-climb indicator
5. Turn indicator
6. Gyro-horizon
7. Pilot direction indicator (PDI)
8. Radio compass
9. Flux gate compass
10. Manifold pressure gages
11. Tachometers
12. Blind-landing indicator
13. Clock
14. Turret warning lights
15. Bomb release indicator light
16. Vacuum warning light

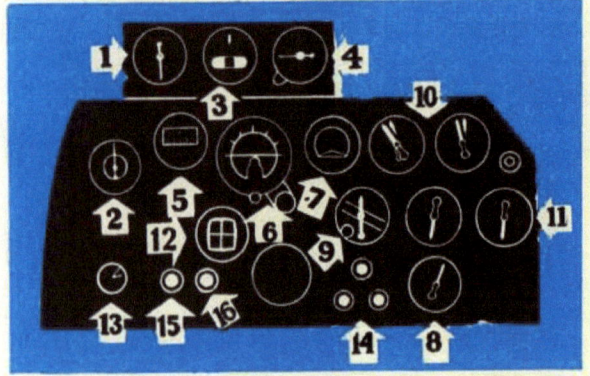

THE INSTRUMENTS MOUNTED ON THE COPILOT'S INSTRUMENT PANEL ARE:

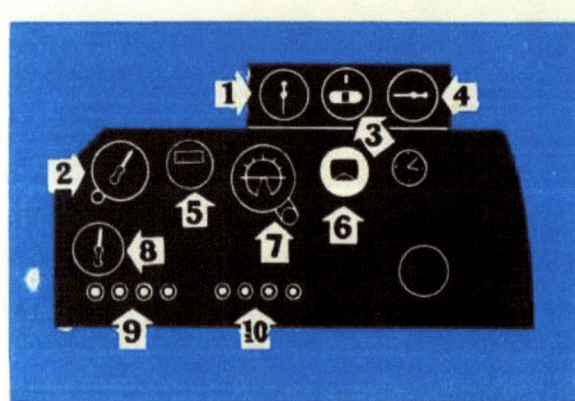

1. Airspeed indicator
2. Altimeter
3. Bank-and-turn indicator
4. Rate-of-climb indicator
5. Turn indicator
6. Magnetic compass
7. Gyro-horizon
8. Flap position indicator
9. Propeller rpm limit indicator lights
10. Landing gear indicator lights

The flight controls are conventional and the forces necessary to move them are light, even at high flying speeds—a surprising fact to most pilots the first time they fly the B-29. **The elevators** are similar to those on the B-17. **The ailerons**, although considerably larger than those on the B-17, are so rigged that they can be easily moved 18° up or down. **The rudder** gives maximum possible control and yet can be moved easily without the use of power boosts.

Wing flaps and **tricycle landing gear** are lowered and raised by reversible electric motors. The Fowler-type flaps, which provide lift and drag, travel on track and roller mechanisms in such a manner that they project beyond the trailing edge of the wing when they are extended. Under normal operation the landing gear can be lowered in 40 seconds.

RESTRICTED

INSPECTIONS AND CHECKS

With any airplane, inspections and checks are important factors in efficient operation. With the B-29, because of its size and complexity, they are more important than ever. Don't ignore them.

Go over your airplane before every mission and after every mission. Make sure each crew member inspects his own station. Check and double-check. As airplane commander you are responsible for all checks.

Before Entering Airplane

Before you climb into your airplane, go over the outside of it thoroughly. Have your copilot make the inspection with you, and pay particular attention to the following:

RESTRICTED

1. Condition of tires—examine carefully for cuts and slippage.

2. Wheel chocks—2 inches in front of inboard tires and 2 inches behind outboard tires.

3. Oleo struts—13¼ inches between pin centers on main gear, 10 inches on nose gear.

4. Hydraulic lines—check for leaks.

RESTRICTED

5. Shimmy dampener—check oil level. Top of pin should be even with groove.

6. Engine fire extinguishers—check red disk at end of line running down from each CO_2 bottle (nosewheel well). If the bottle has been accidentally discharged, the red disk is missing.

7. Gear motor and door motor cannon plugs—check each plug for looseness. If the rotating collar is not screwed tight, engine vibration can shake loose the cannon plug connection.

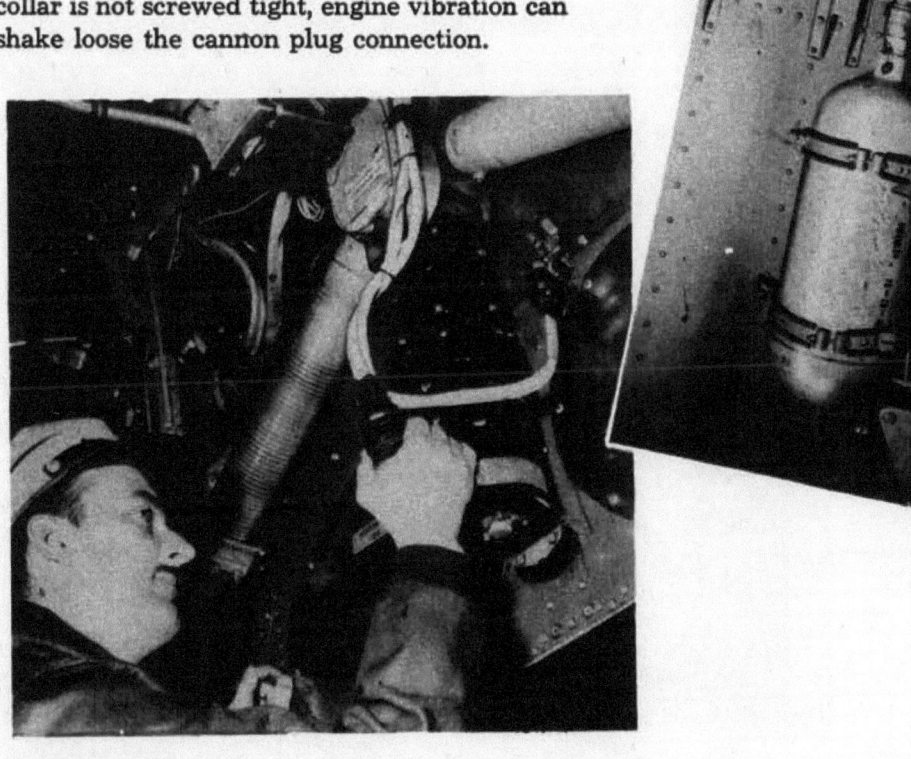

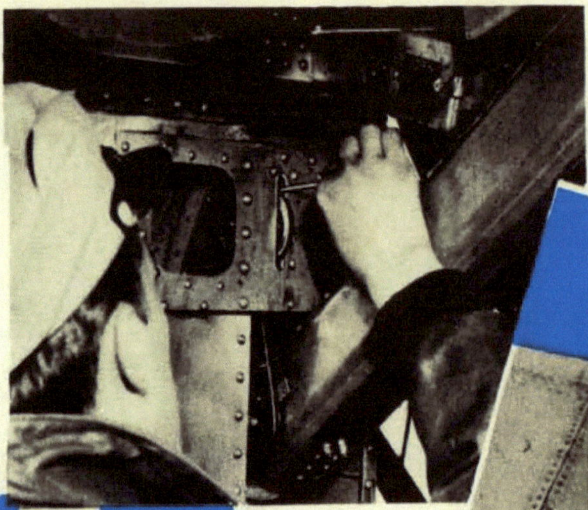

8. Cables on main wheel well doors—cables should be on pulleys and free of obstructions.

9. Pitot tube covers off.

10. All fastenings on inspection plates and engine cowlings should be tight.

11. See that engines and nacelles are free of oil and grease. Oil or grease is a fire hazard. Have it cleaned off before making the flight.

12. Inspect control surfaces and trim tabs for dents or damage.

13. Inspect all windows and blisters for cracks and dirt.

14. Check all seams and connections for fluid leaks.

RESTRICTED

After you have finished the visual outside check and before you perform your crew check, climb into the airplane, make sure that all switches are off, and instruct your crew to pull the propellers through preparatory to starting. If the airplane has been standing more than 30 minutes, each propeller should be pulled through at least 12 blades with no more than two men on each blade. If a propeller sticks, remove the plugs from the bottom cylinders, pull the propeller through to remove the excess oil from the cylinders, install clean plugs, and pull the propeller through again. NEVER attempt to relieve a liquid lock by applying pressure against the propeller or by pulling the propeller backwards.

Note

Prompt detection of liquid lock can prevent a late takeoff. As soon as the crew reaches the airplane they should check the ignition switches and pull each propeller through four blades.

After the propellers have been pulled through 12 blades each, you are ready to inspect your crew. Check each crew member for his physical condition, personal clothing, and equipment. Make this a rigid military inspection. Be sure that each man's parachute fits properly and is in good condition. Check their clothing to make sure it is adequate for the anticipated mission. If an electric suit is to be worn, make sure that the man has checked it for operation. If an altitude mission is contemplated, make sure that each crew member has his oxygen mask. If an overwater flight is contemplated, make sure that each man has his life preserver vest. Each of these articles of clothing and equipment is the crew member's own responsibility, but check and double-check it yourself nevertheless. As airplane commander you are responsible.

At this point, you are ready to check and sign Form 1A and inspect the loading list, the weight, and the center of gravity. Your flight engineer should have the forms ready for you when he reports for the crew check. Make sure that the C. G. is between the allowable limits—minimum 18% to 24%, maximum 34%.

The crew members then enter the airplane and begin going through the check lists for their own stations. These check lists are as follows:

RESTRICTED

PILOT'S B-29 CHECKLIST

BEFORE STARTING ENGINES

1. VISUAL INSPECTION...COMPLETED
2. FORM 1-A, LOADING LIST, WEIGHT & CG....................CHECKED
3. CREW INSPECTION..COMPLETED
4. PARACHUTE...OK, OK
5. CLOTHING..OK, OK
6. LIFE PRESERVER...OK, OK
7. PARKING BRAKES AND CHOCKS................................SET, SET
8. EMERGENCY LANDING GEAR DOOR RELEASE..............IN PLACE
9. EMERGENCY BOMB RELEASE.....................................IN PLACE
10. EMERGENCY CABIN PRESSURE RELEASE.....................IN PLACE
11. LANDING GEAR TRANSFER SWITCH............................NORMAL
12. OVERCONTROL..ENGAGED
13. LANDING GEAR SWITCH AND FUSE............................NEUTRAL, FUSE CHECKED
14. BATTERY SWITCH..ON
15. PUT-PUT...STARTED
16. HYDRAULIC PRESSURE
    (a). MAIN...OK
    (b). EMERGENCY..OK
17. FLIGHT CONTROLS..CHECKED
18. RADIOS..CHECKED, CHECKED
19. ALTIMETERS...SET, SET
20. TURRETS..STOWED
21. SEATS AND PEDALS...OK, OK
22. LIGHTS...CHECKED, CHECKED
23. OXYGEN...OK, OK
24. PROPELLERS...HI RPM
25. TURBOS..OFF
26. ENGINEER'S REPORT..CHECK LIST COMPLETE, READY TO START ENGINES
27. STAND CLEAR — FIRE GUARD ....CLEAR LEFT, CLEAR RIGHT

BEFORE TAXIING

1. VACUUM..OK, OK
2. GYROS..UNCAGED, UNCAGED
3. INSTRUMENTS..CHECKED, CHECKED
4. BOMB BAY DOORS..CLOSED, CLOSED
5. ALARM BELL, ONE CONTACT.....................................OK
6. PHONE CALL SIGNAL LIGHT, ONE CONTACT...............OK
7. COMBAT STATION INSPECTION, ONE CONTACT............OK
8. CHOCKS..OUT LEFT, OUT RIGHT
9. PARKING BRAKES..OFF, STAND BY TO TAXI

RESTRICTED

BEFORE TAKE-OFF

1. EMERGENCY BRAKES..CHECKED
2. NOSE WHEEL..STRAIGHT
3. ENGINE RUN-UP...STAND BY FOR ENGINE RUN-UP
4. WING FLAPS..25 DEGREES
5. TRIM TABS...SET
6. AUTO PILOT..OFF
7. WINDOWS AND HATCHES...CLOSED, CLOSED
8. TURBOS..NO. 8
9. PROPELLERS..HI RPM
10. CREW...PREPARE FOR TAKE-OFF
11. RADIO CALL...COMPLETED
12. THROTTLE BRAKE...OK, STAND BY FOR TAKE-OFF

BEFORE LANDING

1. NOTIFY CREW...PREPARE FOR LANDING
2. RADIO CALL..COMPLETED
3. ALTIMETERS..SET, SET
4. TRAILING ANTENNA..IN
5. AUTO PILOT..OFF
6. TURRETS...STOWED
7. HYDRAULIC PRESSURE
    (a). MAIN..OK
    (b). EMERGENCY...OK
8. PUT-PUT...ON THE LINE
9. PROPELLERS..2400 RPM
10. LANDING GEAR...DOWN AND LIGHTS ON
11. ENGINEER'S REPORT..CHECK LIST COMPLETE:
    WEIGHT_____CG_____
12. STALLING SPEED..._____MPH
13. WING FLAPS...STANDING BY
14. TURBOS...NO. 8

AFTER LANDING

1. HYDRAULIC PRESSURE..OK
2. TURBOS..OFF
3. PROPELLERS..HI RPM
4. WING FLAPS..UP
5. PARKING BRAKES..SET
6. BOMB BAY DOORS..OPEN
7. MAGNETOS..CHECKED
8. ENGINES...CUT
9. RADIOS..OFF, OFF
10. CONTROLS...LOCKED
11. WHEEL CHOCKS...CHOCKS IN PLACE,
    CHOCKS IN PLACE, BRAKES OFF
12. FORM 1 AND 1A..ACCOMPLISHED
13. CREW INSPECTION

FLIGHT ENGINEER'S B-29 CHECK LIST

BEFORE STARTING ENGINES:

1. FLIGHT PLAN..COMPLETED
2. ENGINEER'S PREFLIGHT......................................COMPLETED
3. PARACHUTE..OK
4. CLOTHING..OK
5. LIFE PRESERVER..OK
6. BATTERY SWITCH..ON
7. AUX. P. P...START
8. INSTRUMENTS..CHECKED
9. EMERGENCY HYDRAULIC PRESSURE............................OK
10. FUEL TRANSFER TOGGLE SWITCHES AND TANK
    SELECTOR CONTROLS..OFF
11. INVERTER..ON
12. ENGINEER'S CABIN AIR VALVES AND RELIEF VALVE........CLOSED
13. COWL FLAPS...OPEN
14. INTERCOOLERS..OPEN
15. CABIN PRESSURE WARNING SWITCH.........................ON
16. OIL COOLER FLAPS...AUTOMATIC
17. PITOT HEAT...OFF
18. DE-ICERS..OFF
19. ANTI-ICERS...OFF
20. GENERATORS..OFF
21. FUEL QUANTITY GAGE..RECORD READINGS
22. OIL QUANTITY GAGE..RECORD READINGS
23. EMERGENCY HYDRAULIC SERVICING VALVE..................CLOSED
24. OXYGEN..OK
25. LIGHTS...OK
26. FUEL SHUT-OFF VALVE..CLOSED
27. FUEL BOOST...ON
28. MIXTURE CONTROL..CRACKED
29. FUEL SHUT-OFF VALVE..OPEN
30. MIXTURE CONTROL..IDLE CUT-OFF
31. PUTT-PUTT..CHECK FOR ON THE LINE
32. ENGINEER'S REPORT..READY TO START ENGINES

BEFORE TAXIING:

1. MASTER IGNITION SWITCH....................................ON
2. THROTTLES..SET TO START
3. FIRE EXTINGUISHER..SET TO ENGINE BEING STARTED
4. START ENGINES..1, 2, 3, 4
5. ENGINE INSTRUMENTS..CHECK READINGS
6. CHECK VACUUM...3.8—4.2 IN. HG.
7. BOMB BAY DOORS..CLOSED
8. ENGINEER'S REPORT...ENGINEER READY TO TAXI

BEFORE TAKE-OFF:

1. GENERATORS...CHECKED
2. MAGNETOS...CHECKED
3. INTERCOOLERS..OPEN
4. MIXTURE CONTROLS......................................AUTO RICH
5. FUEL BOOST PUMPS......................................ON
6. GENERATORS..ON
7. ENGINEER'S REPORT.....................................MIXTURE AUTO RICH, FUEL BOOST ON, GENERATORS ON, STANDING BY ON COWL FLAPS, READY FOR TAKE-OFF
8. AT START OF TAKE-OFF ROLL............................PULL COWL FLAPS FROM 15° TO 7½° AT TIME WHEELS LEAVE GROUND

AFTER TAKE-OFF:

1. WHEN GEAR IS COMING UP................................CHECK GENERATORS
2. AFTER FLAPS AND GEAR ARE UP..........................HAVE AUX. P.P. STOPPED
3. COWL FLAPS..ADJUST AS REQUIRED
4. FUEL BOOST PUMPS......................................OFF
5. INTERCOOLERS..CLOSED, WHEN TURBOS ARE OFF

BEFORE LANDING:

1. WEIGHT AND CG...CALL IN TO COPILOT
2. MIXTURE CONTROLS......................................AUTO RICH
3. AUX. P.P...START
4. DE-ICERS..OFF
5. ANTI-ICERS..OFF
6. FUEL BOOST PUMPS......................................ON
7. INTERCOOLERS..OPEN
8. COWL FLAPS..OPEN TO 7½°
9. EMERGENCY HYDRAULIC PRESSURE.........................OK
10. ENGINEER'S REPORT....................................MIXTURE AUTO RICH, FUEL BOOST ON, STANDING BY ON GENERATORS AND COWL FLAPS, READY FOR LANDING

AFTER LANDING:

1. COWL FLAPS..OPEN
2. INTERCOOLERS..OPEN
3. FUEL BOOST PUMPS......................................OFF
4. GENERATORS..OFF
5. MAGNETOS..CHECKED
6. BOMB BAY DOORS..OPEN
7. ENGINES...IDLE CUT-OFF
8. ALL SWITCHES..OFF
9. WHEEL CHOCKS AND DOWN LOCKS..........................IN PLACE
10. BRAKES...OFF
11. CONTROLS...LOCKED
12. FLIGHT LOG...COMPLETE
13. FORMS 1, 1A..COMPLETE
14. GIVE CREW CHIEF REPORT OF MALFUNCTIONS...............
15. ASSIST IN LOCATION OF TROUBLE........................

BOMBARDIER'S B-29 CHECKLIST

BEFORE STARTING ENGINES

1. BOMBSIGHT...PRE-FLIGHTED
2. AUTO-PILOT...PRE-FLIGHTED
3. RACKS..PRE-FLIGHTED
4. BOMB BAY TANK SAFETY SWITCHES......................CHECKED
5. BOMBS..INSPECTED
6. PINS...PULLED
7. OXYGEN AND MASK...CHECKED
8. PARACHUTE..O. K.
9. AB COMPUTER AND SCALES...............................CHECKED
10. FUSES AND SPARES...CHECKED
11. INTERPHONE...CHECKED
12. ALTIMETER AT 29.92......................................SET
13. CLOCK..SYNCHRONIZED
14. INTERVALOMETER PROPERLY SET.......................CHECKED
15. BOMB FORMATION LIGHTS...............................CHECKED
16. TARGET INFORMATION....................................CHECKED
17. BOMBARDIER'S KIT...COMPLETE
18. NOSE COMPARTMENT.....................................CLEAR
19. WINDOWS..CLEAN
20. NOSE SIGHTING STATION................................PRE-FLIGHTED
21. CAMERA VACUUM VALVES...............................ON
22. CHECKED WITH WEATHER OFFICE......................O. K.
23. SWITCHES IN BOMBARDIER'S COMPARTMENT.......OFF

IMMEDIATELY BEFORE I. P.

1. ALL BOMBSIGHT SWITCHES................................ON
2. ALTITUDE COMPUTATIONS.................................COMPLETE
3. DISC SPEED AND TRAIL IN SIGHT.........................O. K.
4. PROPER RACK SELECTOR SWITCHES.....................ON
5. AB COMPUTER PROPERLY SET UP........................O. K.
6. BOMB BAY DOORS...OPEN
7. BOMBSIGHT STABILIZER....................................LEVEL
8. INTERVALOMETER PROPERLY SET........................CHECKED
9. AUTO-PILOT BEING USED..................................O. K.
10. CAMERA INTERVALOMETER..............................ON
11. CAMERA DOORS..OPEN

BEFORE LANDING

1. BOMBSIGHT SWITCHES.....................................OFF
2. BOMBARDIER'S PANEL SWITCHES........................OFF
3. NOSE SIGHTING STATION SWITCHES....................OFF
4. SIGHT..COVERED
5. BOMBING EQUIPMENT MALFUNCTION REPORT......COMPLETE

NAVIGATOR'S B-29 CHECKLIST

PRE-FLIGHT

1. MISSION ORDERS..O. K.
2. NAVIGATION KIT (COMPLETE)..............................O. K.
3. MAPS AND CHARTS...O. K.
4. WEATHER...O. K.
5. FLIGHT PLAN..O. K.
6. TIME TICK..O. K.

BEFORE STARTING ENGINES

1. PERSONAL EFFECTS (CLOTHING, PARACHUTE, OXYGEN MASK, LIFE VEST)..O. K.
2. HEADSET AND MICROPHONE...............................O. K.
3. OXYGEN SYSTEM...O. K.
4. A. P. I. CHECKED FOR COORDINATES OF DEPARTURE AND PROPER COLOR FOR LATITUDE............................O. K.
5. ASTRO-COMPASS..O. K.
6. SYNCHRONIZATION OF ALL TIME PIECES..............COMPLETED
7. CHECK FOR CALIBRATION CARDS..........................O. K.

WHILE TAXIING

1. CHECK OPERATION OF FLUX-GATE COMPASS..........O. K.
2. TURN ON A. P. I. (SET VARIATION ON THE FLUX GATE).....O. K.

DURING FLIGHT

1. USE ALL METHODS OF NAVIGATION
2. ALTITUDE AND AIR-SPEED HANDSET UNIT
   a. SET IN THE FOLLOWING (CHECK EVERY 10 MINUTES)
   TEMPERATURE — (WITHIN 5 DEG.)
   ALTITUDE — (WITHIN 500 FEET)
   INDICATED AIR SPEED — (WITHIN 5 MPH)..............COMPLETED
3. NAVIGATOR'S LOG...COMPLETED

AFTER LANDING

1. SWITCHES..CHECKED
2. CREW INSPECTION

RADIO OPERATOR'S B-29 CHECKLIST

BEFORE STARTING ENGINES

1. AERIAL RADIO OPERATOR'S KIT..................COMPLETE
2. ANTENNAS..CHECKED
3. FUSES...CHECKED
4. PLUGS...CHECKED
5. TUNING CABLES..CHECKED
6. FORM 1A..CHECKED
7. SCR-578...CHECKED
8. FACILITY CHARTS....................................COMPLETE
9. CREW INSPECTION...................................
10. PARACHUTE..CHECKED
11. CLOTHING...CHECKED
12. LIFE PRESERVER......................................CHECKED
13. OXYGEN..CHECKED
14. BATTERY SWITCH....................................ON
15. COMMAND SET..CHECKED
16. INTERPHONE..CHECKED
17. ALDIS LAMP...CHECKED

BEFORE TAXIING

1. LIAISON SET...CHECKED
2. RADIO COMPASS.......................................CHECKED
3. SCR-522..CHECKED
4. RC-103..CHECKED
5. FORM 1A..SIGNED
6. INTERPHONE..STAND BY
7. BOMB BAY DOORS.....................................CLOSED
8. CREW REPORT...O. K.

BEFORE LANDING

1. STATION...CLOSED
2. TRAILING ANTENNA.................................IN
3. INTERPHONE..STAND BY

AFTER LANDING

1. RADIO...OFF
2. BOMB BAY DOORS.....................................OPEN
3. FORM 1A..COMPLETE
4. CREW INSPECTION...................................

TOP GUNNER'S B-29 CHECKLIST

BEFORE STARTING ENGINES

1. PRE-FLIGHT INSPECTIONS: SIGHTS, TURRETS, GUNS, AMMUNITION, CAMERA, ETC.
2. CREW INSPECTION
3. INTERPHONE
4. PARACHUTE AND OXYGEN
5. CLOTHING

BEFORE TAXIING

1. ENGINE ALERT
2. ALARM BELL
3. PHONE CALL SIGNAL LIGHT
4. COMBAT STATION INSPECTION

BEFORE TAKE-OFF

1. TAXI ALERT
2. PREPARE FOR TAKE-OFF

AFTER TAKE-OFF

1. IN THE AIR CHECKS OPERATIONAL, SIGHTS, TURRETS AND GUNS
2. ENEMY AIRCRAFT ALERT

BEFORE LANDING

1. EQUIPMENT STOWED AND SWITCHES OFF, WHEN CO-PILOT GIVES ORDER, "PREPARE FOR LANDING"

AFTER LANDING

1. GUNS CLEARED
2. FIELD STRIP GUNS FOR CLEANING
3. MALFUNCTION REPORT

LEFT OR RIGHT GUNNER'S B-29 CHECKLIST

BEFORE STARTING ENGINES

1. PRE-FLIGHT, INSPECTION (SIGHTS, TURRETS, GUNS, AMMUNITION, CAMERA, ETC.)
2. CREW INSPECTION
3. INTERPHONE CHECK
4. FLIGHT CONTROLS
5. PARACHUTE AND OXYGEN
6. CLOTHING

BEFORE TAXIING

1. ENGINE ALERT
2. BOMB BAY DOORS CLOSED
3. PHONE CALL SIGNAL LIGHT
4. COMBAT STATION INSPECTION

BEFORE TAKE-OFF

1. TAXI ALERT
2. WING FLAP REPORT (25 DEG.)
3. PREPARE FOR TAKE-OFF

AFTER TAKE-OFF

1. LANDING GEAR AND FLAPS (FULL UP)
2. IN THE AIR CHECKS OPERATIONAL, SIGHTS, TURRETS, AND GUNS
3. ENEMY AIRCRAFT ALERT

BEFORE LANDING

1. EQUIPMENT STOWED AND SWITCHES OFF, WHEN CO-PILOT GIVES ORDER, "PREPARE FOR LANDING"
2. LANDING GEAR REPORT (DOWN AND LOCKED)
3. FLAP REPORT

AFTER LANDING

1. BOMB BAY DOORS OPEN
2. GUNS CLEARED
3. FIELD STRIP GUNS FOR CLEANING
4. MALFUNCTION REPORT

TAIL GUNNER'S B-29 CHECKLIST

BEFORE STARTING ENGINES

1. PRE-FLIGHT INSPECTION: (SIGHTS, TURRETS, GUNS, AMMUNITION, CAMERA, ETC.)
2. CREW INSPECTION
3. START PUT-PUT (WHEN BATTERY SWITCH IS TURNED ON)
4. INTERPHONE CHECK
5. PARACHUTE AND OXYGEN
6. CLOTHING

BEFORE TAXIING

1. PHONE CALL SIGNAL LIGHT
2. COMBAT STATION INSPECTION

BEFORE TAKE-OFF

1. TAXI ALERT
2. PREPARE FOR TAKE-OFF

AFTER TAKE-OFF

1. PUT-PUT OFF (AFTER GEAR AND FLAPS ARE REPORTED UP)
2. IN THE AIR CHECKS OPERATIONAL, SIGHTS, TURRETS AND GUNS
3. ENEMY AIRCRAFT ALERT

BEFORE LANDING

1. EQUIPMENT STOWED AND SWITCHES OFF, WHEN CO-PILOT GIVES ORDER, "PREPARE FOR LANDING"
2. PUT-PUT STARTED (AS SOON AS ABOVE IS ACCOMPLISHED)
3. NOTIFY CO-PILOT WHEN PUT-PUT IS ON THE LINE

AFTER LANDING

1. PUT-PUT OFF AT FLIGHT ENGINEER'S COMMAND
2. GUNS CLEARED
3. FIELD STRIP GUNS FOR CLEANING
4. MALFUNCTION REPORT

RESTRICTED

AIRPLANE COMMANDER'S AMPLIFIED B-29 CHECKLIST

When you have completed your visual check (items 1 to 3 on your checklist) and have climbed into your seat beside your copilot, you are ready for the rest of the *Before Starting Checklist*

4. PARACHUTE O.K.

Airplane commander and copilot put on parachutes at this time, and check for location of their seat-type dinghies if the airplane carries them.

5. CLOTHING O.K.

Airplane commander and copilot check their clothing and the operation of their electric suits. Also adjust helmet, throat microphone, and attach oxygen mask to left side of helmet.

6. LIFE PRESERVER O.K.

On all over-water flights, airplane commander and copilot check to see if their life vests are fitted with cartridges. Wear parachute harness over life vest.

7. PARKING BRAKES AND CHOCKS SET

Airplane commander depresses rudder pedals and pulls out the parking brake lever. He and the copilot look out the windows on their respective sides to see that chocks are in place as explained in the Visual Inspection.

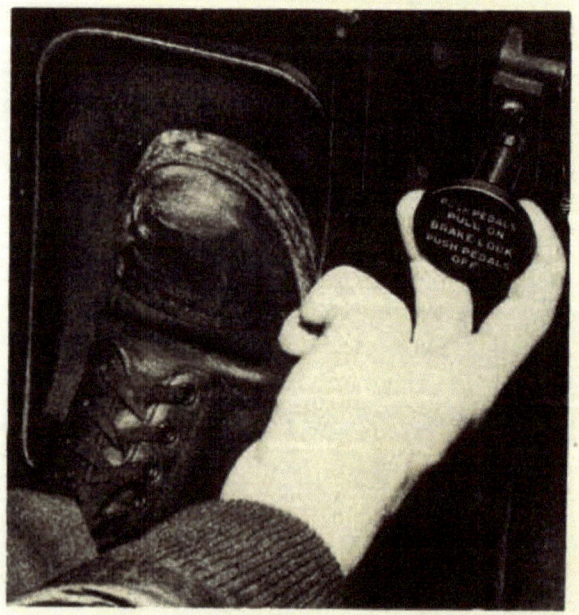

◄ SET PARKING BRAKES

RESTRICTED

8. EMERGENCY LANDING GEAR DOOR RELEASE IN PLACE

Airplane commander sees that the T-handle is in its proper position. Pulling this handle releases the nacelle doors only.

9. EMERGENCY BOMB RELEASE IN PLACE

T-handle on airplane commander's control stand.

10. EMERGENCY CABIN PRESSURE RELEASE IN PLACE

T-handle on airplane commander's control stand.

11. LANDING GEAR TRANSFER SWITCH—NORMAL

Airplane commander sees that switch (airplane commander's control stand) is in the NORMAL position. In this position, the main landing gear and nosewheel are operated by the landing gear switch on the aisle stand. When the landing gear transfer switch is in the EMERGENCY position, power from the engine-driven generators goes to the emergency bus and the emergency landing gear motors can be actuated by the emergency landing gear switches.

RESTRICTED

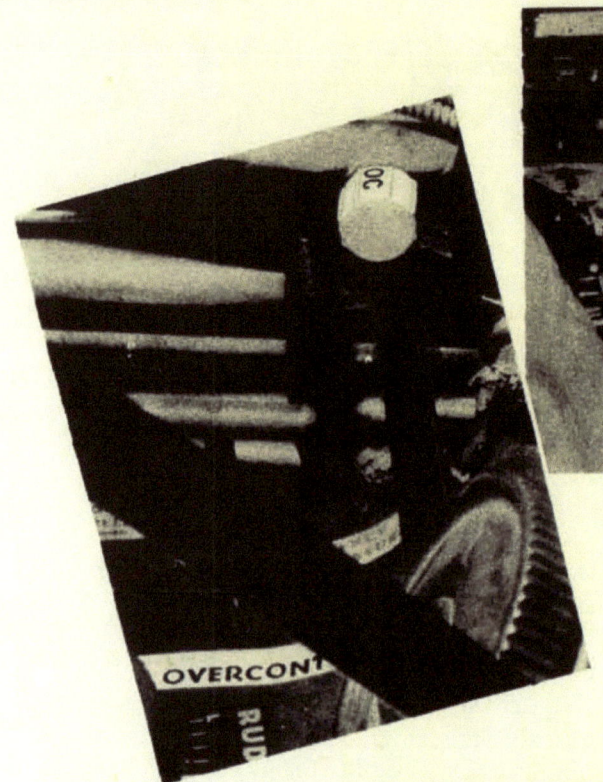

12. OVERCONTROL ENGAGED

Airplane commander sees that the lever (on airplane commander's control stand, but eliminated in later models) is in the ENGAGED position (full forward). This engages the flight engineer's throttles.

13. LANDING GEAR SWITCH NEUTRAL AND FUSE CHECK

Switch (airplane commander's aisle stand) should be neutral. Check to see that fuse in airplane commander's aisle stand is in place and not burned out.

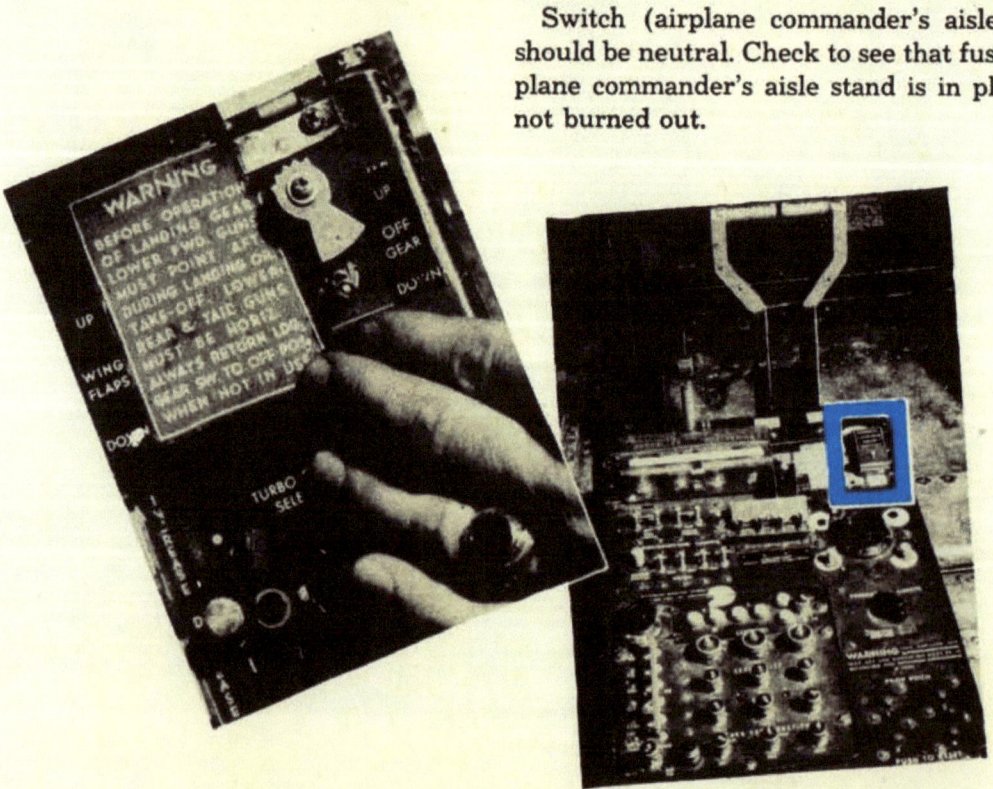

RESTRICTED

14. BATTERY SWITCH ON

Flight engineer flips battery switch ON and notifies the airplane commander. All electrical circuits are energized by either the battery or the auxiliary power unit, or both. Both are used for normal ground operation on loads up to 200 amperes. For additional power, use an external power source or engine-driven generators.

15. PUTT-PUTT STARTED

Copilot tells tail gunner to start the putt-putt.

16. HYDRAULIC PRESSURE O.K.

The copilot asks the flight engineer to check the emergency hydraulic pressure on engineer's panel (900-1075 psi) and checks the hydraulic pressure gage on his own instrument panel for a pressure of between 800 and 1000 psi. A fluctuating needle indicates a faulty pressure regulator. If the hydraulic pump overheats and smokes, remove the fuse on the flight engineer's aft fuse panel. To prevent overheating, make sure that pump stops when pressure reaches 1000 psi.

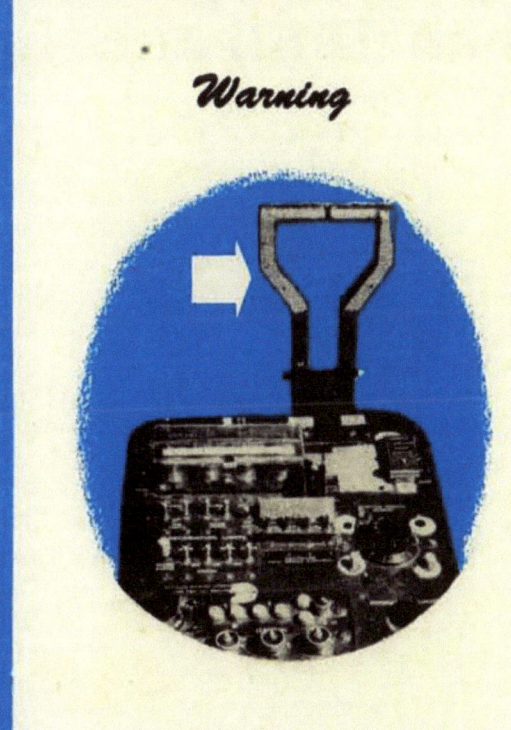

Warning

If an expander tube breaks while taxiing, use the emergency brakes only. Use of both normal brake pedals at the same time provides no braking on either side and allows all fluid and pressure in the normal system to drain through the broken tube. Use of both emergency brakes at the same time provides 100% braking on the good side (left gear, for example) and 50% braking on the bad side (right gear, for example). By switching the hydraulic servicing valve (flight engineer's panel) to emergency, you can maintain pressure and fluid indefinitely in both the normal and emergency systems. In those cases where you lose all fluid and pressure in the normal system, check valves prevent loss of fluid in the emergency lines, regardless of the position of the hydraulic servicing valve, and these lines hold enough fluid for approximately three applications of the emergency brakes.

RESTRICTED

Note
Make sure control lock is pushed all the way down and locked. Check to make sure it is locked.

17. FLIGHT CONTROLS CHECKED

Airplane commander pushes down locking lever located at forward end of airplane commander's aisle stand. This also unlocks the throttles, which a lock bar holds in the closed position when the control lock is on. This lock bar is linked to the control lock in such a way that strong forward pressure on the throttles forces the control lock off and eliminates the possibility of locked controls on takeoff. The copilot makes the control check. In making the check, the copilot announces over the interphone, "Copilot to gunners, stand by to check controls." He then pulls the control column back and says on interphone, "Check elevators." Left gunner answers, "Left elevator up, sir." Right gunner answers, "Right elevator up, sir." The copilot then pushes the column forward and completes his check on the elevators. Ailerons and rudder are checked in the same manner.

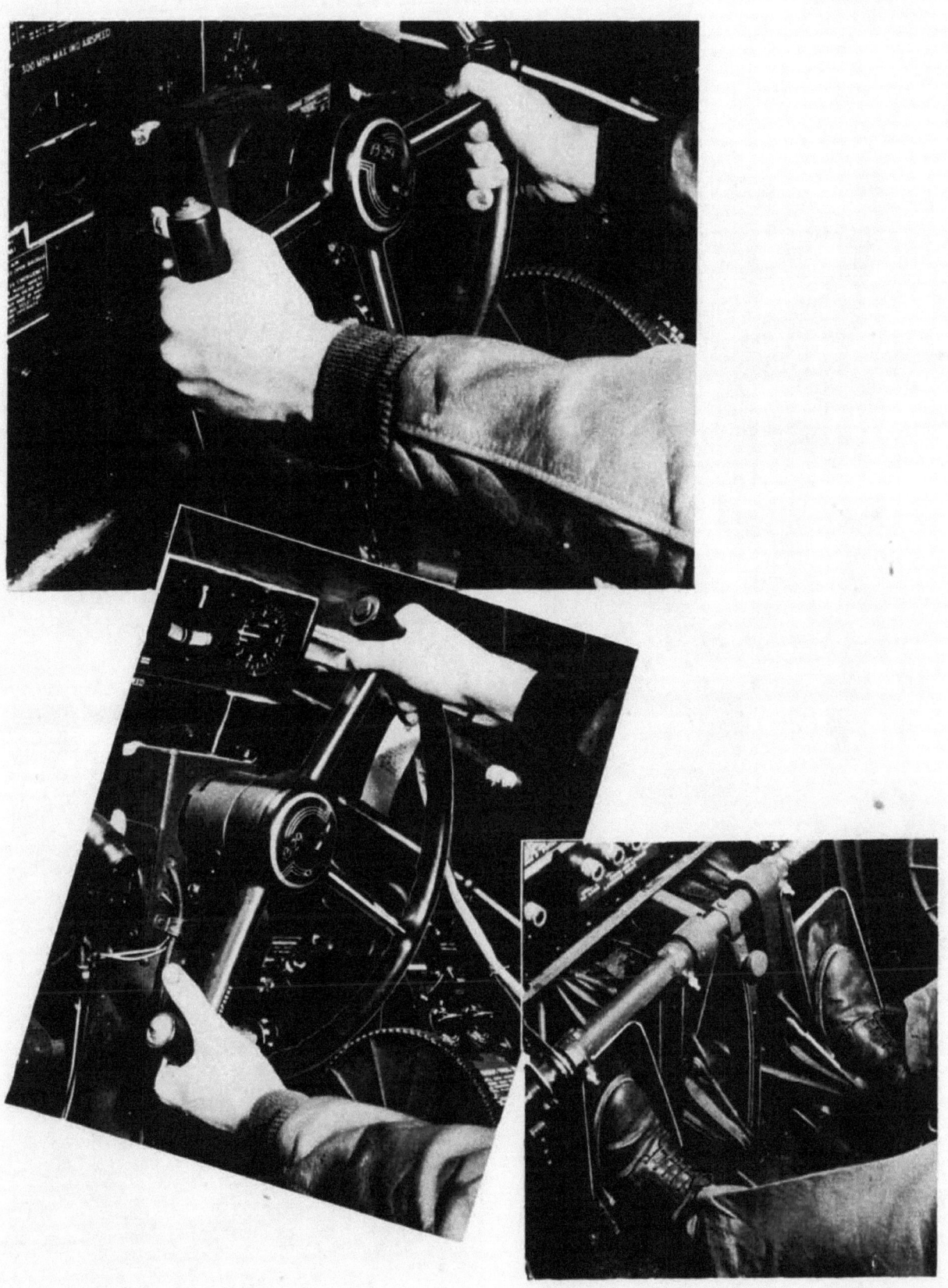

RESTRICTED

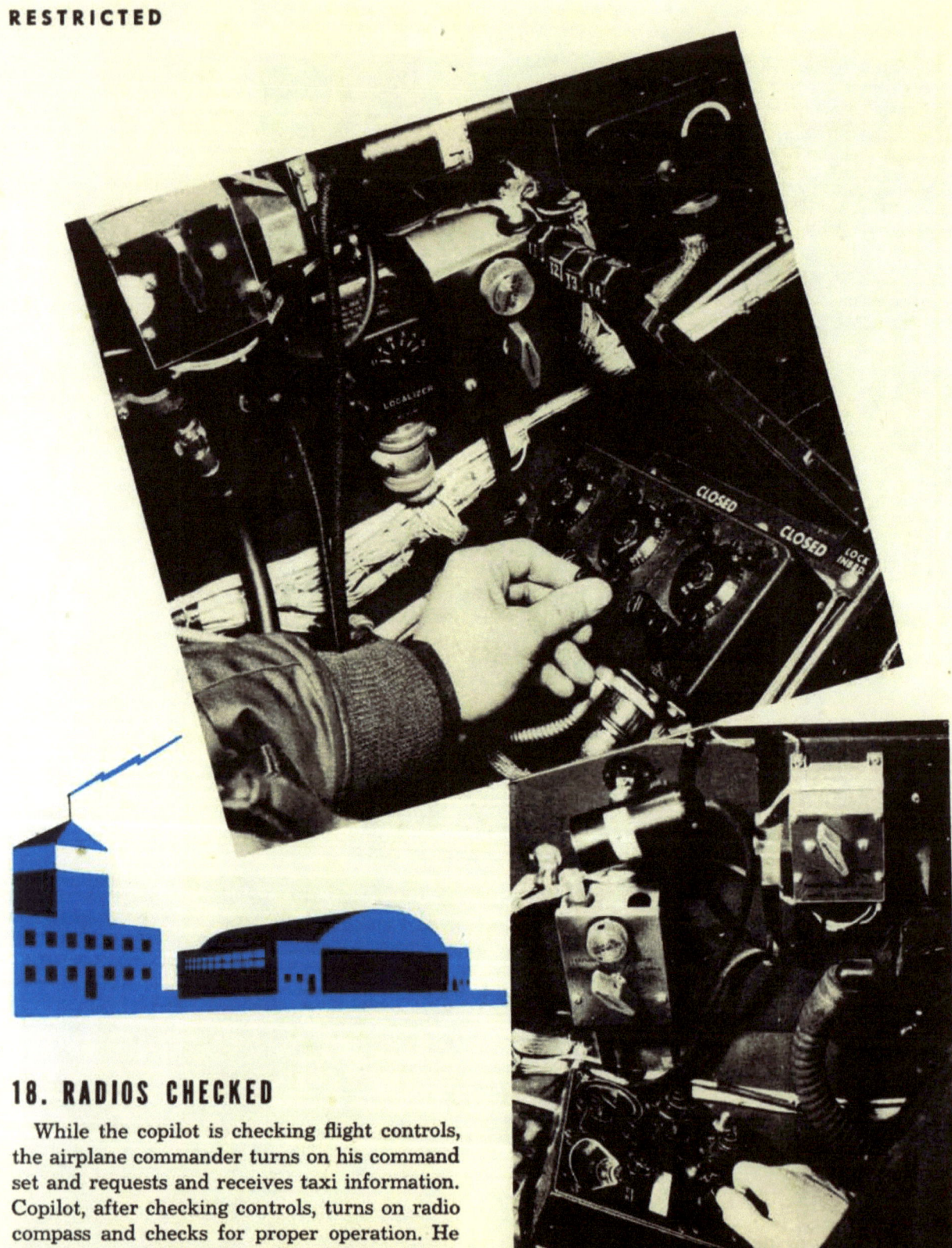

18. RADIOS CHECKED

While the copilot is checking flight controls, the airplane commander turns on his command set and requests and receives taxi information. Copilot, after checking controls, turns on radio compass and checks for proper operation. He then turns radio compass off and stands by on the interphone so that he can be in continuous contact with the crew.

RESTRICTED

19. ALTIMETERS SET

Airplane commander and copilot set their altimeters by the tower altimeter setting. Check the altitude reading against the known field elevation. If the altimeter setting given by the tower indicates an altitude different from the known field elevation, check the setting again and note the difference in elevation so you can use it in correcting the reading when landing.

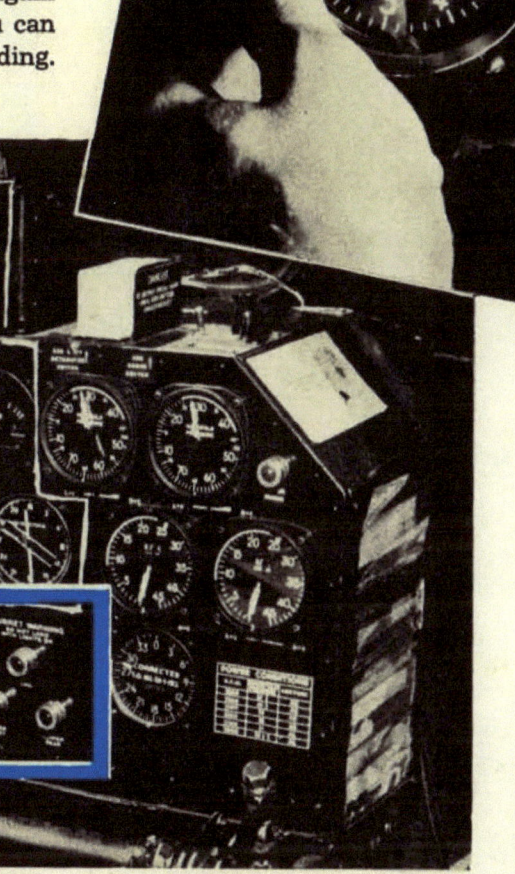

20. TURRETS STOWED

Airplane commander checks the three turret warning lights on his instrument panel to see that all turrets are properly stowed. Turret lights should be **out**.

21. ADJUST SEATS AND PEDALS

22. LIGHTS-CHECKED

If any night operation is contemplated on the flight, check all lights—fluorescent lights, identification lights, landing lights, and position lights (switches on control and aisle stands). A member of the ground crew should be instructed to check the landing lights and position lights. Wing position lights are not visible from the airplane in flight. They can be inspected at night from inside the airplane only by checking the reflection on the ground under the wing.

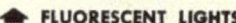

◄ FLUORESCENT LIGHTS

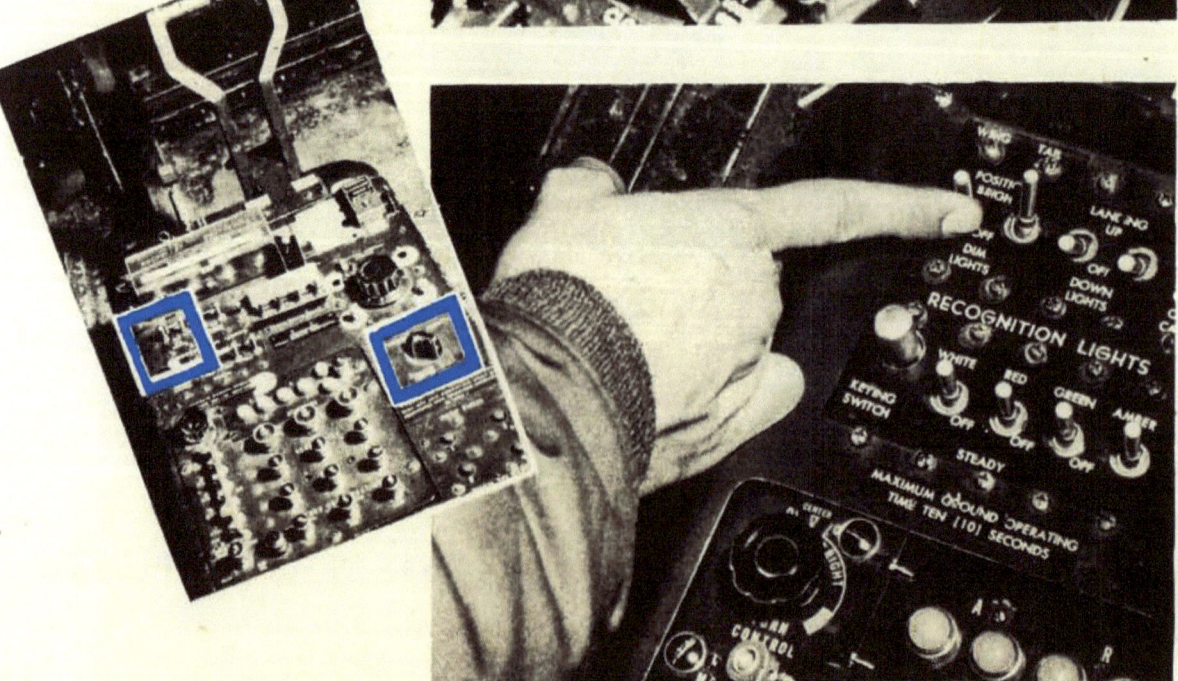

RESTRICTED

23. OXYGEN O.K.

Airplane commander and copilot check their oxygen pressure gages for proper pressure (400 to 425 psi) and their walk-around bottles (should have same pressure as in system). Auto mix should be on ON, emergency valve OFF.

RESTRICTED

RESTRICTED

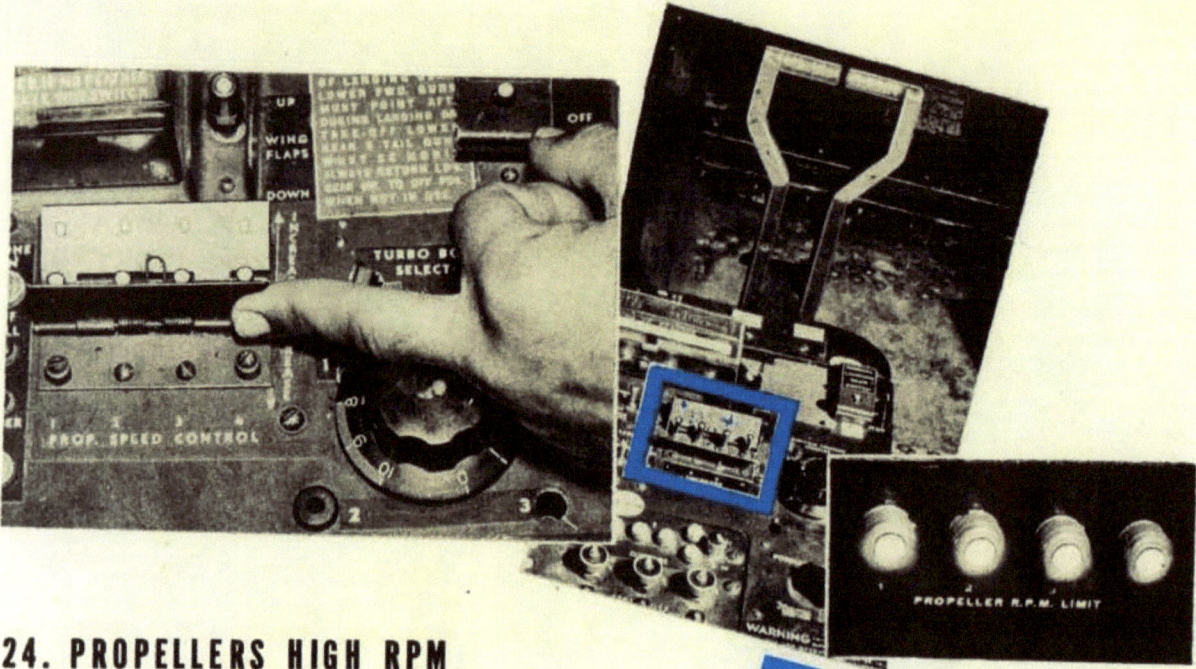

24. PROPELLERS HIGH RPM

Copilot pushes the propeller switches (aisle stand) to INCREASE RPM and holds them there until the propeller limit lights on his instrument panel flash on. The propellers then will be in high rpm.

25. TURBOS OFF

Airplane commander checks to see that the turbo selector dial is set at 0. Turbo-supercharger regulators are ready for instant operation at any time since amplifier tubes remain on even with selector dial at 0.

26. FLIGHT ENGINEER'S REPORT - CHECKLIST COMPLETE, READY TO START ENGINES

At this point, if the flight engineer has not completed his checklist, the airplane commander waits before giving the command to start engines.

27. STAND CLEAR - FIRE GUARD - CLEAR LEFT - CLEAR RIGHT

When ready to start the engines both the airplane commander and the copilot give the command "Stand clear" to the ground crew (clear right, clear left). When the fire guard is ready, copilot says on interphone, "Stand by to start engines."

RESTRICTED

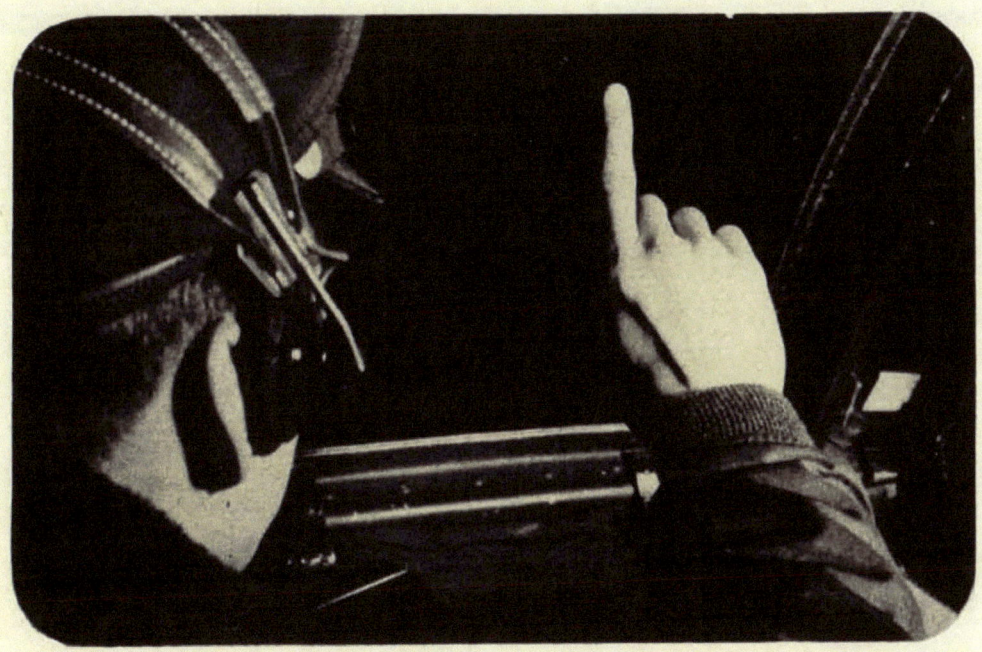

Starting the Engines

The engines are started in 1, 2, 3, 4 order. The airplane commander tells the flight engineer to start No. 1 engine and signifies to the ground crew that No. 1 engine is ready to be started. The number of fingers held up by the airplane commander in case of engines 1 and 2 and the copilot in case of engines 3 and 4 signifies the number of the engine to be started. When the engine starts, the flight engineer ordinarily reports "Engine operating normally" and announces that he is "Ready to start No. 2 engine." Follow a similar procedure for the other engines.

In starting each engine, the flight engineer uses the following procedure:

a. Turns fire extinguisher to the engine being started.
b. Turns master ignition switch on.
c. Turns the boost pump on.
d. Energizes starter for from 12 to 16 seconds.
e. Moves starter switch to START position.
f. After propeller has made one revolution, turns ignition switch on and holds the primer down as needed to start and smooth out engine at 800-1000 rpm.
g. Moves mixture control to AUTO-RICH.

The flight engineer handles the throttles throughout the starting procedure, keeping the rpm between 1,000 and 1,200. When an engine is running, the flight engineer sets the throttle at 700 rpm (1,000 rpm if the cylinder-head temperature is below 150°C). Thereafter, the airplane commander will control the throttles except when asking for engine-driven generators and during the engine run-up. If either the copilot or the flight engineer sees that an engine is loading up (black smoke or rpm drop or both) he informs the airplane commander. Do not idle engines below 700 rpm.

STARTING DONT'S

1. **Don't** start the engines until the before-starting check has been covered item by item.

2. **Don't** start the engines until the propellers have been pulled through to eliminate any possibility of liquid locks.

3. **Don't** jam throttles forward at any time, especially during the starting procedure.

4. **Don't** start your engines until a fire guard is posted.

5. **Don't** continue to run an engine if the nose oil pressure and rear oil pressure do not build up within 30 seconds after starting.

RESTRICTED

Before Taxiing

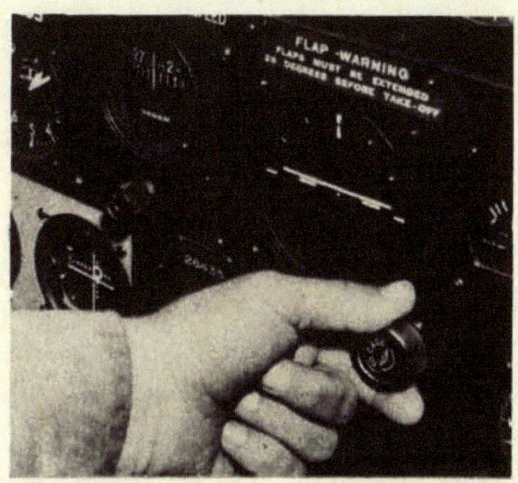

CHECK GYRO INSTRUMENTS

1. VACUUM

The copilot asks the flight engineer to check vacuum reading. The flight engineer, after checking the vacuum reading for both pumps (gage on engineer's panel should read 3.8" to 4.2" Hg), reports this check to the copilot.

WARNING: Do not move the vacuum selector valve (engineer's control stand), except when making this check. Frequent use of the valve will cause unnecessary wear.

2. GYROS

Airplane commander and copilot check their gyro instruments to make sure that they are uncaged and operating correctly. At this time, set the directional gyros to agree with the magnetic compass reading.

3. INSTRUMENTS

Airplane commander and copilot check their respective instrument panels for proper readings and operation of all instruments.

RESTRICTED

47

4. BOMB BAY DOORS CLOSED

After the copilot has instructed the gunners and radio operator to check and see that all members of the ground crew are clear of the bomb bay doors, he says to the flight engineer, "Generators on," and tells the bombardier to close the bomb bay doors. Flight engineer has meantime set throttle on coolest engine to 1400 rpm and turned generators on. The radio operator and one of the gunners check through the pressure doors and report to the copilot that the bomb bay doors are closed. Flight engineer returns throttle to 700 rpm when copilot says, "Generators off." (Eliminate generator procedure on airplanes with snap-opening bomb bay doors.)

ON ONE INTERPHONE CALL CHECK
{
5. ALARM BELL
6. PHONE CALL SIGNAL LIGHT
7. COMBAT STATION INSPECTION
}

Airplane commander switches on alarm bell (aisle stand) and phone call signal light (aisle stand), then calls for combat station inspection. Copilot repeats this command on interphone and receives acknowledgment in the following manner: Bombardier, navigator, flight engineer, radio operator, top gunner, left gunner, right gunner, and tail gunner (in that order) acknowledge that they have completed a check of their stations by saying, for example, "Bombardier O.K." Top gunner says, "Alarm bell O.K., light O.K., top gunner O.K." Left and right gunners say, "Left (or right) gunner O.K." Tail gunner says, "Light O.K. (radar compartment), tail gunner O.K."

ALARM BELL

PHONE CALL

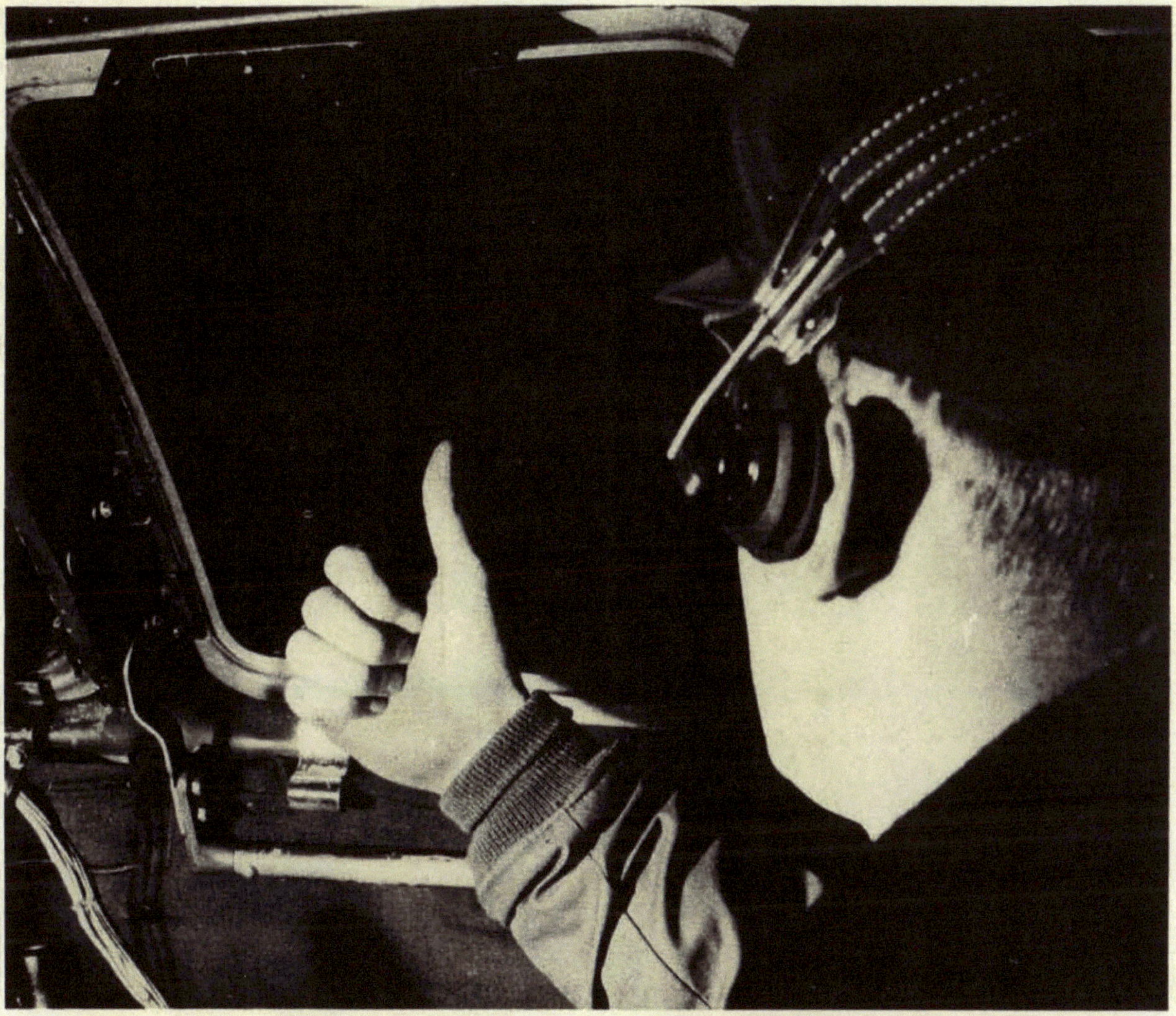

8. CHOCKS OUT

Airplane commander and copilot check to see that chocks have been pulled.

9. PARKING BRAKES OFF, STAND BY

After releasing the parking brakes, the airplane commander gives the command "Stand by to taxi." The copilot repeats the command over the interphone.

RELEASE PARKING BRAKES ▶

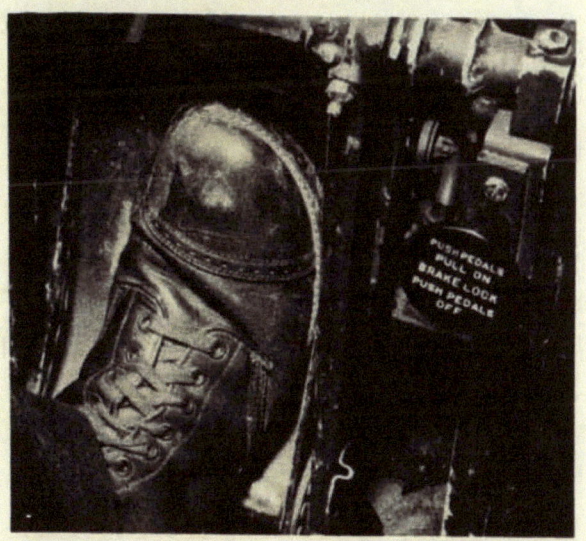

TAXIING PROCEDURE

Like all tricycle-landing-gear aircraft, the B-29 taxis easily. Brakes are good—four expander tubes per wheel. Remember, however, that it is a big, heavy airplane. It gains momentum rapidly and, because of its size, you have to depend on your side and top gunners to act as observers to warn you of obstacles.

For all ground operations, set the rpm at 700 (after cylinder-head temperatures reach 150°C) and the mixture in AUTO RICH. Never use AUTO LEAN for taxiing. If the carburetors are set properly, the engines idle as low as 550 rpm without loading up. When taxiing uphill or in hot weather, 700 rpm may not keep the airplane rolling. Under these conditions, increase all throttle settings, but not more than necessary to continue taxiing. Always return throttles to 700 rpm when parked.

For maximum cooling and prevention of backfires, it is recommended that the airplane be taxied with brakes alone, controlling both speed and direction with brakes. Entering a taxi turn with outside throttle doesn't save your brakes, in the long run, because the speed of the airplane accelerates quickly with this extra power and you must use the brakes to slow down. If you gain too much speed, bring the airplane almost to a stop, straight ahead, then stay off the brakes as long as possible to let them cool. Don't ride your brakes.

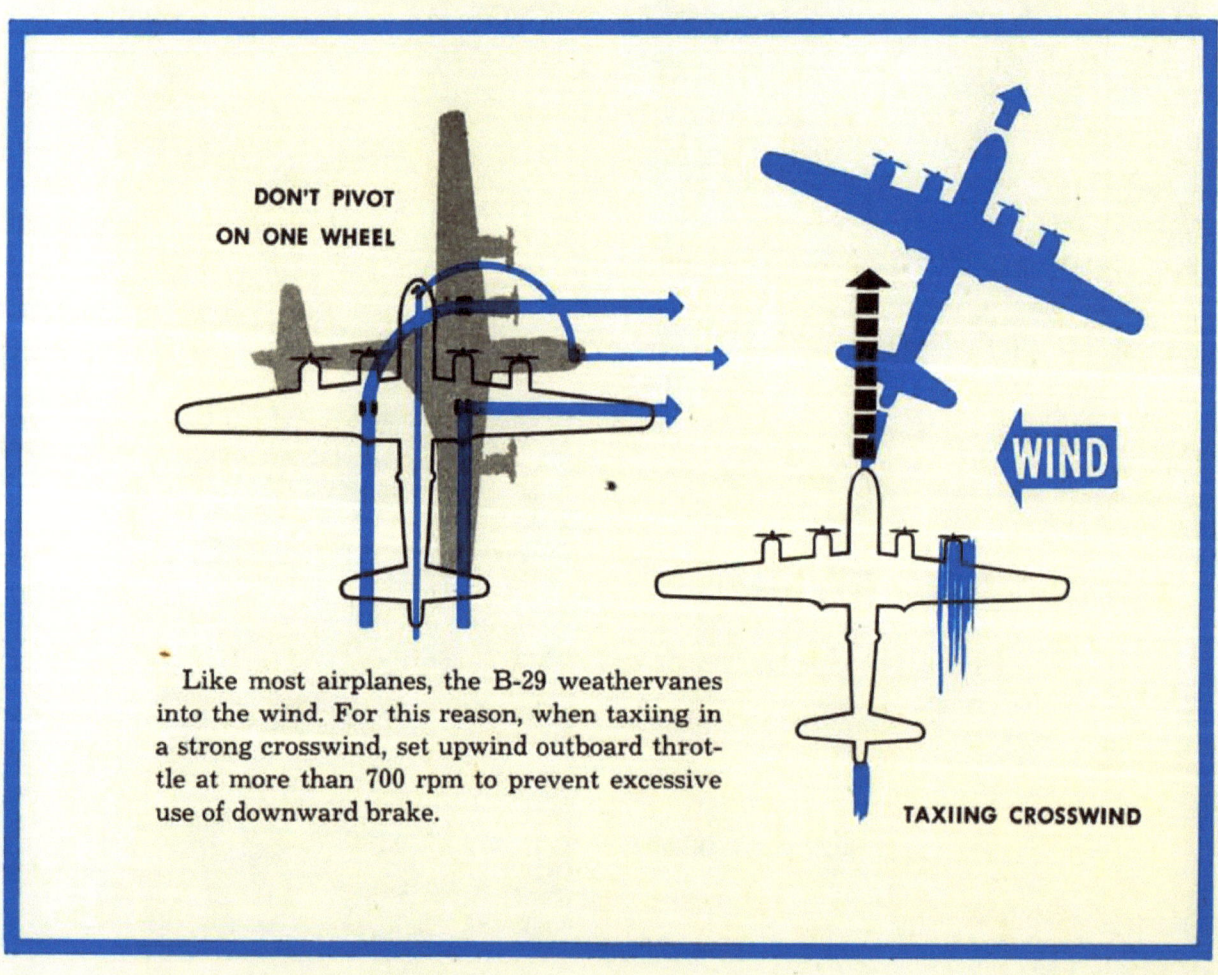

DON'T PIVOT ON ONE WHEEL

TAXIING CROSSWIND

Like most airplanes, the B-29 weathervanes into the wind. For this reason, when taxiing in a strong crosswind, set upwind outboard throttle at more than 700 rpm to prevent excessive use of downward brake.

Before Takeoff

1. EMERGENCY BRAKES CHECKED

After parking brakes are released, when starting to taxi, copilot says, "Emergency brakes." Airplane commander then pulls the emergency brake hand metering levers (aisle stand) to see that emergency brakes are operating properly on both sides. Copilot then tells flight engineer to recharge emergency system. Normal brakes may be safely used while recharging the emergency system, since the electric hydraulic pump recharges both systems with the hydraulic servicing valve on emergency.

2. NOSEWHEEL-STRAIGHT

Copilot checks through cockpit floor observation window to make sure the nosewheel is straight before engine run-up.

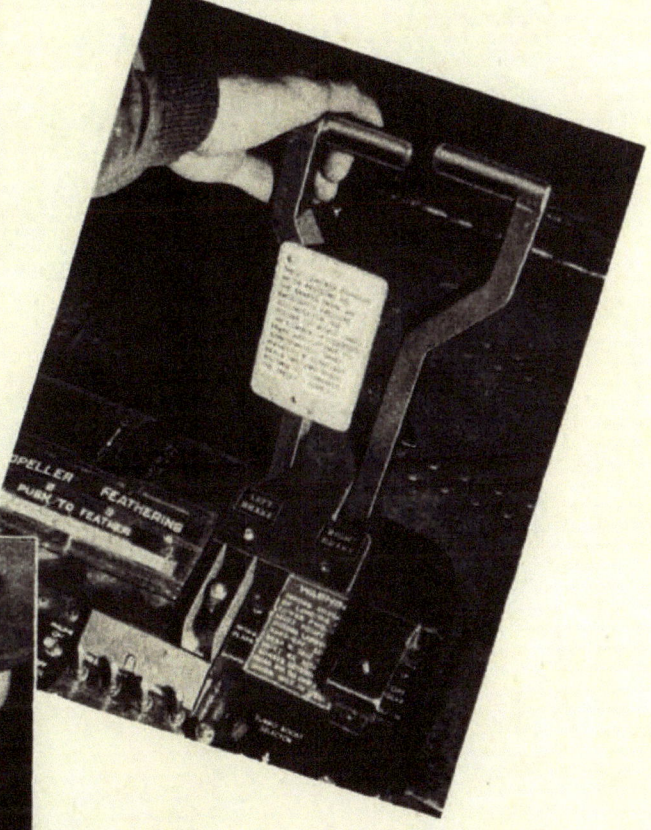

CHECK EMERGENCY BRAKES

CHECK TO SEE NOSEWHEEL IS STRAIGHT

ENGINE RUN-UP

The airplane commander gives the command "Stand by for Engine Run-up," and the copilot repeats the command over the interphone. The engine run-up for first take-off should be accomplished in the following manner: (For subsequent takeoffs, eliminate entire procedure, items a. through f.)

a. Airplane Commander increases all throttles to 1500 rpm and commands "Check generators." Copilot starts flaps down (switch on aisle stand) and tells Flight Engineer to check generators. Copilot holds switch DOWN until flaps have reached full down position then returns them to 25°. Flight Engineer will have generators checked by the time the flaps have been run to the full down position and back to 25°.

NOTE: Flaps are run down at this time in order to have an electrical load on the normal

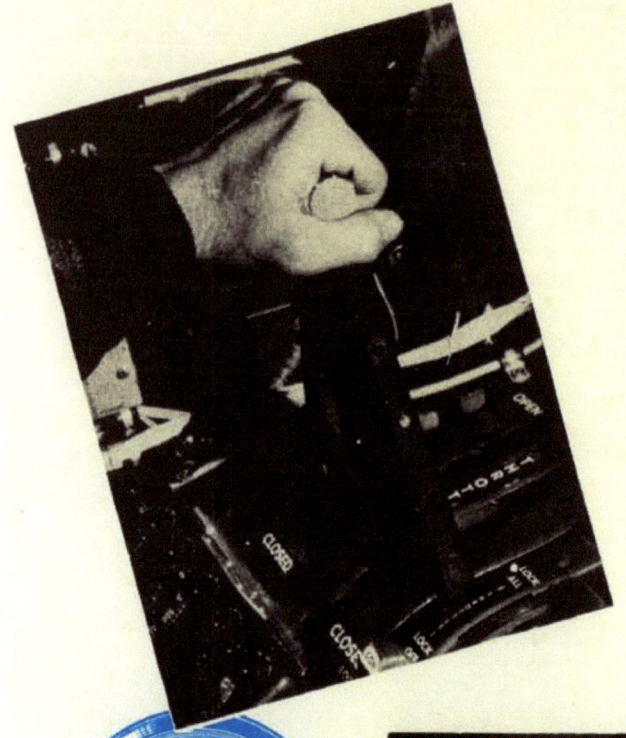

INCREASE ALL THROTTLES TO 1500 RPM

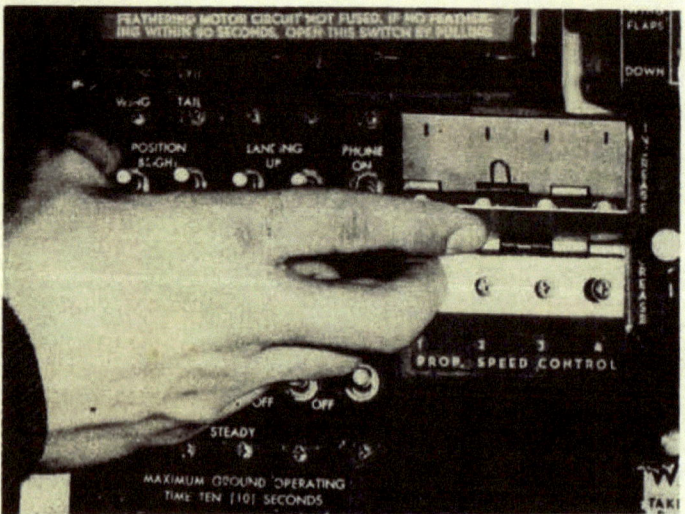

AT FULL DECREASE RPM, TACHOMETER SHOULD READ 1200-1300 ►

WITH PROPS BACK TO HIGH RPM, TACHOMETER SHOULD READ 1500 ►

bus so the Flight Engineer can properly check the generators. Gunners check the lowering of the flaps by reporting "Left flap down 25°, sir" and "Right flap down 25°, sir."

b. Airplane Commander operates all four propeller switches to full decrease then to full increase (from limit warning light to limit warning light) to test the propeller governors. At full decrease rpm, before returning switches to increase rpm, check tachometers for stable, uniform readings of 1200-1300 rpm. When propellers are again returned to high rpm, tachometers should all read 1500 as before. Any propeller overshooting the original setting is not being properly governed and this must be corrected before takeoff.

c. When propellers and generators are checked, airplane commander pulls all throttles back to 700 rpm and tells flight engineer to check magnetos.

d. Flight engineer advances No. 1 throttle to 2000 rpm, checks magnetos, and calls out, "Right, both, left, both." Flight engineer then returns throttle to 700 rpm. At this time, check each engine for manifold pressure necessary to get 2000 rpm. At sea level, approximately 30 inches is normal. Above sea level, subtract one inch for each thousand feet of altitude. Changes in temperature will vary these settings, but the variation will be the same for all engines. Excessive manifold pressure on one engine is an indication of a bad cylinder, a bad valve, or some other engine malfunction.

e. Magneto check is made for each engine. Allowable drop at 2000 rpm is 100.

f. If rpm drop on any engine is more than 100, caused by fouled plugs, proceed with full-power check for that engine. Then check magnetos (turbos off) on bad engine again. If rpm drop is still above 100, return ship to the line.

g. After magnetos are checked, airplane commander sets turbo selector on No. 8 and advances throttles one at a time full open to check manifold pressure and rpm. For this ground check gages should read between 2500 and 2600 rpm and 46½ and 47½ inches of manifold pressure—deduct ½ inch manifold pressure for each 50 rpm.

Warning

Do not check magnetos with turbos on. A backfire at this time (with turbos on) can damage turbo and waste gate assembly.

Do not park airplane at 45 deg. to runway for engine run-up.

Head airplane directly into wind for maximum cooling.

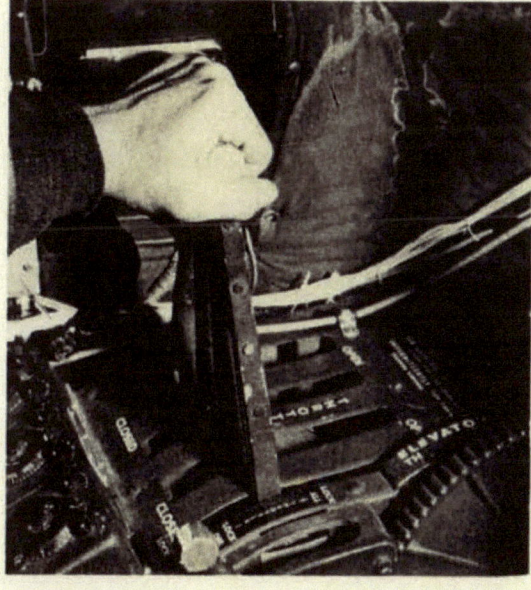
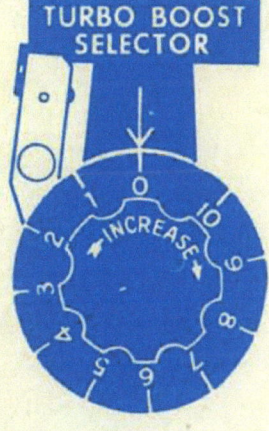

RESTRICTED

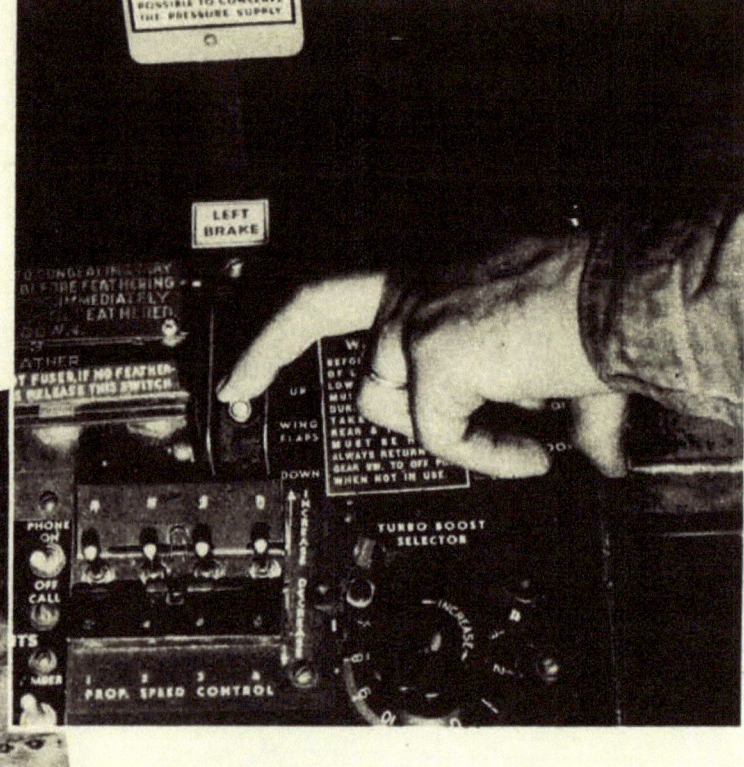

4. WING FLAPS 25°

Gunners have already checked the lowering of the flaps by reporting "Left flap down 25°, sir," "Right flap down 25°, sir."

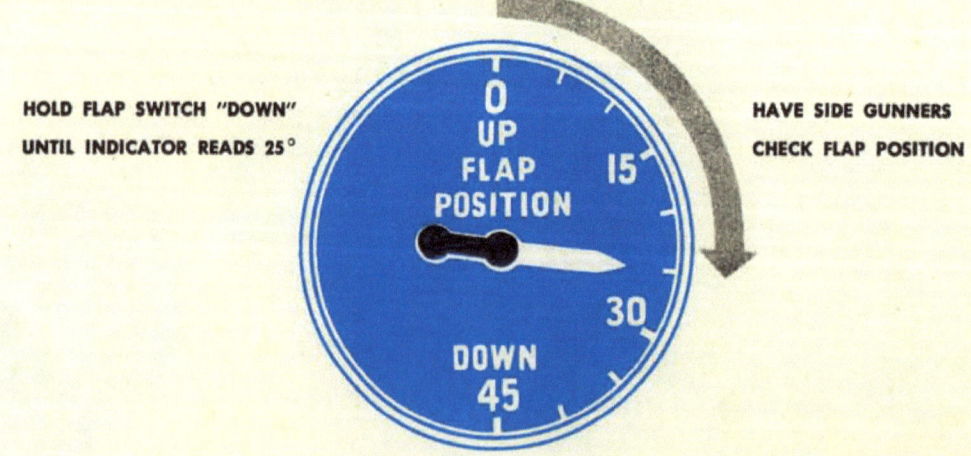

HOLD FLAP SWITCH "DOWN"
UNTIL INDICATOR READS 25°

HAVE SIDE GUNNERS
CHECK FLAP POSITION

RESTRICTED

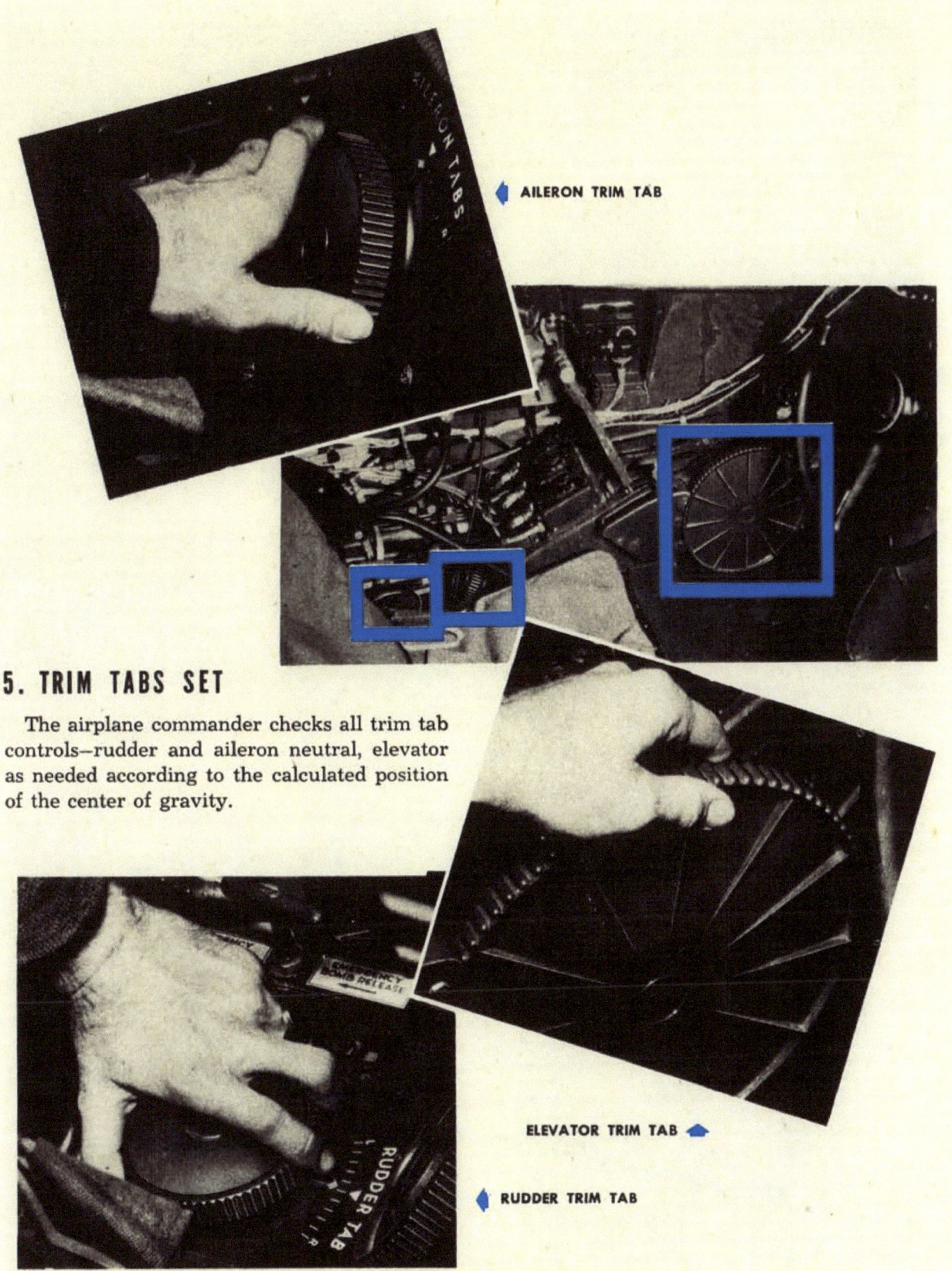

◀ AILERON TRIM TAB

5. TRIM TABS SET

The airplane commander checks all trim tab controls—rudder and aileron neutral, elevator as needed according to the calculated position of the center of gravity.

ELEVATOR TRIM TAB ◀

◀ RUDDER TRIM TAB

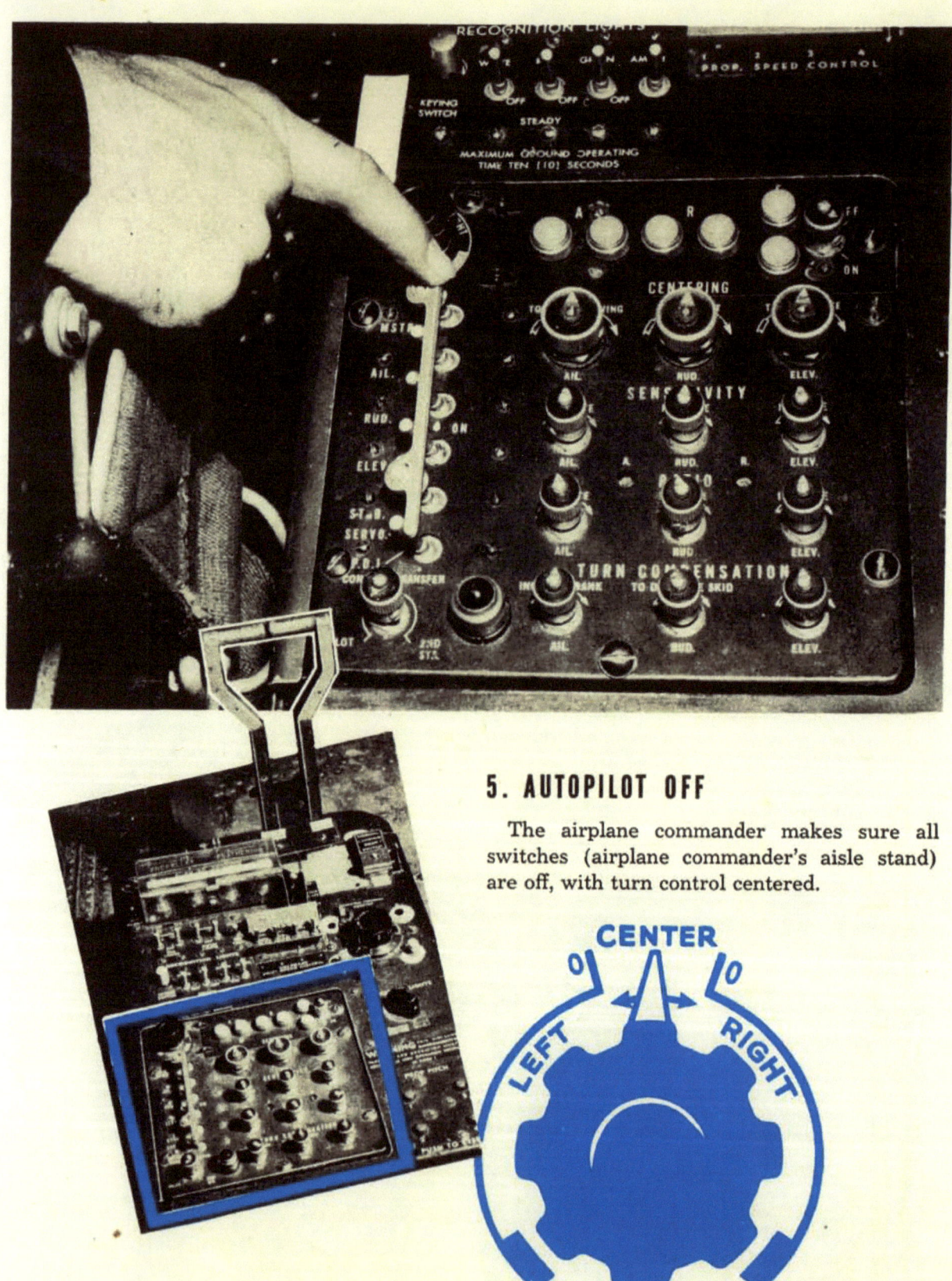

5. AUTOPILOT OFF

The airplane commander makes sure all switches (airplane commander's aisle stand) are off, with turn control centered.

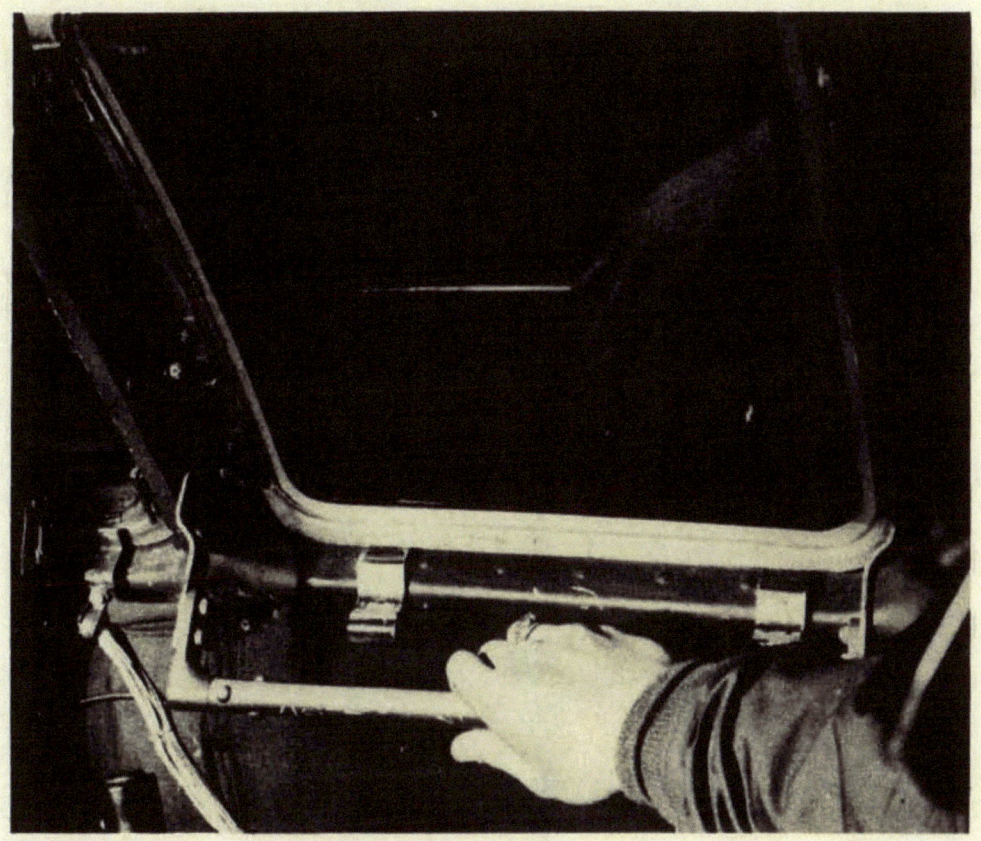

7. WINDOWS AND HATCHES CLOSED

As the airplane commander closes and secures his window, the copilot closes his, checks to see that the forward compartment entrance hatch is closed, and checks over the interphone with the tail gunner to make sure that the rear entrance door and rear escape hatch are closed.

8. TURBOS ON No. 8
9. PROPELLERS HIGH RPM
10. CREW READY

The copilot says on interphone, "Prepare for takeoff."

11. RADIO CALL COMPLETED

Airplane commander calls tower and requests permission to take off.

12. THROTTLE BRAKE O. K.

Airplane commander adjusts his throttle brake for desired friction to prevent slipping.

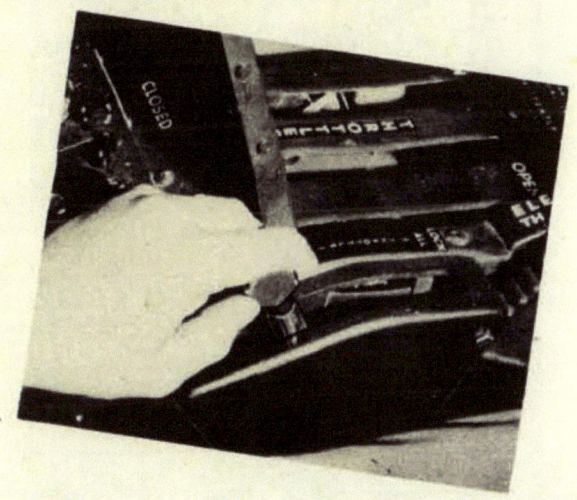

Stand by for Takeoff

RESTRICTED

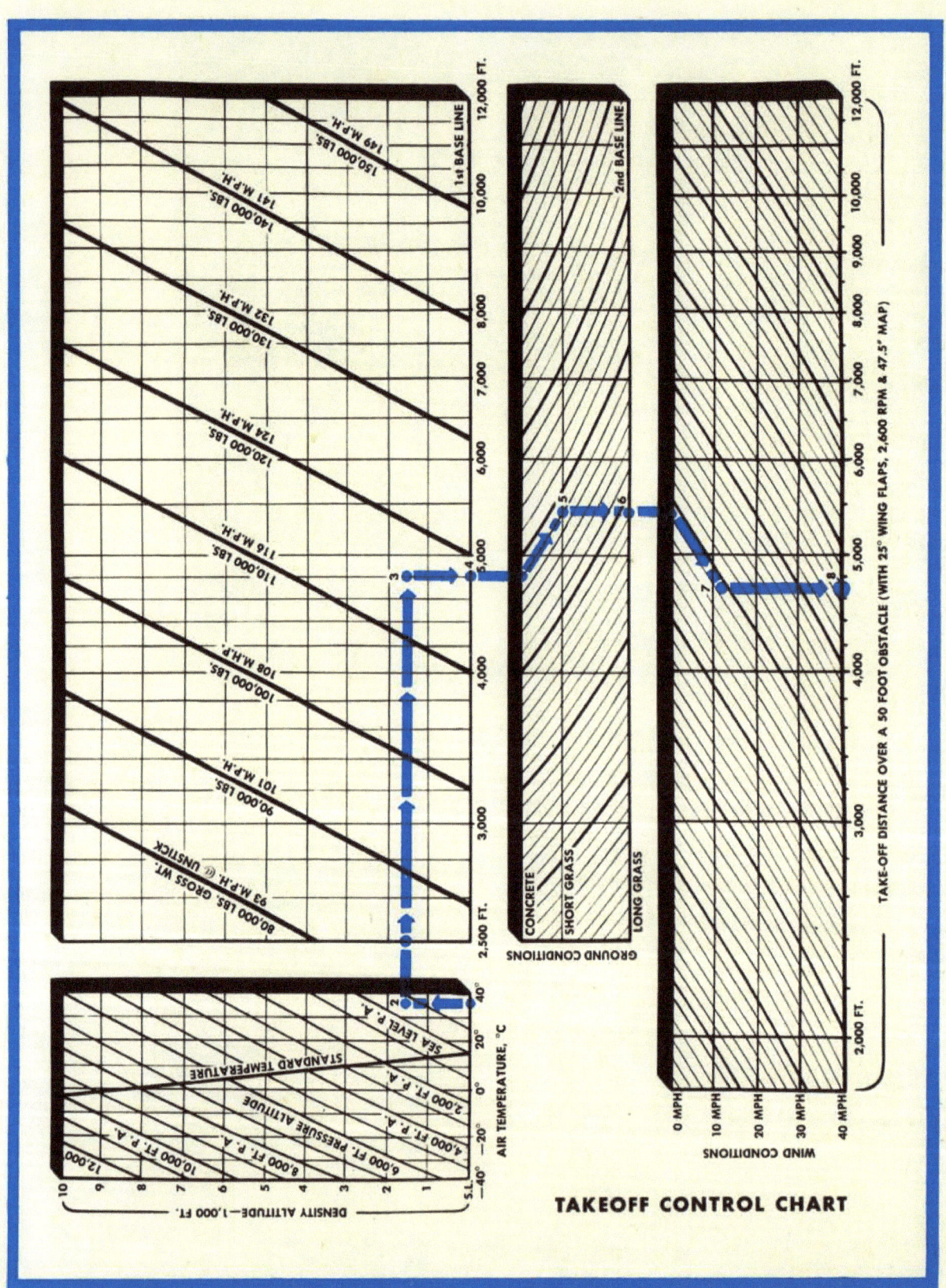

TAKEOFF CONTROL CHART

58

RESTRICTED

Takeoff Procedure

Keep the cylinder-head temperatures (CHT) at a minimum before takeoff. Never take off with any CHT above 220°C.

Use the throttles (**not the brakes**) to line up with runway, then as the airplane starts to roll, walk the throttles forward slowly until there is rudder control at 60 to 65 mph. You then can move the throttles steadily forward to the full open position. In this way, you can maintain directional control first with throttles, then with rudder. Don't use the brakes to hold the airplane straight on the runway, except in emergencies, since this increases the takeoff distance and wears out the brakes. If you are careful not to use brakes, the airplane will gain speed continuously from the point of run-up (off the runway) to the point where the wheels leave the ground. If you advance the throttles to 40" at a standstill for power check, or move the throttles forward too quickly at the beginning of the roll, you won't have the reserve power necessary to hold the airplane straight with throttles. So until the airplane picks up speed you must use brakes to stay on the runway. This lengthens the time required to get rudder control, and lengthens the takeoff roll and heats up the brakes.

The copilot makes a continuous power check as the throttles are advanced during the initial takeoff roll. Full power (47½" and 2600 rpm) (Few airplanes 49" and 2800 rpm) should be obtained during the roll down the first third of the runway. If any unusual power conditions are noted, the copilot notifies the airplane commander who still has time to cut throttles if he decides continued takeoff is inadvisable.

USE THROTTLES TO LINE UP WITH THE RUNWAY

Never attempt takeoff with less than full takeoff power. Full-power takeoffs are not harmful to the engines as long as the CHTs stay within their limits. Takeoffs with reduced power prolong the time required to reach 195 mph. Flying the B-29 below this speed after takeoff is hazardous and does not properly cool the engines.

When adjusting propeller rpm, make sure that none of the propeller rpm switches sticks in the full rpm position. To be sure, always use both metal tabs when operating the switches.

At 90 mph, relieve pressure on the nosewheel by easing the control column back. The airplane then flies itself off the ground at 115 to 130 mph, depending on the gross weight. As soon as the ship is safely off, brake the wheels and call for gear up.

◀ NOTES ON TAKEOFF CONTROL CHART

1. Distance to leave ground is approximately 70% of the total
2. Use first base line to determine takeoff distance when using concrete runways (no wind)
3. Example: 35°C O.A.T., 1,500 ft., 115,000 lbs., short grass runway, 12 MPH headwind

   1. Select ground temp. °C
   2. Determine pressure altitude
   3. Select takeoff weight point
   4. Drop vertically to first base line
   5. Move parallel to surface correction lines to ground condition line
   6. Drop vertically to 2nd base line
   7. Move parallel to wind correction lines to 12 mph line
   8. Drop vertically and read takeoff distance on bottom scale

RESTRICTED

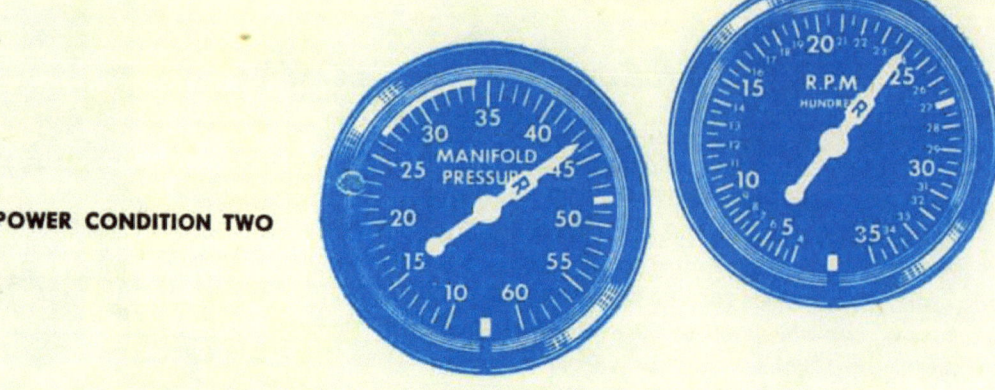

POWER CONDITION TWO

At 140 mph, the airplane commander calls for Power Condition 2 (43½" and 2400).

At 150 mph, the airplane commander calls for flaps up easy. Flaps may be raised 5° at a time if copilot waits for the airplane to fly out of the tendency to settle, before raising the flaps another 5°. Gear and flaps pull a total of 965 amperes and may be safely raised together, provided the switches are not tripped simultaneously.

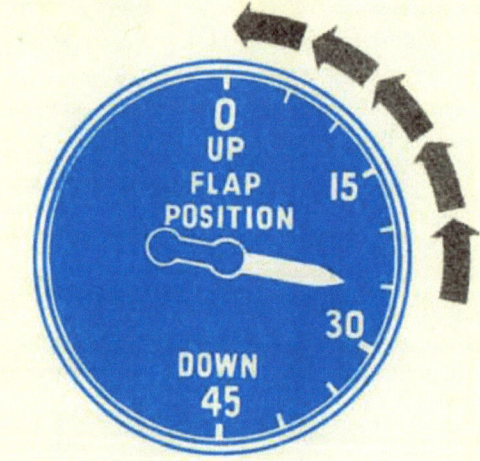

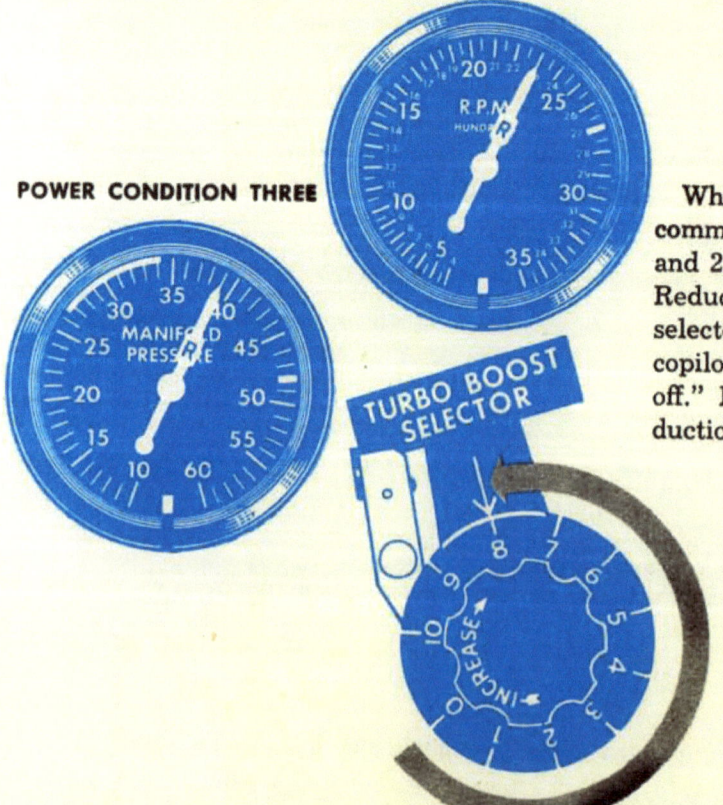

POWER CONDITION THREE

When gear and flaps are full up, the airplane commander calls for Power Condition 3 (39" and 2300) if gross weight is under 115,000 lbs. Reduce the manifold pressure with the turbo selector dial until turbos are off, at which time copilot announces to flight engineer, "Turbos off." Make subsequent manifold pressure reductions with the throttles.

REDUCE MANIFOLD PRESSURE WITH TURBO

CONVERSION TABLE ON SHORT-CHORD

Cowl Flap Openings

12½° same as 3¾ inches
10°   same as 3⅜ inches
7½°   same as 3   inches
5°   same as 2½ inches
2½°   same as 2⅛ inches
0°   same as 1¾ inches

WATCH YOUR CYLINDER-HEAD TEMPERATURES!

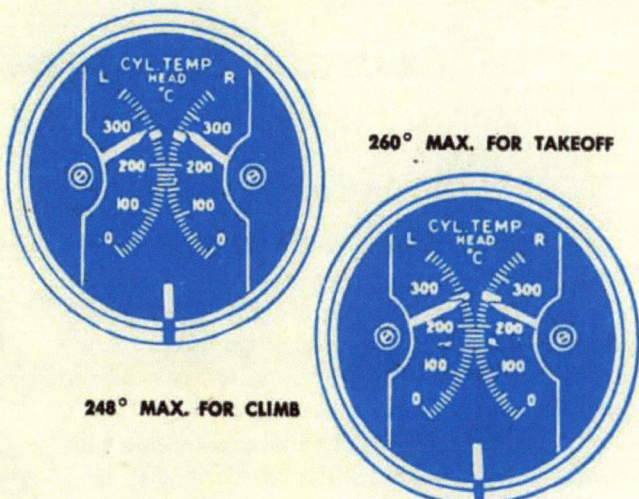

260° MAX. FOR TAKEOFF

248° MAX. FOR CLIMB

Cowl flaps, which are 15° open as the ship takes the runway, are closed to 7½° by the time the airplane leaves the ground. This setting permits rapid acceleration of airspeed and should keep all cylinder-head temperatures below 260°.

If cylinder-head temperatures rise above 260° on takeoff, or stay above 248° after the second power reduction, the flight engineer informs the airplane commander. The airplane commander can then order cowl flaps on the hot engine opened to a maximum of 10°. (Never open cowl flaps more than 10° in flight. Larger openings provide little, if any, additional cooling and reduce cruising ranges considerably.) Or, the airplane commander can pull back the throttle on the hot engine to about 25". The throttle should not be pulled back unless the airplane has reached 170 mph.

Cowl flaps should be set at the smallest opening which keeps cylinder-head temperatures below the required maximum (260° for takeoff; 248° for climb; 232°-248° for cruising—continuous).

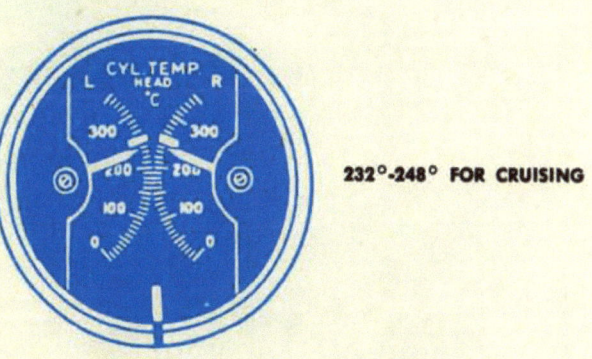

232°-248° FOR CRUISING

NOTE: For night and instrument take-offs, first climb to 500 feet above the terrain with a minimum airspeed of 160 MPH. Then, before continuing the climb, level off until reaching climbing airspeed (195 to 205, depending on weight) and until CHT fall below 248°C.

Takeoff Emergencies

ENGINE FAILURE ON TAKEOFF

Just remember these points if an engine fails on takeoff:

1. Get directional control first (balancing power if necessary), then pick up airspeed before trying to climb.

Because of the large flap area on the B-29, the total or partial loss of an engine on one side creates an unbalanced blast against the flaps which tends to raise one wing and lower the other. Unless you balance power immediately, the ailerons may not be effective enough to counteract this tendency to roll.

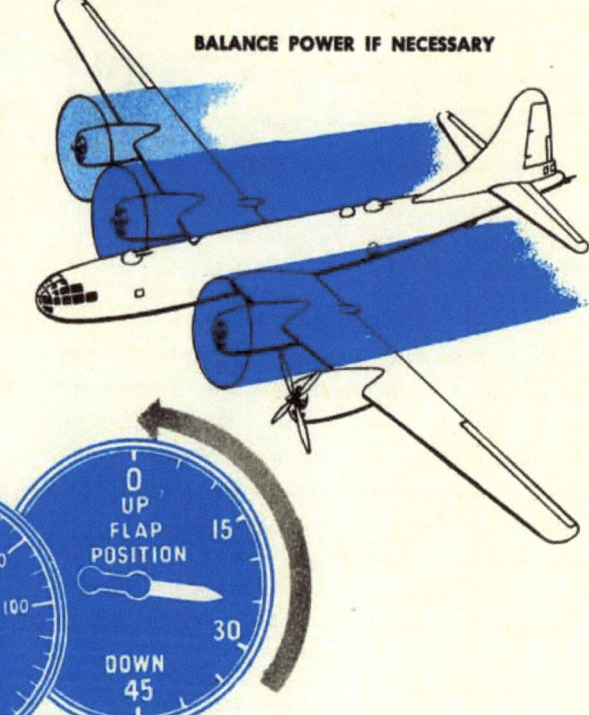

BALANCE POWER IF NECESSARY

RAISE GEAR IMMEDIATELY, RAISE FLAPS AT 150 MPH

2. Drag with gear and flaps down is excessive, so raise gear immediately and bring up flaps at 150 mph, even if gear is not all the way up.

3. If you use turbo position No. 10, reduce power as soon as possible.

4. If two engines fail on takeoff, be prepared to crash land straight ahead.

RESTRICTED

UNDER NO CONDITIONS ATTEMPT A TURN..

until you have balanced power and attained a safe flying speed. If there is no alternative, crash land straight ahead.

RUNAWAY PROPELLER

1. Throttle back.
2. Keep rpm down by using feathering button intermittently and feather propeller completely as soon as a safe altitude is reached.

Note: Don't confuse normal overspeeding of the propellers up to 3150 rpm, caused by a power surge, with a runaway propeller. The governor normally returns an overspeeding propeller to the set speed within a few seconds. Sometimes, after the feathering button has been used to return the propeller to normal rpm, the governor controls the propeller, if the airplane commander is careful not to apply sudden power to the engine. In this case, do not feather the propeller. Just handle the throttles carefully and come in for a landing as soon as possible.

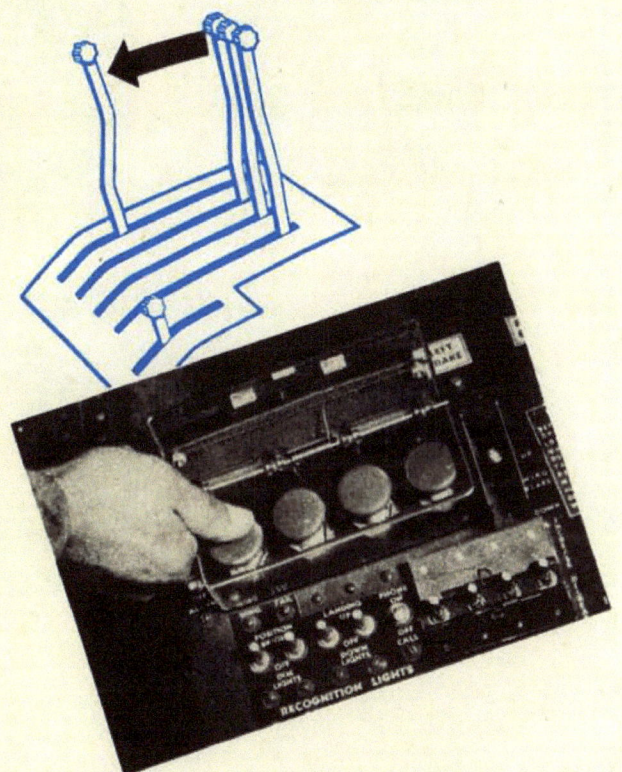

RUNAWAY TURBO

1. Throttle back.
2. Change amplifier (amplifiers mounted forward of navigator's seat).

RESTRICTED

RESTRICTED

CLIMB AND CRUISING

FOR GROSS WEIGHTS UNDER 115,000 LBS. CLIMB AT

39"   2300 RPM   195 MPH

FOR HIGHER GROSS WEIGHTS CLIMB AT RATED POWER:

43½"   2400 RPM   195 TO 205 MPH

Climb

If all cylinder head temperatures run high during a sustained climb, hold the climbing power setting and level off until the cylinder head temperatures return to normal, then start climbing again.

On long-range cruising missions, climb at rated power, regardless of the gross weight. Rated-power climbs use less fuel than climbs at 39" and 2300, provided the cylinder-head temperatures can be maintained within limits during a sustained climb.

If when climbing at high altitudes, 39" and 2300 will not maintain a satisfactory rate of climb, change over to rated power (43½" and 2400).

For takeoff, intercooler flaps are full open. For climb and cruise, open the intercooler flaps enough to get the lowest possible carburetor air temperature. However, if conditions are likely to produce ice, adjust the intercooler flaps to hold the carburetor air temperatures to between 25° and 38°C. With turbos off, intercooler flaps should be completely closed.

RESTRICTED

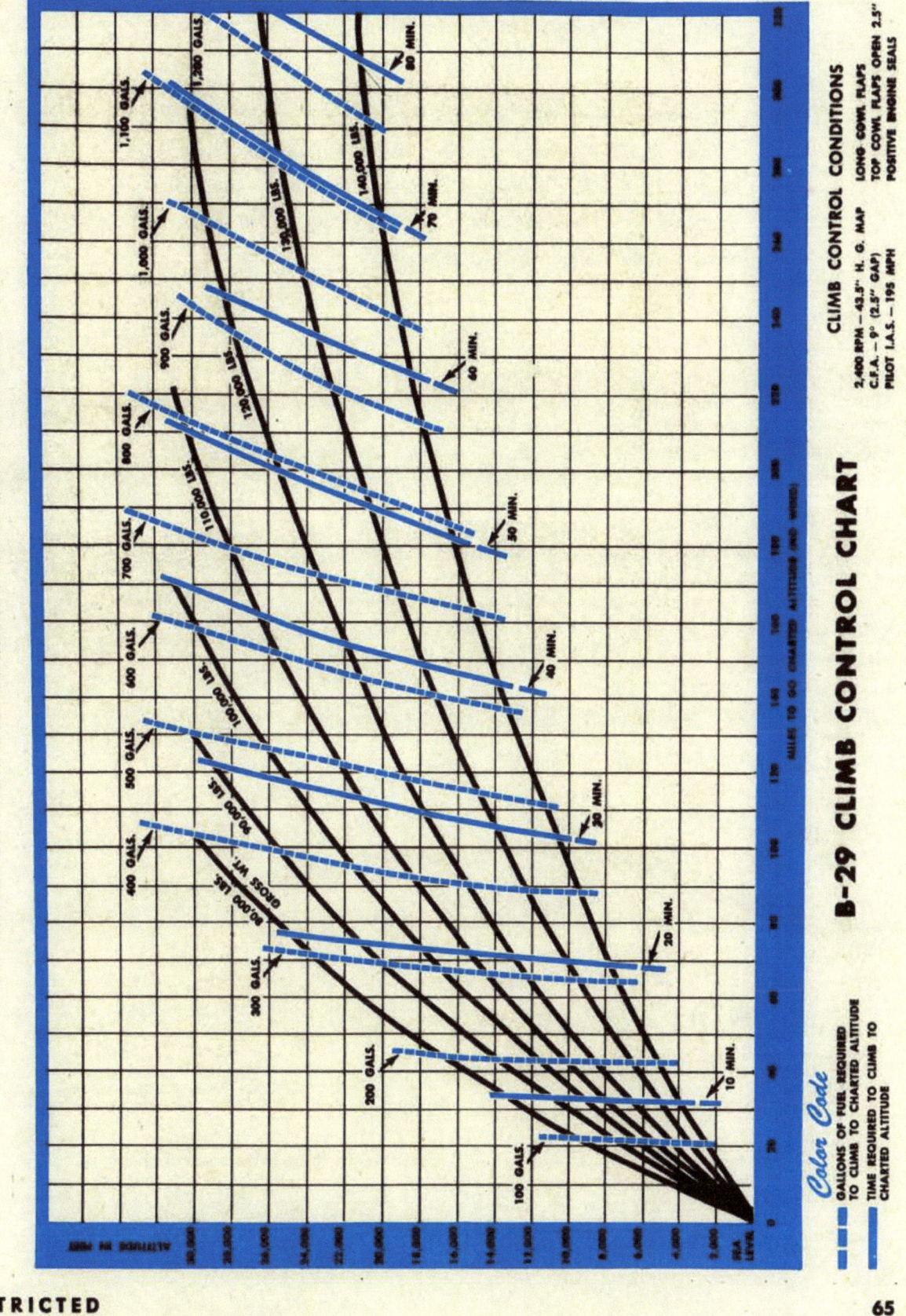

Cruising

For each rpm setting, whether climbing or cruising, there is a definite manifold pressure setting. Using more manifold pressure leads to detonation; using less manifold pressure wastes fuel. Form the habit of using related power settings at all times, and control your cylinder-head temperatures with airspeed.

Before cruising, climb above your desired altitude (500 feet above for altitudes below 10,000; 1,000 feet above for altitudes between 10,000 and 20,000 feet; 1500 feet above for altitudes above 20,000 feet), then hold your climbing power settings at zero rate of climb until reaching 210 mph. An airspeed of 210 mph will put the airplane **on the step.** Then set the predetermined cruising power setting, nose the airplane down slightly, open the cowl flaps to 10°, and descend to desired altitude at 210 mph. When reaching the desired altitude, close the cowl flaps to 3° and use elevators to hold the predetermined cruising airspeed. Vary power setting slightly to maintain your altitude. After you establish airspeed, the cowl flaps may be opened or closed individually to maintain the head temperatures within the safe limits.

The B-29 does not reach its maximum airspeed for a given power setting unless you fly it **on the step.** By setting cowl flap openings as small as possible, by closing the intercooler flaps as soon as turbos are off, and by flying on the step, you should cruise at indicated airspeeds running from 180 to 210 mph, depending on your power settings, gross weight, and altitude. Use mixture control settings of AUTO RICH for power settings above 35" and 2200 rpm or whenever CHT are above 232°. At 35" and 2200 or less, use AUTO LEAN. Never, under any circumstances, set the mixture on MANUAL LEAN—the position between IDLE CUT-OFF and AUTO LEAN.

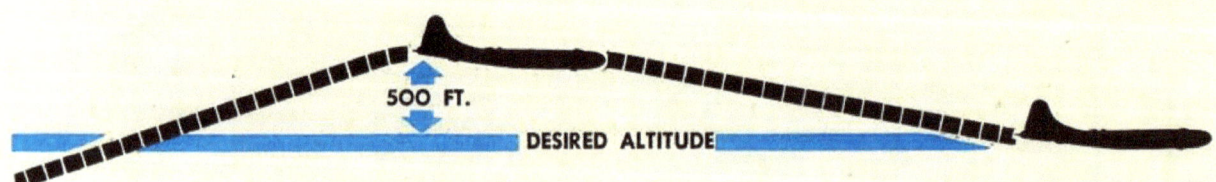

KNOW HOW TO USE YOUR CRUISE CONTROL CHART ▶

To fly your B-29 efficiently, use the power settings indicated in this cruise control chart. Check your flight engineer frequently to make sure he knows how to use it and does use it.

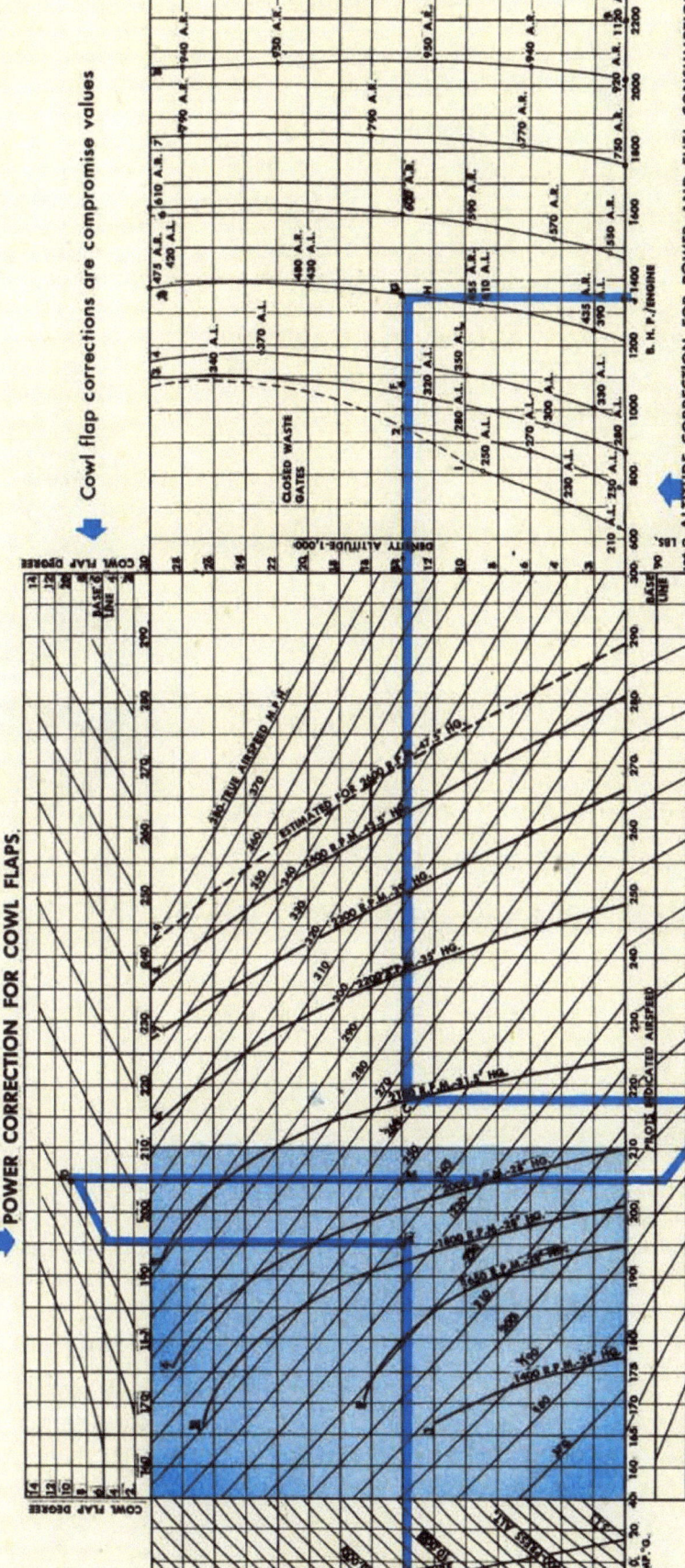

Maximum Endurance

The way to stay in the air the longest possible time is to fly the airplane at the speed where the engines use gasoline at the lowest possible rate. That condition exists when you use the smallest amount of engine power to keep the airplane flying.

Actually the B-29 endurance speed is much higher than the B-17 long-range cruising speed. To get good performance, fly the airplane at a **constant indicated airspeed (IAS).** This means that you must adjust the power to maintain altitude.

The less the airplane weighs and the lower the altitude flown, the longer the airplane stays in the air.

You can obtain maximum endurance by trimming the airplane for the best speed (slightly nose-down) and dropping below the normal cruising power by reducing the rpm and holding the manifold pressure to 28" (plus or minus 2"). Hold 1400 rpm as the absolute minimum. The main reason for using a minimum of 1400 rpm is to avoid losing current from the generators on the engines when flying at low rpm.

TRIM AIRPLANE SLIGHTLY NOSE-DOWN
REDUCE RPM
HOLD MANIFOLD PRESSURE TO 28"

Maximum Range

The B-29 is built to do one particular job well: to fly a long way with a big load of bombs. It has excellent abilities to fly fast and high, but its outstanding tactical ability is long-range bombing.

Maximum range is flown at the speed and altitude that give the greatest mileage from each gallon of gasoline consumed. This is a higher speed than that for maximum endurance. Adding a little more power to the minimum power needed to stay in the air (which also increases fuel flow) produces a fairly large increase in speed and therefore an increase in miles traveled for each gallon of fuel used. As you increase the power further and further, both the speed and the fuel consumption increase. There is one range of speeds in this process, however, where the speed has increased the most while the rate of using gasoline has not increased as much. The middle of this range is about 15 mph, indicated, above the minimum power speed. Going above this speed, the airplane gets fewer miles per gallon of gasoline. Actually, it works out so that there is a fairly wide speed band within which you can obtain maximum miles per gallon. This speed band is normally at least 15 mph, indicated, wide in terms of IAS.

If you fly the airplane within this speed band, you obtain maximum range. The lower portion of this band is difficult to use in formation, and there is no reason to fly at a low speed when a higher one carries the airplane just as far and does it in a shorter time. A headwind decreases the range by its mph value for every hour the airplane flies. You obtain a greater range when flying at the higher end of the speed band in a headwind. For this reason, it is best to cruise at the upper 5-mph portion of this band. The weight of the airplane materially affects the speed, but altitude has no effect upon the indicated speed at which you obtain maximum range.

INDICATED SPEED AT WHICH MAXIMUM RANGE IS OBTAINED WITH HEADWINDS

GROSS WEIGHT	INDICATED AIRSPEED
80,000–90,000 LBS.	180–185 mph
90,000–100,000 LBS.	185–190 mph
100,000–110,000 LBS.	190–195 mph
110,000–120,000 LBS.	195–200 mph
120,000–130,000 LBS.	200–205 mph

When flying for maximum range, hold the speed within one of these speed bands. Obtain the power by adjusting the rpm while holding the manifold pressure to 35" (plus or minus 2") in AUTO LEAN, at 2200 rpm (and below). When in formation, the formation leader should hold the speed at the bottom of the band in order to allow the other airplanes, which will have to make some changes in speed to keep formation, to stay within the economical speed band.

Maximum range, like maximum endurance, is obtained at low altitudes. However, if you operate at powers of 2200 rpm and 35" in AUTO LEAN (or less) in the desired speed band, there is no gain in range by flying at a lower altitude. The range loss at high altitudes is caused almost entirely by the rich mixtures required at high powers and the larger cowl flap openings needed to cool the engines at high altitudes. In general, there is no loss in range up to 15,000 feet and the range losses at higher altitudes occur almost entirely when flying at the highest weights. You can avoid them, to a considerable extent, by flying at low altitudes until fuel has been used and a moderate weight has been obtained and then climbing to a higher altitude.

To obtain maximum range it is necessary to control the airplane's drag and weight. For each 6 lbs. added to the empty weight of the airplane, it is necessary to add one gallon of fuel to get the same range. This increases the gross weight 12 lbs. Every degree of cowl flap opening used above that required to cool the engines increases the fuel used by at least 15 gallons per hour. The airplane is clean and added drag affects it considerably. Everything added to the outside of the airplane, whether it is streamlined or not, adds drag and decreases the range and maximum speed.

If you have difficulty keeping up with the others, it is probably because of extra drag or extra weight. Do not have one of the airplanes which takes more power and gas.

To extend the maximum range, make descents with the recommended long-range cruising speeds and the lowest recommended power setting at the end of a long-range flight.

KEEP YOUR AIRPLANE CLEAN AND LIGHT.

KEEP THE COWL FLAPS AS NEARLY CLOSED AS POSSIBLE AND USE AUTO LEAN IF ENGINE POWERS PERMIT.

USE RECOMMENDED AIRPLANE SPEEDS AND ENGINE POWERS.

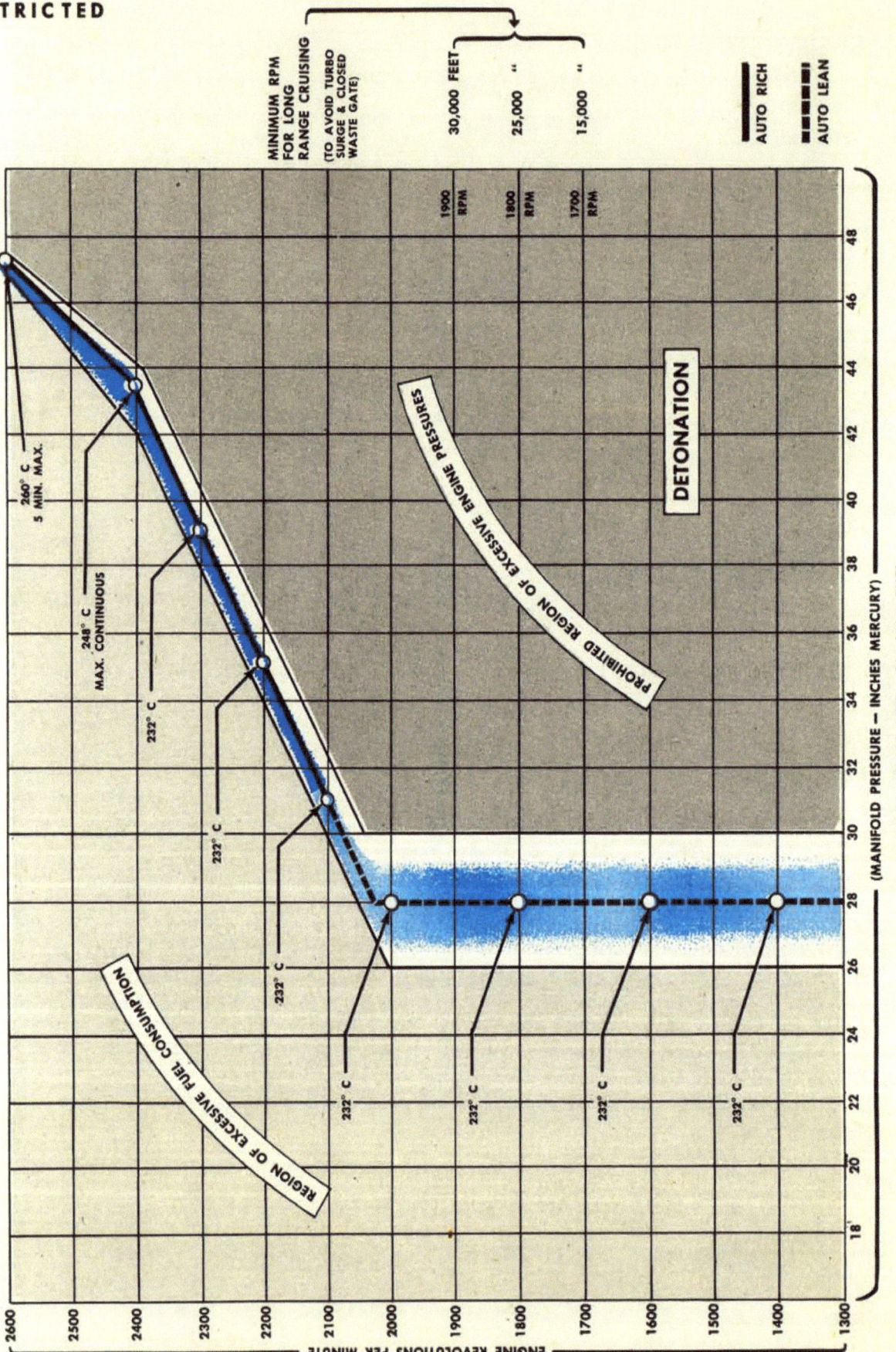

FLIGHT CHARACTERISTICS

Even with its large size and weight, the B-29 has just about the same flying qualities as smaller aircraft. Large aircraft are usually slower in responding to the pilot's controls because of their larger inertia. The control forces on the B-29 are light, and even at low flying speeds the combination of light forces with the high inertia of the airplane seldom gives the pilot any impression of sluggishness or lack of control. Just after taking off, and again during the short interval of time while landing, the rudder and the aileron control response is slow but it is still positive. The controls are as good and in many ways better than those of many small aircraft.

ELEVATORS

The elevator control is almost exactly like that on the B-17. The size of the horizontal tail is exactly the same except that the B-29 elevators have a little more balance and the nose of the tail airfoil section is turned up so that the tail does not stall when making a power-on approach to a landing with the flaps full down. Elevator trim tab is extremely sensitive in high-speed dives, and you must be careful not to over-control the airplane when flying with the trim tab. Overloading of the tail surfaces and other portions of the airplane may occur. Also, avoid diving in rough air.

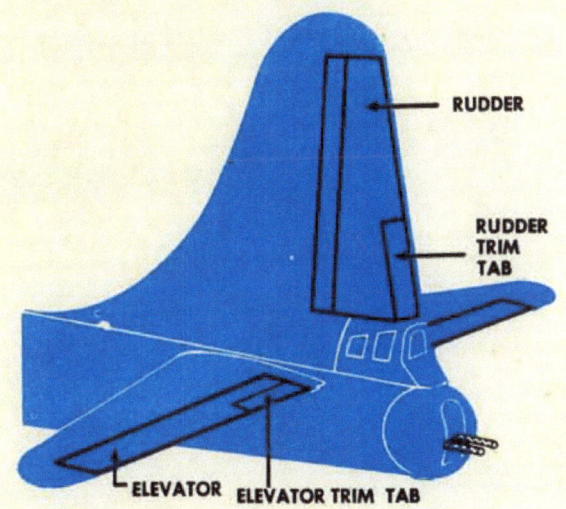

RESTRICTED

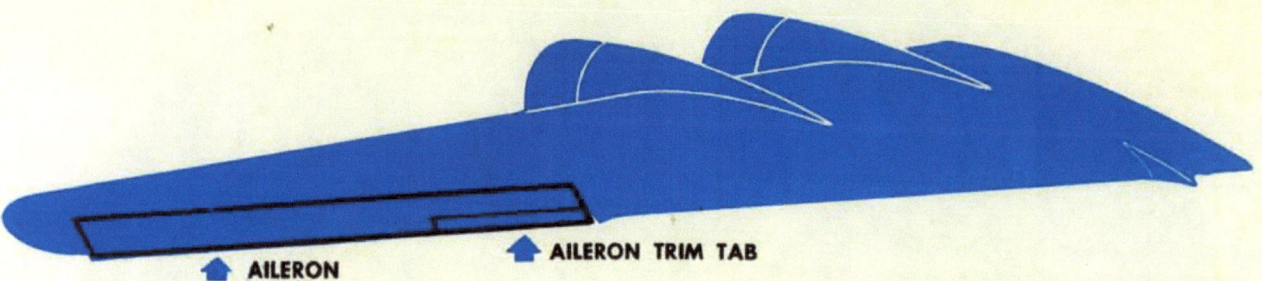

AILERONS

The ailerons are large and can move the largest possible amount (18° up or down), so that the pilot has good control. The control wheel travel is greater than that now on the B-17. This extra control is valuable if an engine fails just after takeoff; or when, for some reason, fuel is used on one side of the airplane only and the other wing gets heavy. The effect of unbalanced amounts of fuel in the two sides is noticeable in the aileron control when flying straight and level. If you allow the speed to approach the stalling speed, the amount of aileron needed to offset uneven wing weights increases rapidly. Don't attempt a landing when this unevenness exists until you check the aileron control in flight at the landing speed.

The aileron trim tabs are geared to move when the ailerons move. The shape of the wing airfoil contour is such that the part covered by the ailerons has a hollow on top and is full on the bottom. If the control cables are cut during combat, the ailerons would ordinarily trim down because of this shape. To avoid this, the trim tabs are rigged down 1 inch at the trailing edge to trim the ailerons more nearly neutral if a cable is cut or broken.

RUDDER

The rudder gives the maximum possible control and stability, yet it can be moved without the help of power boosts. The diamond shape of the rudder is the result of studies made to find a rudder which behaves normally under all flight conditions. A good rudder is one that can be moved with a small amount of effort when an engine fails at any speed and does not become overbalanced or locked. Don't be confused by the light B-29 rudder forces—they do

PRACTICE STALLING AT NOT MORE THAN 15" HG.

ALTITUDE AND FLIGHT PATH OF A B-29 IN A STALL

RESTRICTED

not tell you what the rudder is doing to the airplane. In landing approach conditions, it is possible to get an appreciable amount of skid with slight effort. Remember, it takes a certain amount of time to skid a large airplane and also to stop the skid.

When you trim the rudder, trim it to obtain equal pedal pressures.

STABILITY

The longitudinal stability of the B-29 is normal for all conditions. For good flying characteristics, however, the center of gravity (CG) must be kept within the allowable limits. The forward center of gravity limits are fixed by structural strength, and the elevator control for these forward limits is good for all normal operations. The most rearward center of gravity limit is determined by the longitudinal instability which occurs at climbing power. Going aft of this limit makes the airplane difficult to fly and decreases the safety of the airplane.

Make every possible effort to keep the center of gravity within the design limits and to keep the gross weight of the airplane to the absolute minimum for the mission to be performed. Use a weight-and-balance slide rule before and during every flight.

Stalls

The stall characteristics of the B-29 airplane are entirely normal. In practice, stall the airplane at not more than 15″ Hg. As it approaches the stall, a noticeable lightening of the elevator loads occurs. It is necessary to move the controls an appreciable amount to get a response from the airplane. There is rudder and elevator control during the actual stall, but no aileron control. Just before the full stall is reached, a shuddering and buffeting of the airplane occurs. The airplane recovers from the stall normally and has no excessive tendency to drop off on one wing when the stalls are properly controlled. Power reduces the stalling speed but, in general, has no great effect upon the stall.

Never fly below the power-off stalling speed, since any loss in power when flying below this speed is likely to put the airplane into a violent stall. On all landing approaches, be extremely careful not to allow the speed to fall below the power-off stalling speed. Try power-off approaches whenever possible in order to become familiar with the airplane under emergency conditions. Never use power to reduce your landing speed.

When the airplane stalls, always recover by **first nosing the airplane down** and then increasing the power. Never apply power at the stall without first dropping the nose. In most aircraft, it is possible to obtain a high rate of descent by applying power during the power-off stall without dropping the nose. **Avoid these conditions in the B-29.**

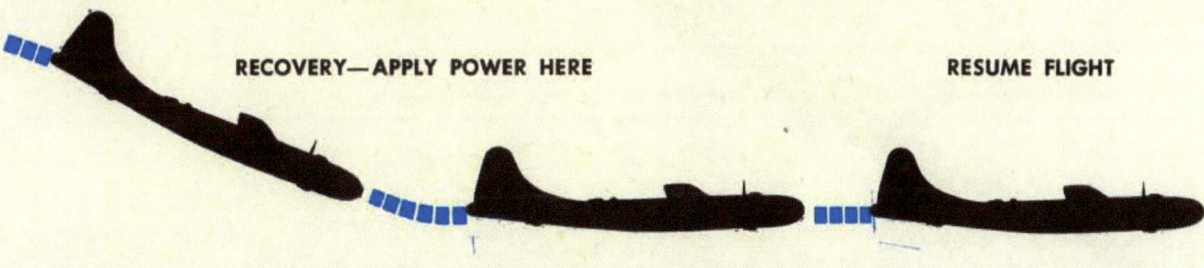

RECOVERY—APPLY POWER HERE   RESUME FLIGHT

POWER-OFF STALLING SPEEDS

GROSS WEIGHT	INDICATED STALLING SPEEDS		
	FLAPS UP	FLAPS 25°	FLAPS FULL
140,000 POUNDS	145 mph	131 mph	119 mph
130,000	140	125	114
120,000	135	121	110
110,000	129	115	105
100,000	123	110	100
90,000	117	104	95
80,000	110	98	89
70,000	103	92	84

WARNING: DO NOT STALL THE AIRPLANE WITH THE COWL FLAPS OPEN MORE THAN 10°

Turns

In spite of its size and weight, the B-29 has good maneuverability. It controls easily and turns easily:

SHALLOW TURN .. ½ NEEDLE ... 12 to 15°

STEEP TURN .. FULL NEEDLE ... 25 to 30°

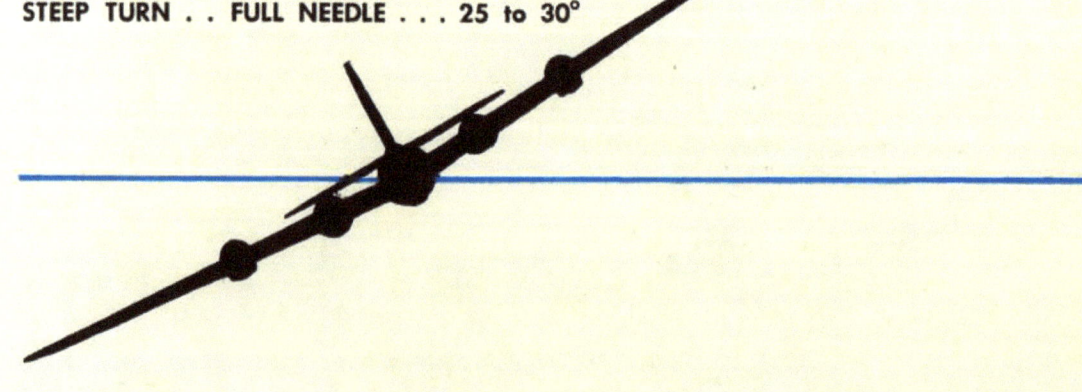

Dives

The B-29 is limited in its allowable diving speed by both strength limitations and control characteristics. Again, remember that this is a big, heavy airplane. As the speed increases, the loads carried by nearly every part of the airplane increase rapidly. This is especially true of the horizontal tail surfaces.

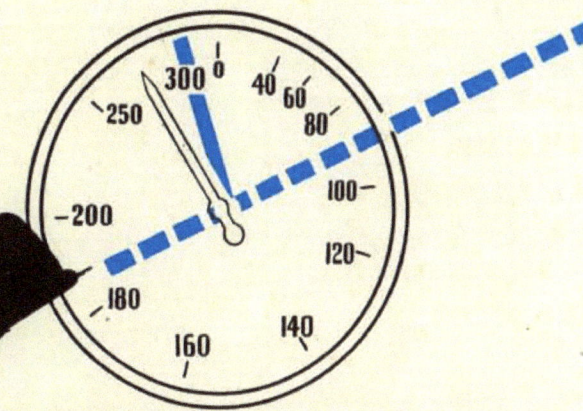

It is red lined at 300 MPH indicated

It is red-lined at ...... 300 mph, indicated.
This speed is sufficiently above the level-flight, top speed of the airplane to cover most diving needs.

At high altitudes, you experience compressibility effects such as buffeting of wings and tail, extremely large elevator trim changes, and control ineffectiveness. For this reason, when flying at high altitude, reduce the red-line speed in accordance with the "altitude-in-thousands—maximum airspeed" table mounted beside the airspeed indicator.

Dead-Engine Characteristics

In straight and level flight, normal power, with one engine feathered and power balanced, the flight characteristics of the B-29 differ little from those of normal 4-engine operation. When turning into a dead engine to the extent of a 180° full needle-width turn, maintain a speed at least 20 to 25 mph, indicated, greater than the power-off stalling speed of the airplane. To avoid trouble, never turn into a dead engine at less than 150 mph, indicated.

If two engines on the same side are out, the airplane has a tendency to roll and yaw. To keep lateral trim, apply aileron; the airplane then crabs, necessitating the use of rudder. It is possible to fly with two dead engines with good control at low weights at speeds down to 150

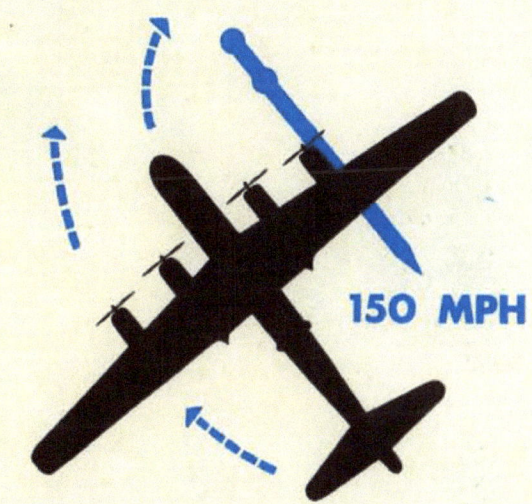

150 MPH

RESTRICTED

mph. However, at slower speeds full rudder is necessary to control the crab. In general, always stay at least 10 mph, indicated, above the power-off stalling speed. Keep the drag of the airplane as small as possible. At 100,000 lbs. gross weight it is just possible to maintain level flight on two engines with two propellers feathered and with the landing gear down and flaps in the approach position.

At 130,000 lb. a similar condition exists with three engines and one feathered.

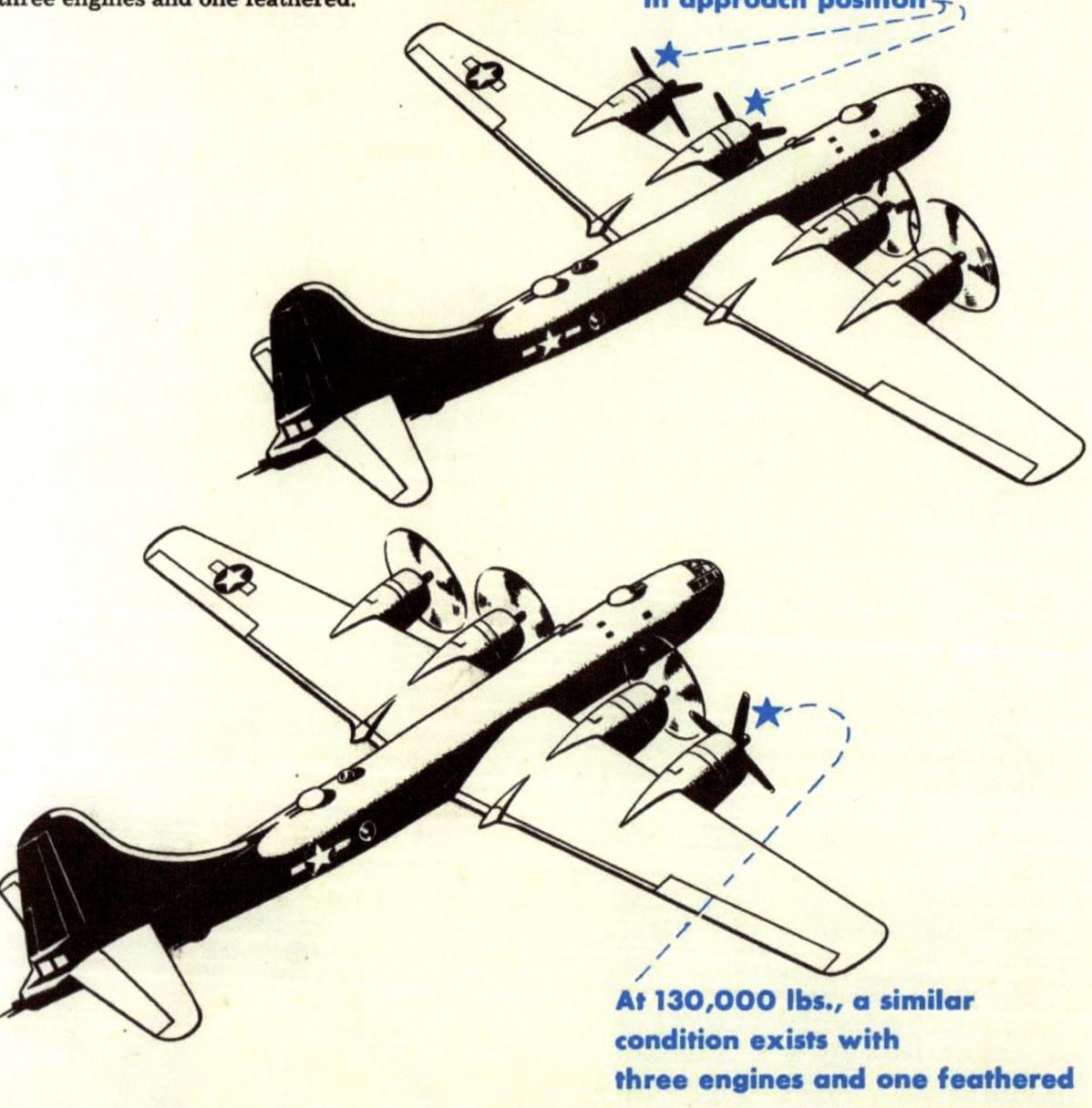

At 100,000 lbs. gross weight it is just possible to maintain level flight on two engines with two propellers feathered and the landing gear and flaps in approach position

At 130,000 lbs., a similar condition exists with three engines and one feathered

RESTRICTED MANEUVERS

The following maneuvers are prohibited:

LOOP   SPIN   IMMELMANN

INVERTED FLIGHT

ROLL    VERTICAL BANK

DIVE 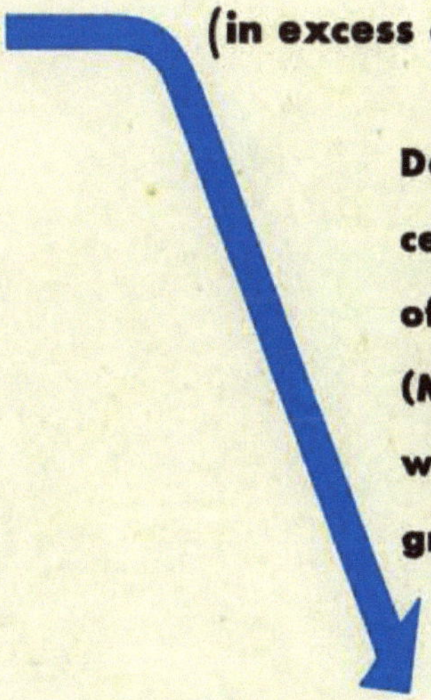   (in excess of red-line speed for the altitude).

Don't fly the airplane with the center of gravity (CG) behind 34% of the mean aerodynamic chord (MAC) at any time, and don't fly with it ahead of 24% except at low gross weights (120,000 lbs.).

LANDING

Before Landing Checklist

1. NOTIFY CREW — PREPARE FOR LANDING

The before-landing check starts on aircraft returning from a mission about 8 to 10 minutes before landing. For transition missions, take-offs can be spaced 10 minutes apart so that the airplane will not have to leave the traffic pattern. The airplane commander announces, "Prepare for landing." Copilot repeats the command over the interphone, at which time the tail gunner starts the putt-putt. Crew members acknowledge in the following order: Bombardier, navigator, flight engineer, radio operator, top gunner, left gunner, right gunner, and tail gunner.

2. RADIO CALL COMPLETED

The airplane commander calls the tower for landing information.

3. ALTIMETERS SET

Airplane commander and copilot set their altimeters to the altimeter setting given by the tower.

4. TRAILING ANTENNA IN

5. AUTOPILOT OFF

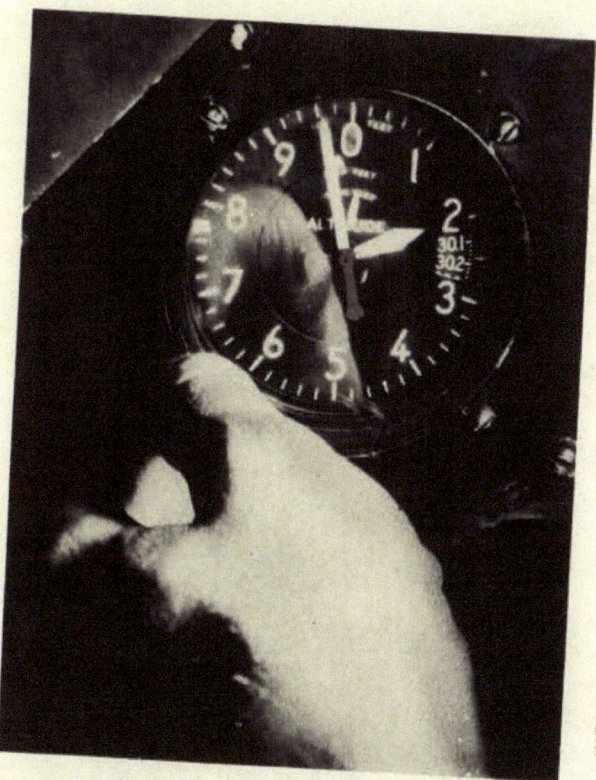

RESTRICTED

6. TURRETS STOWED

7. HYDRAULIC PRESSURE OK

The copilot meters the brake pedals until the pressure falls below 800 psi and checks to see that pressure returns to 1000 psi. Any difference in final pressure should be reported to the flight engineer, as copilot asks him to check emergency hydraulic pressure.

8. PUTT-PUTT ON THE LINE

The copilot checks with the tail gunner to make sure that the putt-putt is on the line.

9. PROPELLERS 2400 RPM

The copilot adjusts propellers to 2400 rpm before airplane commander reduces power.

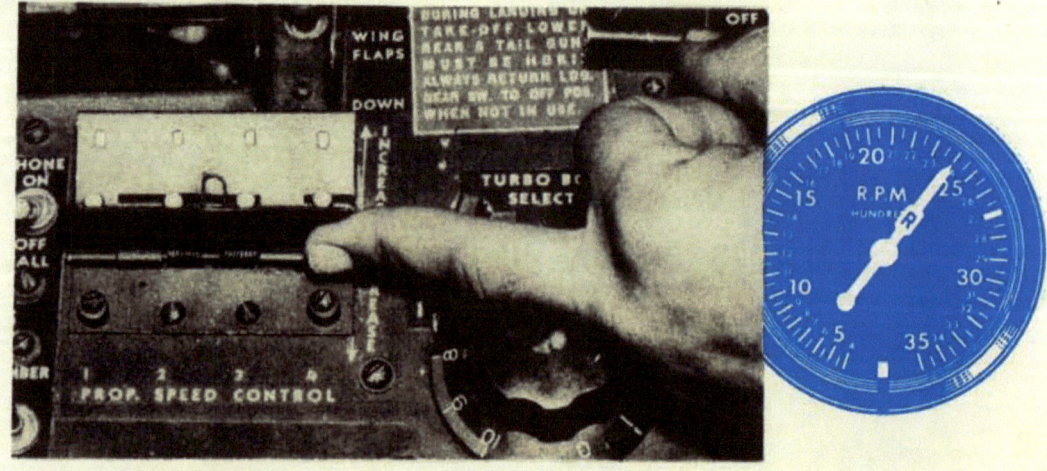

10. LANDING GEAR DOWN AND LIGHTS ON

The copilot, on command of the airplane commander, lowers the landing gear. The side gunners check the main gear and announce in order, "Left gear down and locked," and, "Right gear down and locked." The copilot checks the nosewheel through the observation window in the floor of the cockpit and checks the landing gear warning lights on his instrument panel. Copilot announces, "Nosewheel down and locked."

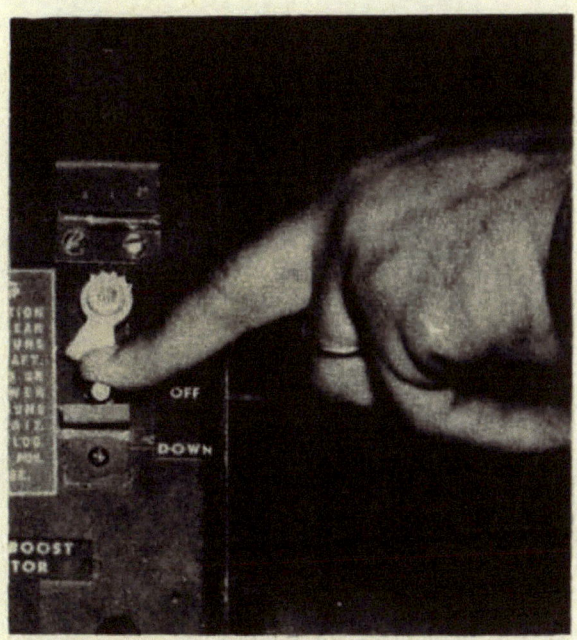

Note: The IAS must be less than 180 mph before the gear is lowered.

The visual check by the gunners and the copilot is most important. The red warning light and the green down and locked lights (and the landing gear warning horn, on early models) all operate from the gear-motor limit switches. Remember this—the lights and the horn are not position indicators. They mean only that the limit switches have stopped the operation of the gear motors. If the switches open the circuits too soon, the gear is only partly down and warning of this danger can come only from the visual check. The gear supports the weight of the airplane if the retracting screw is not more than 4 inches from the full-down position (the screw itself retracts as the gear lowers). The gear is not designed to support the airplane if the screw is extended more than 4 inches.

11. FLIGHT ENGINEER'S REPORT

The flight engineer gives the weight and center of gravity (CG) figures to the copilot.

12. STALL SPEED

The copilot finds the stalling speed based on the weight by referring to the table mounted on his instrument panel and informs the airplane commander.

13. WING FLAPS

At the airplane commander's command, the copilot extends the wing flaps 25° just before turning into the base leg. Later, on the final approach and at the airplane commander's command, he extends full flaps, at which point the airplane commander retrims the elevators. The side gunners check position of flaps and inform the copilot over the interphone.

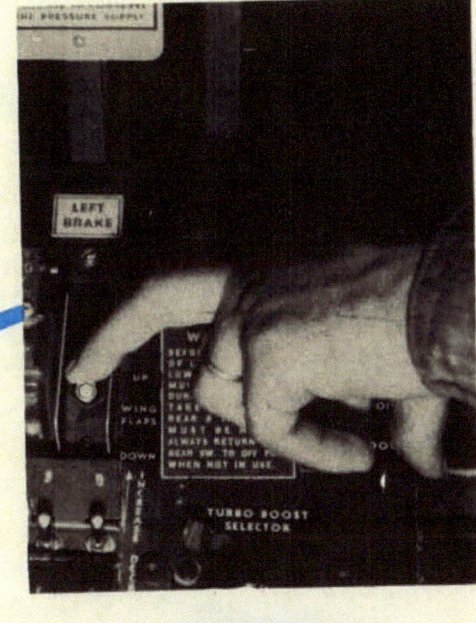

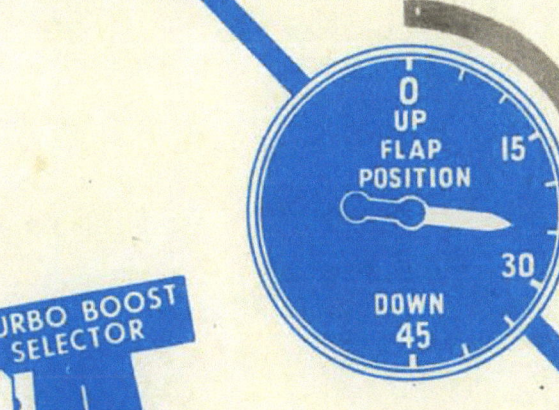

14. TURBOS ON NO. 8

Airplane commander calls for turbos on base leg. Copilot announces, "Turbos on," to flight engineer and turns selector dial to 8.

Landing Procedure

Don't put down full flaps until you are lined up with runway and sure of making the field. Go-arounds are difficult only when full flaps are down. After putting down full flaps, maintain an airspeed of 30 mph, indicated, above the power-off stalling speed. Don't chop the power at any point on the approach.

Long approaches are not necessary, even when landing on narrow runways, but the base leg is normally placed farther out than for a B-17 or a B-24.

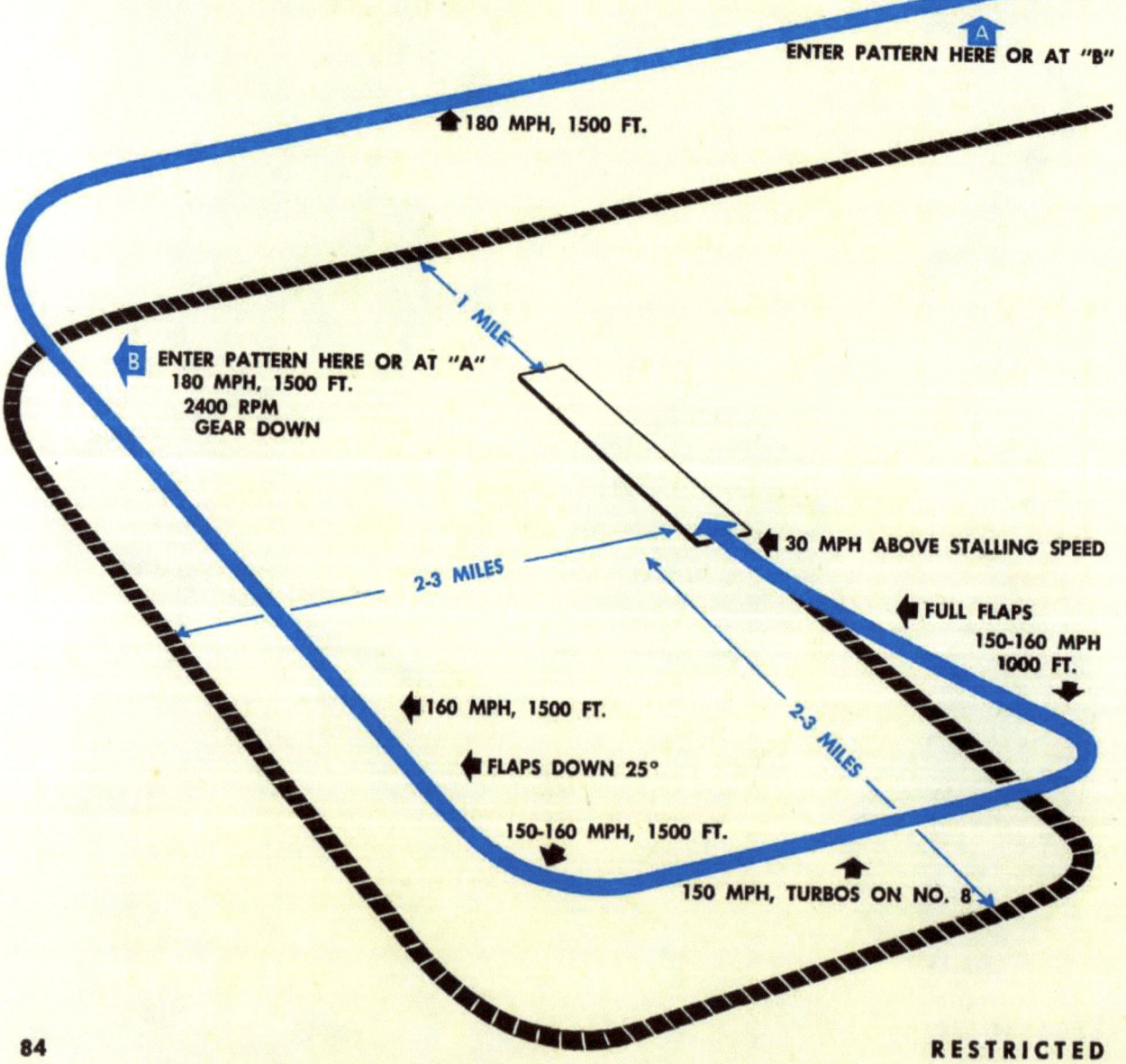

CROSSWIND LANDINGS

Although there is good aileron, rudder, and elevator control throughout the landing approach, remember that the B-29, because of its weight and size, is slow to respond to control movements. When making a crosswind landing, lower the wing on the upwind side and then raise it just before the wheels touch by applying a little throttle to the outboard engine on the low side. Make fairly long approaches on crosswind landings to give ample time to make drift corrections.

LANDING ROLL

Don't use your brakes more than necessary after the wheels touch the ground. On a long runway, let the airplane roll until it loses speed. Lower the nose gently at 90 mph, and when nearing end of runway, apply brakes evenly and smoothly. Toward the end of the landing roll, the copilot sets the turbo selector to 0, sets high rpm, and sets throttles at 700 rpm for taxiing.

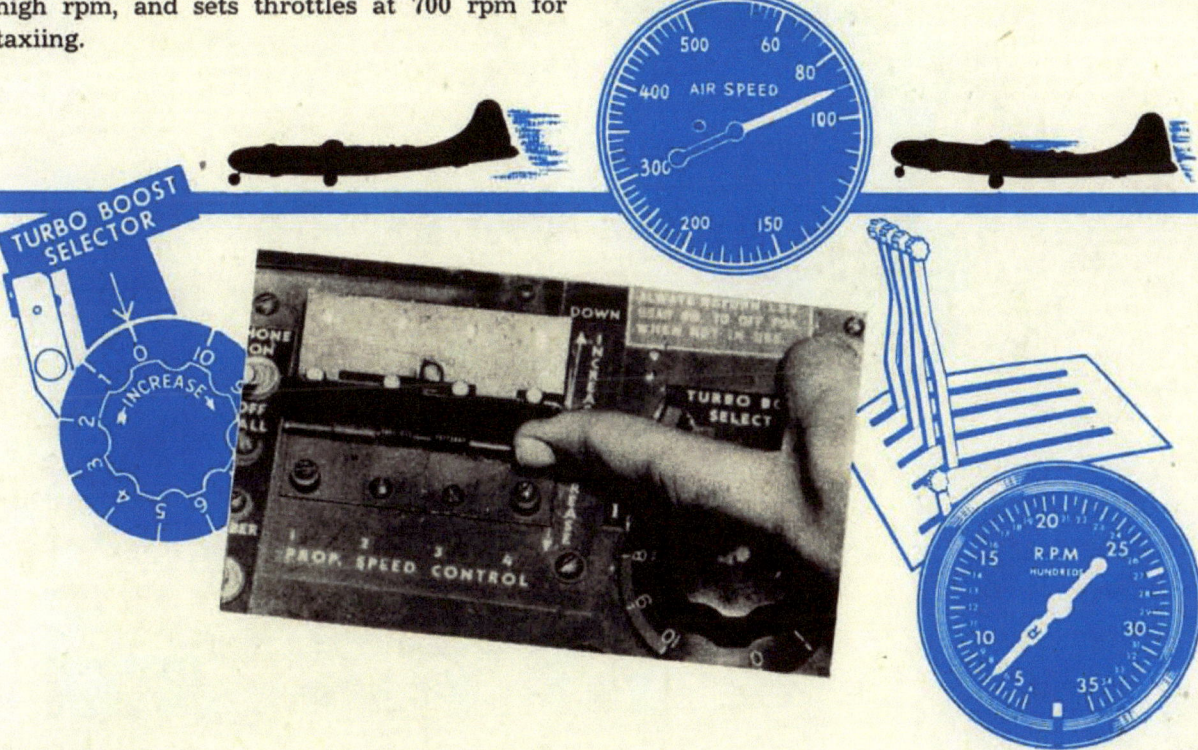

RESTRICTED

After Landing

1. HYDRAULIC PRESSURE

Copilot checks normal pressure gage for reading between 800 and 1000 psi.

2. TURBOS OFF

3. PROPELLERS IN HIGH RPM

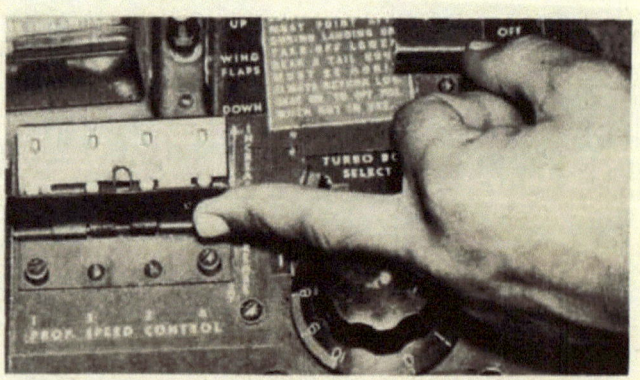

RESTRICTED

RESTRICTED

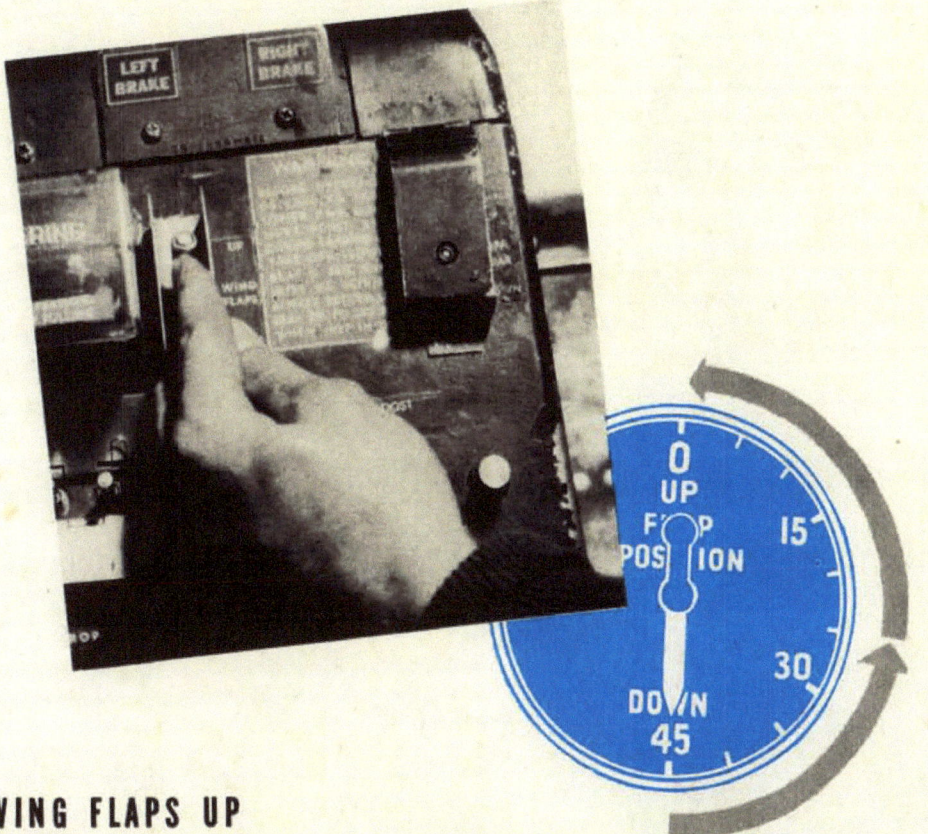

4. WING FLAPS UP

At the airplane commander's command, near the end of the landing roll, copilot raises flaps (all the way, if this is the last landing; to 25° if planning to make another takeoff). Side gunners report on position of wing flaps.

5. PARKING BRAKES SET

6. BOMB BAY DOORS OPEN

Copilot calls for bomb bay doors open. Copilot says on interphone, "Open bomb bay doors." Flight engineer sets throttle on coolest engine to 1400 rpm. The radio operator and one of the gunners check through the pressure doors and report to pilot that doors are open. Flight engineer then returns throttle to 700 rpm and turns all generators off. (Generator procedure unnecessary with snap-opening bomb bay doors.)

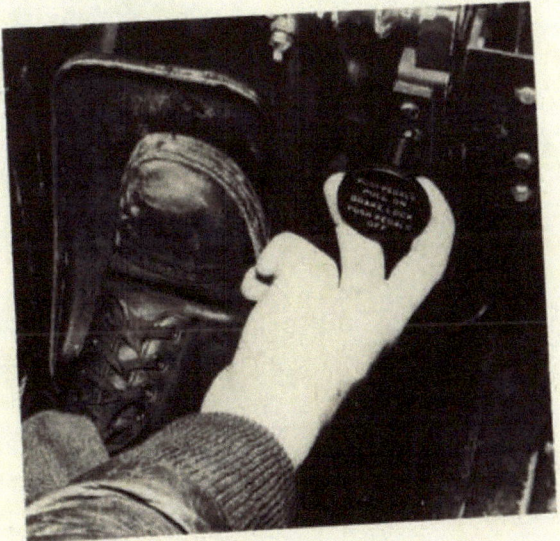

7. MAGNETOS CHECKED

The flight engineer checks all magnetos at 2000 rpm.

RESTRICTED

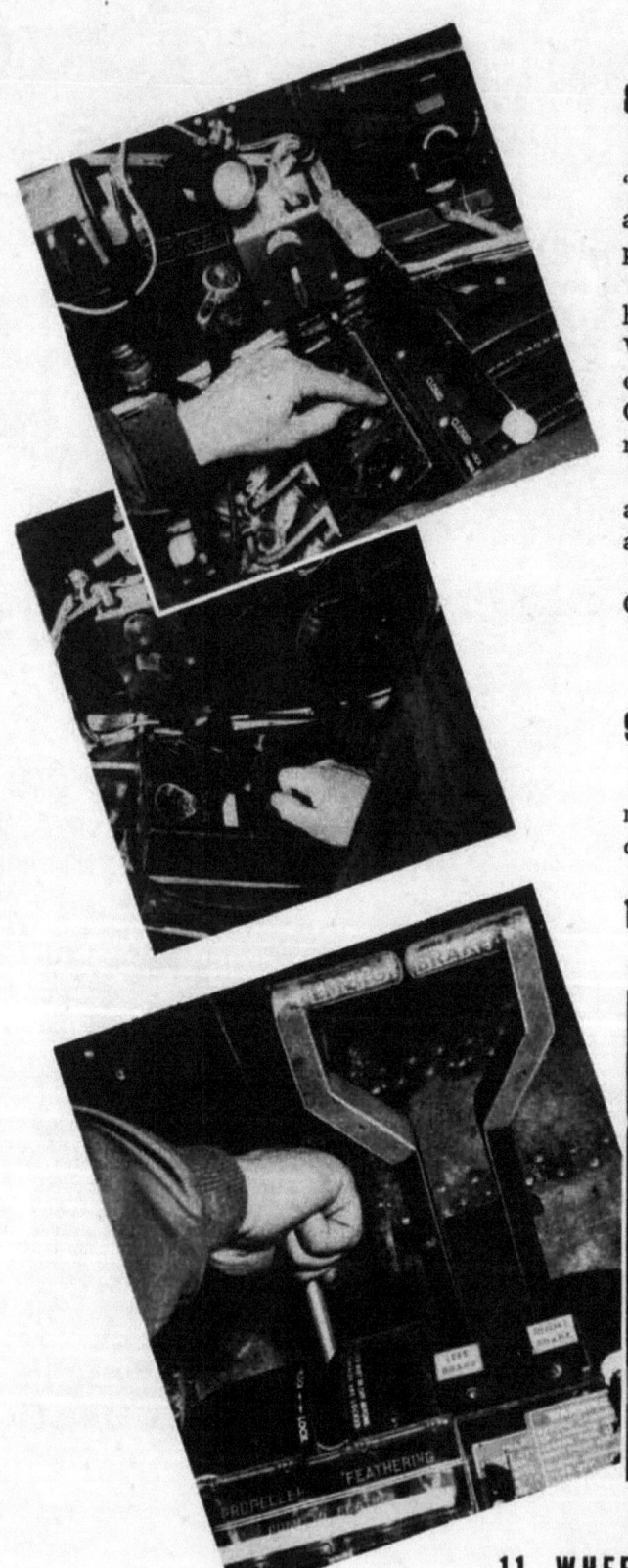

8. ENGINES CUT

The airplane commander gives the order, "Cut engines," to the flight engineer, who cuts all engines simultaneously, using the following procedure:

a. Runs engines at 700 rpm until cylinder-head temperatures drop (190°C, if possible). While engines are cooling at 700 rpm, flight engineer flips master ignition switch to the OFF position momentarily to see that all magnetos are grounded out.

b. Increases throttle settings to 1200 rpm and runs each engine for at least 30 seconds at this speed.

c. Moves the mixture controls to IDLE CUT-OFF.

d. Cut switches after propellers stop turning.

e. Orders tail gunner to stop putt-putt.

9. RADIOS OFF

The airplane commander turns off the command set and the copilot switches off the radio compass.

10. CONTROLS LOCKED

11. WHEEL CHOCKS IN PLACE—BRAKES OFF

12. FORMS 1 AND 1A ACCOMPLISHED

The flight engineer completes Forms 1 and 1A and presents them to the airplane commander for check.

13. CREW INSPECTION

Crew members leave the airplane and line up as before to be checked by the airplane commander. At this time, defects in the airplane not already noted are reported to the flight engineer.

Go-Around

The procedure for a normal go-around is not complicated. Raise the flaps from the full-down position to 25° as power is applied and continue on the same approach angle until a safe flying speed is reached. Then raise the gear as soon as you are sure that the runway will not be touched, and ease the nose of the airplane up. Raising the flaps all in one movement to 25° is important. Don't wait for a safe flying speed—with the flaps full down, you cannot attain a safe flying speed because of the high full-flap drag and reduced acceleration. Follow this procedure:

1. Notify flight engineer that you are going around.
2. Apply throttle gradually as needed.
3. Raise flaps to 25°.
4. Set full high rpm.
5. Don't try to climb until reaching a safe flying speed.
6. Raise gear when safely clear of the ground.
7. Proceed as in a normal takeoff.
8. If needed, apply emergency power by advancing the turbo selector knob to No. 10.

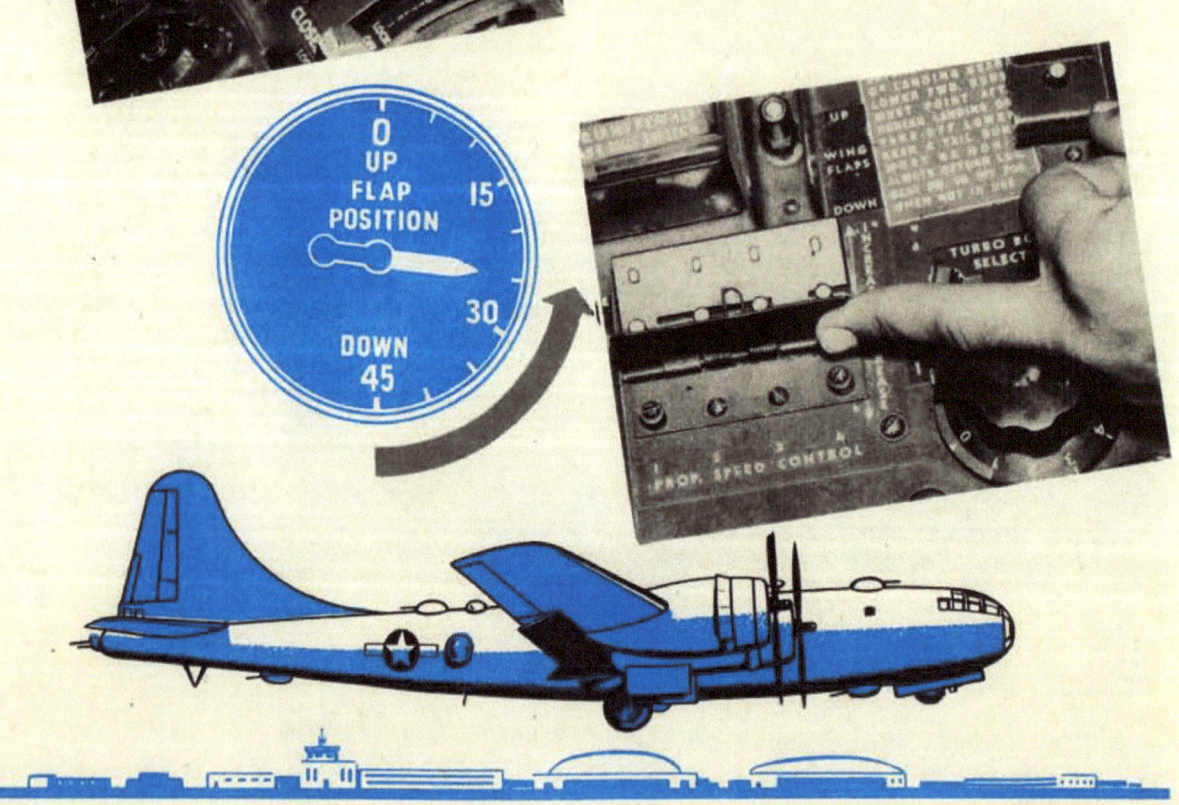

NIGHT FLYING

Don't fall for the belief, common among less experienced fliers, that "night flying is no different from day flying." Night flying **is different** from day flying. Your vision at night is different because you are using a different part of your eye (see **Physiology in Flight** and AAF Memorandum 25-5). Unless lights are properly grouped (as on runways) or easily identifiable (horizons, large cities, towns, etc.), your visual references are diminished considerably. Finally, when visibility is reduced and you have no clearly defined horizon, night flying is **instrument flying.**

ILLUSIONS IN NIGHT FLYING

Night flying can be much more confusing than simple instrument flight through clouds. Probably many of the accidents and fatalities that occur in night flying result from the fact that pilots rely too much on their vision and other senses rather than upon instruments. (See T.O. 30-100A-1.)

The inexperienced pilot is continually looking for some light on the ground by which he can orient himself. Unless he is flying near a large city where there are enough lights to make a good pattern, this practice of trying to orient himself in relation to the terrain is extremely hazardous. Many experienced pilots can tell how they have mistaken a star for a light beneath them, or how they thought lights were moving past when actually their airplane was turning about the lights.

The reason for the particular confusion in night flying is that a pilot's eyes may deceive him. He does not have any definite horizon to use as a plane of orientation; he has only isolated points of light. His sensations may tell him that these light-points are in a certain position in relation to the airplane, when in fact they are in a completely different relation. As a result, when the airplane does not react as he expects it to, he becomes completely confused. In addition, the inexperienced pilot usually forgets his instruments and is so busy looking around that he glances at the instrument panel only after he has become confused and is already in a bad situation.

The only solution for this is to watch the instrument panel, with only occasional glances out at the visual reference points. In night flying, use instruments as your major reference, scattered lights as a secondary reference.

TIPS ON NIGHT VISION

Before flight don't subject your eyes to any bright lights: brightly lighted rooms, wing light beams, bright cockpit lights, etc.

Turn out all unnecessary cockpit lights, dim instrument panel lights.

Read instruments, maps, charts rapidly; then look away.

RESTRICTED

Know your field layout, the proper relationship of taxi strips to runways, etc. It is easy to become confused at night.

NIGHT VISION PRECAUTIONS

Be sure that goggles, side windows, and wind screens are kept scrupulously clean. Scattered light on unclean surfaces reduces the contrast between faint lights and their background.

Be sure that all fluorescent lights, wing lights, navigation lights, passing light, cockpit light and individual instrument lights are in operating order.

Be sure that you, the copilot, and flight engineer have individual flashlights.

Check radio operation and set proper frequencies. You need your radio, especially at night.

TAKEOFF

On all night takeoffs climb to 500 feet above the terrain before levelling off to build up airspeed.

Obtain clearance from the tower before taxiing to the runway. Line up in the center of the runway and select a distant light as a reference point.

If visibility is poor and no horizon is visible, prepare to take off on instruments.

Maintain proper airspeed and a constant heading. It is imperative to hold a constant heading until you reach sufficient altitude for the turn.

Top and side gunners should warn you if you are turning into the path of other aircraft.

RESTRICTED

NIGHT LANDINGS

1. Fly compass headings on the different legs of the traffic pattern.

2. To line up properly with the runway and avoid overshooting or undershooting, begin a medium turn on the final approach **when the runway lights seem to separate.** On the downvents stalling out high. Carry power until you are sure of making contact with the ground. Avoid cutting power too high or too soon.

7. Check generators and batteries for proper operation. They carry a heavier load at night.

8. Check putt-putt for operation in possible emergency. It should be on for all takeoffs and landings.

TURN INTO APPROACH FROM BASE LEG WHEN RUNWAY LIGHTS SEPARATE INTO TWO ROWS

wind and base legs, the runway lights seem to be in a single row. As the airplane comes nearer to the runway on the base leg, the lights begin to separate into two rows. **This is the time to start the turn onto the approach.**

3. Avoid a low approach at night. Maintain constant glide, constant airspeed, constant rate of descent by making slight changes in power and attitude.

4. Don't turn on landing lights while too high; they become effective at 500 feet.

5. Don't try to sight down the landing light beam. Use the whole lighted area ahead and below for reference. Don't rely on landing lights alone; use runway lights as secondary reference. Wing lights alone may induce you to level off for landing too late. Runway lights alone may cause you to level off too high, especially if there is haze or dust over the field.

6. If you are uncertain of your final approach, carry a little more power. This pre-

TAXIING PRECAUTIONS

1. When taxiing use the landing lights alternately as needed. This reduces the load on the electrical system imposed by both lights. Also, continuous gound operation of the lights burns them out quickly. However, don't hesitate to use both lights if necessary.

2. Make frequent checks of wheels and tires.

3. Check for signs of engine roughness.

4. When taxiing close to obstructions or parked aircraft, see that members of the ground crew walk ahead of each wing and direct taxiing by means of light signals.

5. Be particularly careful in judging distance from other taxiing aircraft. Sudden closure of distance is difficult to notice at night.

6. In case of failure or weakening of brakes, stop immediately and have the airplane towed to the line. Faulty brakes are always hazardous. They are certain to cause accidents when taxiing at night.

FORMATION FLYING

Skillful flying in large formations requires the airplane commander to be alert at the controls at all times. To foresee and anticipate each movement of the formation calls for teamwork. Smooth operation of the flight controls is important. Each member's motion in the team depends on the changing speeds of the others in the formation ahead. Overcome the tendency to over-run or fall behind by anticipating the action of your airplane and the others in the formation.

For increasing speed there are two methods at the airplane commander's disposal: First, to increase the power; second, to dive the airplane slightly. For decreasing the speed, reduce the power or climb the airplane. Never use the cowl flaps, wing flaps, or landing gear to increase the drag for slowing down.

In some cases, it is necessary to increase power. In formation flying, the lead plane must set up the cruising conditions according to the operating charts. The bottom end of the long-range speed band, explained under long-range flying, is the correct place for the lead plane. The wing planes should set their rpm from 100 to 200 higher than the lead plane at manifold pressures recommended for these rpm and then reduce the manifold pressures with the boost control to get the desired speed. In high altitude formations, reductions in turbo boost are limited by the amount of boost required for cabin pressure. Set the boost and the inboard throttles to give the desired power, then use the outboard throttles to stay in formation. The mixture control should be set the same for all airplanes and it should be the setting recommended for the power setting of the lead airplane except when the lead plane is using 2200 rpm or more; then it should be AUTO RICH.

The response of the airplane to changes in power varies considerably with different loadings and different altitudes. Supposing a formation of B-29's, average weight of 105,000 lbs.,

TO GAIN SPEED, INCREASE THROTTLE...

...OR DIVE SLIGHTLY.

is cruising for a long range at 25,000 feet altitude, and after a maneuver, one airplane finds itself 100 yards behind its assigned position. In order to catch up, the airplane commander may apply rated power. The total time for him to gain 100 yards and get back into position is 35 seconds. Under similar conditions, he is able to repeat the same maneuver at 5000 feet in 25 seconds. The reason for the difference in time is that there is more power available for accelerating at low altitudes than at high altitudes since less of the available power is required to cruise at low altitudes than at high altitudes. When flying with 130,000 lbs. at 25,000 feet, it is difficult to accelerate the airplane rapidly.

Changes in altitude are helpful in changing the speed only when the change is needed momentarily. For instance, if a large formation makes a turn where inside planes must slow down and the outside planes must speed up, the outside planes can gain speed by diving slightly and the inside planes can lose speed by climbing slightly. Coming out of the turn, the outside plane may still have too much speed and that can be eliminated by climbing a little more. However, the wing planes are not able to get back to their former level until a turn is made in the opposite direction. Such a procedure may not always work; but it should be used, if at all possible, for such maneuvers as flak evasion. It is believed that this procedure provides better fuel consumption. A gain or loss in altitude of 100 feet momentarily drops or picks up speed from 3 to 5 mph, indicated. Of course, such altitude changes can be only used in large or reasonably open formations.

Formation Signals

ASSUME NORMAL FORMATION

SIGNAL: Rock the wings. A slow, repeated rocking motion of the airplane around its longitudinal axis. Wing movement to be slower and of greater amplitude than in "Flutter Ailerons."

MEANING: Assume normal formation. From any other formation, go into normal closed-up formation.

OPEN UP FORMATION

SIGNAL: Fishtail or yaw. By rudder control, cause the airplane to move alternately and repeatedly right and left.

MEANING: Open up formation. Where applicable, this signal may be used to order a search formation.

ATTENTION

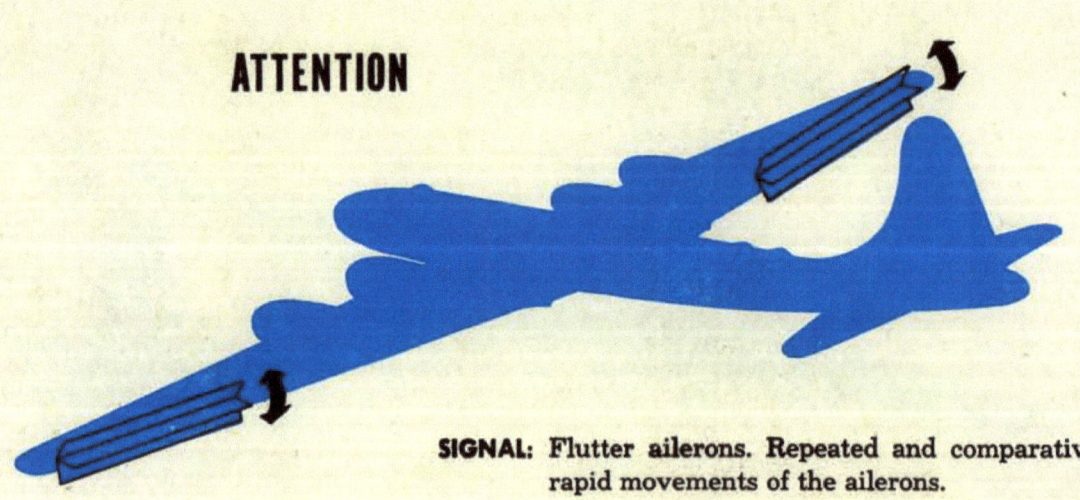

SIGNAL: Flutter ailerons. Repeated and comparatively rapid movements of the ailerons.

MEANING: Attention. This signal is used on the ground and in the air to attract the attention of all pilots. Airplane commanders should stand by for radio messages or further messages. When on the ground in proper position to take off, the signal means "Ready to take off."

CHANGE FORMATION

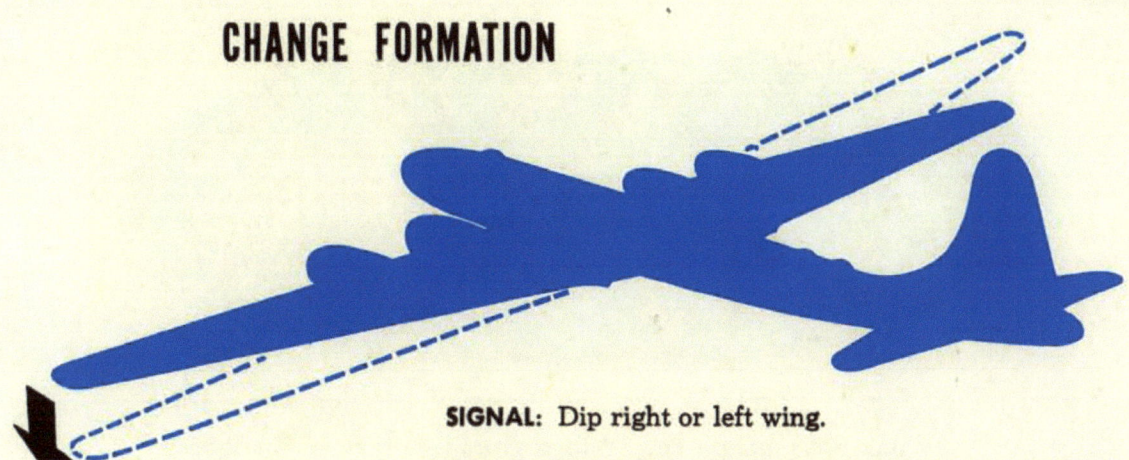

SIGNAL: Dip right or left wing.

MEANING: Change formation. (a) From any formation other than echelon, go into echelon of flights to the right or left. (b) If in echelon of flights, right or left, go into echelon of individual airplanes to the same side. (c) If in echelon of individual airplanes, go into echelon of flights on the same side if the wing is dipped to the side on which the aircraft are echeloned. (d) If in echelon of flights or individual airplanes and wing is dipped on side away from echelonment, form same echelon to the opposite side.

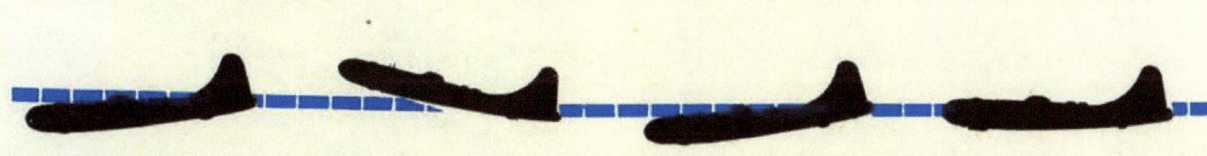

PREPARE TO LAND

SIGNAL: Series of small dives or zooms.

MEANING: Prepare to land. This signal is an order to each airplane commander in the formation to take the necessary steps preparatory to landing. In the absence of additional signals, land in the normal landing formation of the unit. Any change in the landing formation is given by radio or Aldis lamp.

PROPELLER FEATHERING

Think twice before you feather a propeller under emergency conditions, such as engine failure on takeoff or landing. Feather a propeller only when you are sure that the engine is creating a drag. Remember, even an idling engine delivers some thrust at relatively low speeds. On take-off it may be delivering just enough to mean the difference between crash landing and going around. Even if a crash landing is inevitable, do not feather propellers. Balance the power and land straight ahead.

The B-29 propeller feathering system uses engine oil pumped by an electric motor into the propeller dome. If the damaged engine loses oil to the extent that there is a drop in oil pressure, a 3-gallon oil reservoir installed on later B-29's supplies enough oil for feathering and unfeathering once. (An airplane that has this reservoir is easily identified by the fact that the feathering pump is directly beneath the main oil tank.) Under normal flight conditions, feather the propeller at the first visual signs that an engine is losing all of its oil.

Remember, when engine oil is lost, the propeller governor ceases to function and centrifugal force automatically moves the blades into low pitch. The propeller then windmills in low pitch and the speed at which it rotates depends on the altitude and the airspeed.

As an example, if you are operating on three engines at 25,000 feet and 233 mph, true airspeed, and the dead-engine propeller is windmilling in low pitch, it is turning approximately 4000 rpm. (See accompanying chart for vari-

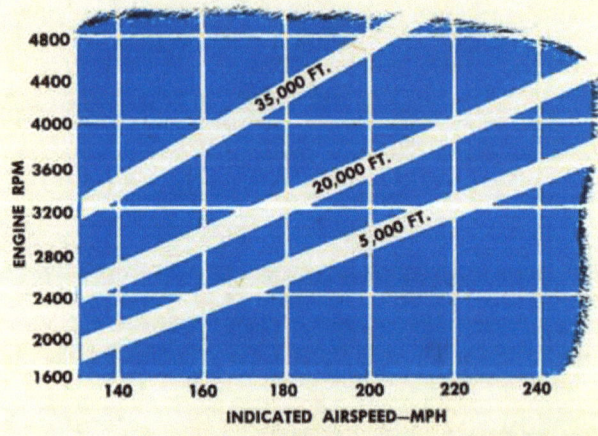

APPROXIMATE PROPELLER WINDMILLING SPEED

ances caused by altitude and airspeed.) Since high windmilling speeds can cause centrifugal explosion of the propeller or destruction of the engine, a combination of reduction in power and altitude is necessary. When you reach a lower altitude, you can resume cruising speed for safe flight back to the base without undue fear that the windmilling propeller will exceed the normal rpm limits.

Feathering

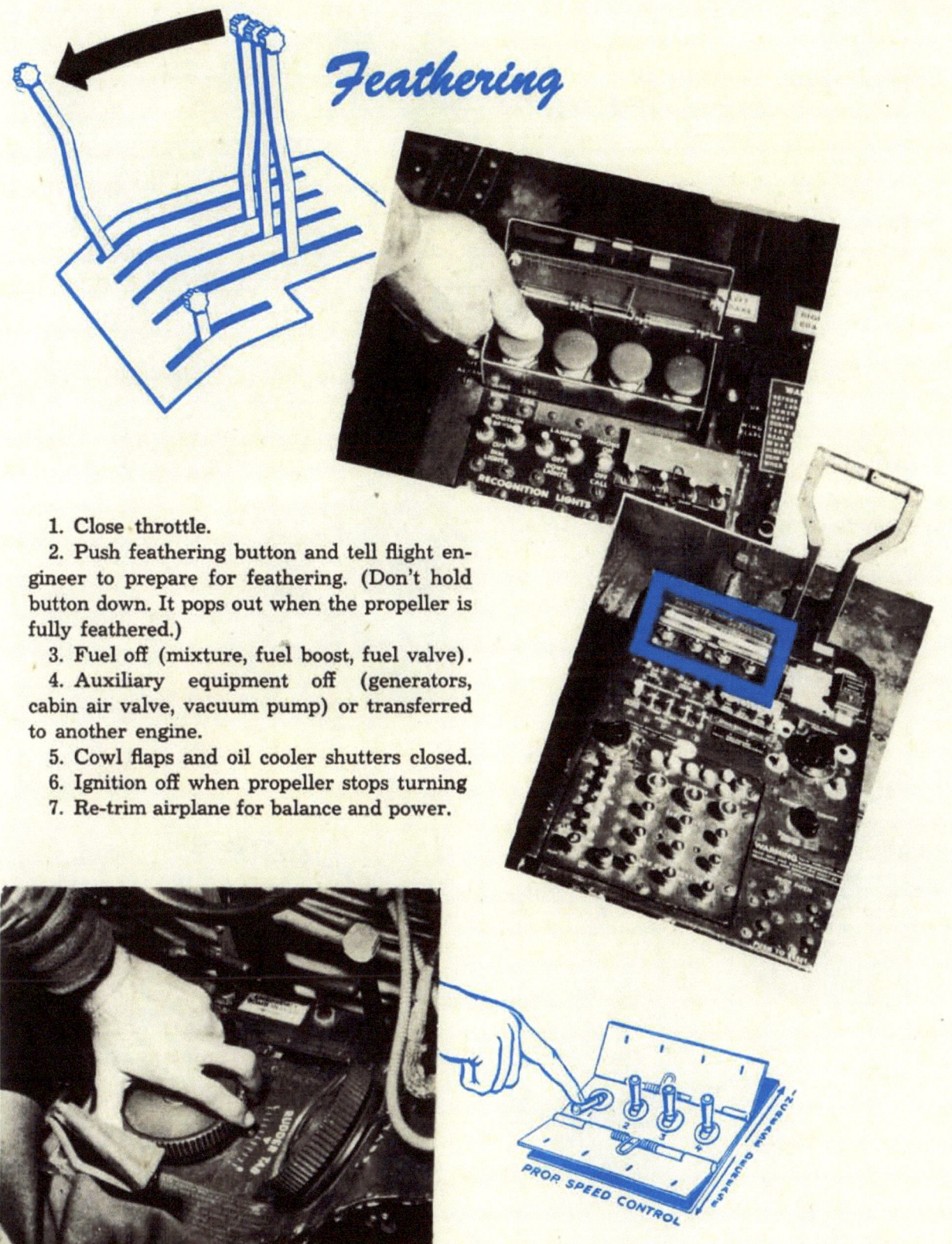

1. Close throttle.
2. Push feathering button and tell flight engineer to prepare for feathering. (Don't hold button down. It pops out when the propeller is fully feathered.)
3. Fuel off (mixture, fuel boost, fuel valve).
4. Auxiliary equipment off (generators, cabin air valve, vacuum pump) or transferred to another engine.
5. Cowl flaps and oil cooler shutters closed.
6. Ignition off when propeller stops turning
7. Re-trim airplane for balance and power.

Unfeathering

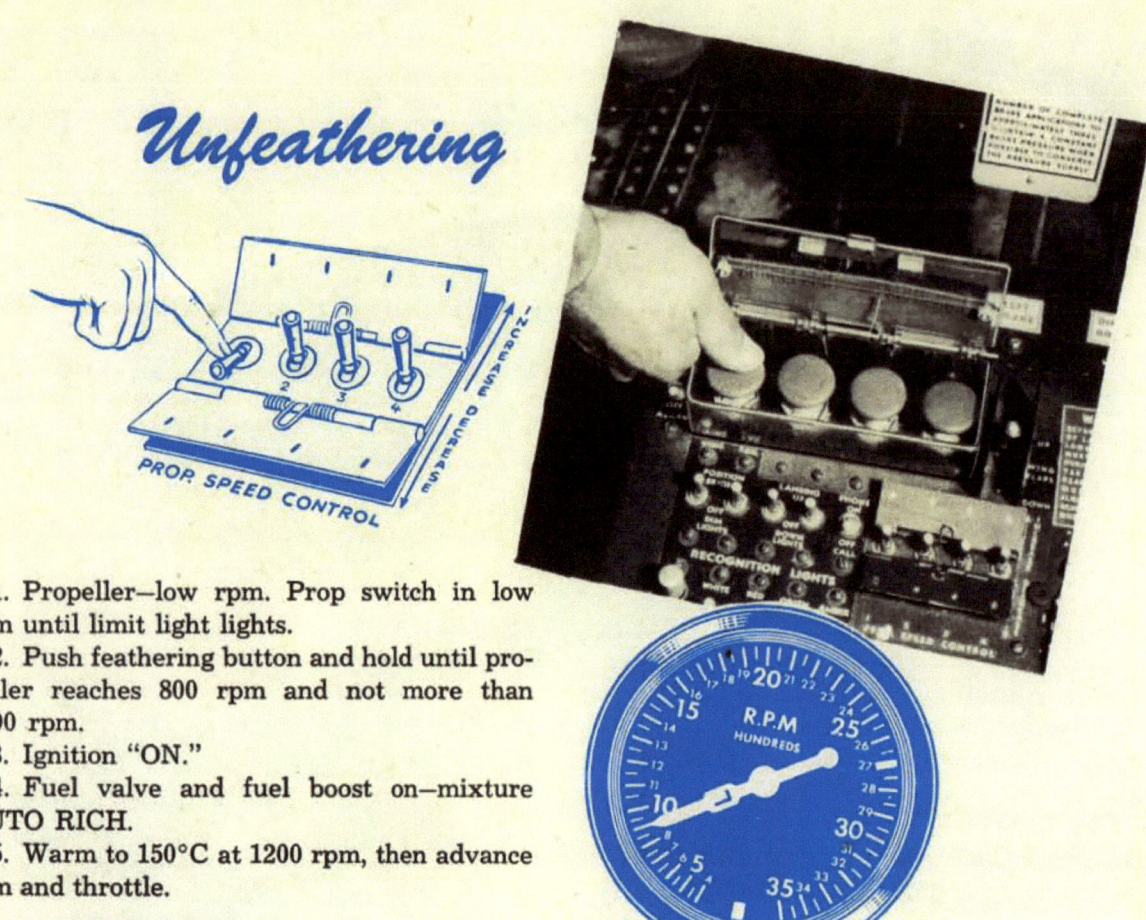

1. Propeller—low rpm. Prop switch in low rpm until limit light lights.
2. Push feathering button and hold until propeller reaches 800 rpm and not more than 1000 rpm.
3. Ignition "ON."
4. Fuel valve and fuel boost on—mixture AUTO RICH.
5. Warm to 150°C at 1200 rpm, then advance rpm and throttle.

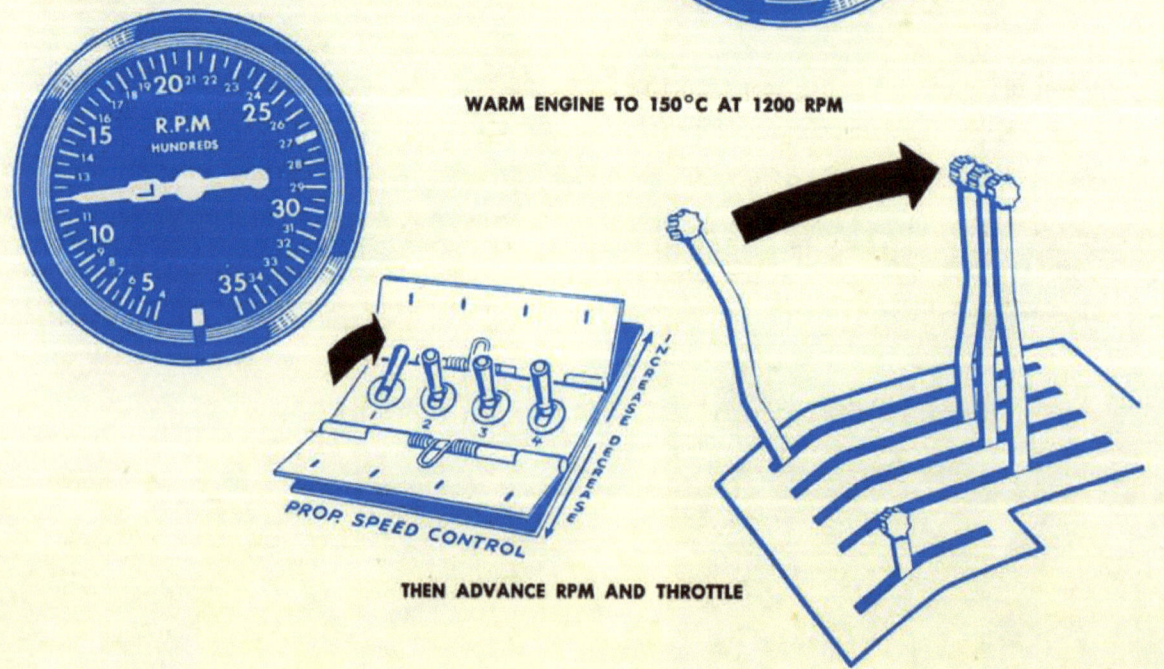

WARM ENGINE TO 150°C AT 1200 RPM

THEN ADVANCE RPM AND THROTTLE

RESTRICTED

EMERGENCIES

Emergency Flap Operation

A portable emergency motor in the bomb bay permits the emergency lowering of the flaps or the emergency operation of the bomb bay doors. It is normally stowed in position to operate the flaps and must be moved to another position to operate the bomb bay doors.

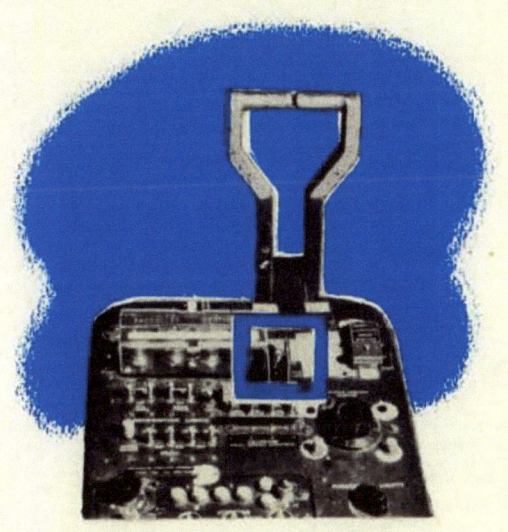

◀ If the normal flap system fails and it is impossible to operate the flaps by operating the normal flap switch, follow the emergency procedures given on the next page: ▶

RESTRICTED

101

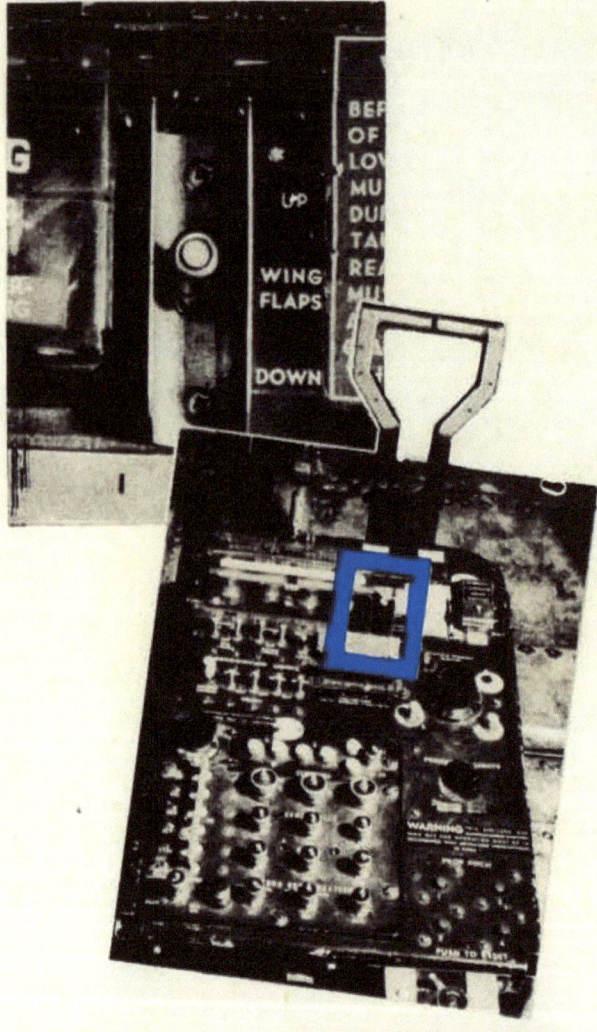

TO LOWER FLAPS:

1. Place the flap switch neutral.
2. The landing gear transfer switch and the bus selector switch should be in NORMAL.
3. Put switch on top of emergency motor down. Motor is normally stowed in flap socket in center wing section and plugged into the emergency bus.
4. Lower flaps by placing the landing gear transfer switch (airplane commander's aisle stand), or the bus selector switch (battery solenoid shield) in the EMERGENCY position. If the bus selector switch is used, the putt-putt must be on the line and the tail gunner operating the bus selector switch must return the switch to NORMAL as soon as informed by the blister gunners that the flaps are down as desired. To be safe in case of the necessity of a go-around, don't lower the flaps more than 30°
5. As a last resort, put the normal flap switch down with the landing gear transfer switch on NORMAL. Then put the bus selector switch on EMERGENCY. The switch on top of the emergency motor must be in the same corresponding position as the normal flap switch, or the normal and emergency motors will work against each other.

THE REVERSE PROCEDURE is used to raise the flaps.

Warning

Do not run the motor beyond the upper and lower flap limits. This burns out the motor, as it has no limit switch. For emergency flap operation, don't depend on the hand crank stowed forward of the rear entrance door. This crank is for starting the engines and does not fit the flap socket.

Emergency Procedures

LANDING GEAR

1. Make sure all operating generators and the putt-putt are turned on. It is erroneously believed that some generators should be turned off in the air. This is a fallacy and a dangerous practice.

2. Check fuse in airplane commander's aisle stand. If this fuse is burned out, both the normal gear switch and the landing gear transfer switch are inoperative. Replace fuse and try normal gear switch again. If fuse burns out again, return gear switch to NEUTRAL, replace fuse and continue with emergency procedures as follows:

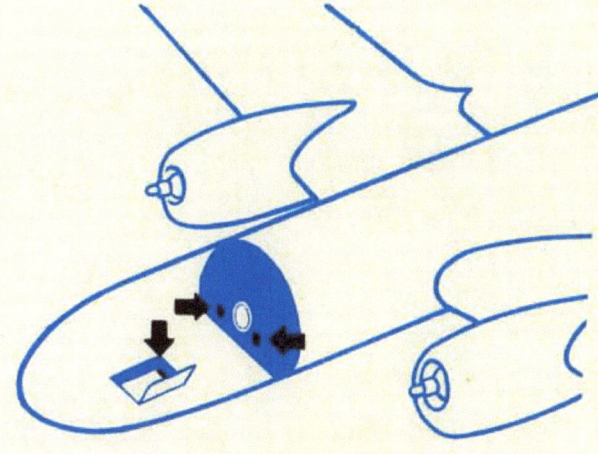

a. Move landing gear transfer switch to EMERGENCY. Make sure that the bus selector switch is in the NORMAL position.

b. Pull the emergency landing gear door release handle and hold until doors are fully open. If doors do not open when handle is pulled, emergency gear motors will in some cases drive the gear through the doors, provided the release handle is held out during operation of emergency motors.

CAUTION: If more than one gear is defective,

RESTRICTED

operate only ONE emergency gear switch at a time. After gear is down and locked, do not operate the emergency motor. There are no limit switches in the emergency system.

3. Operate the emergency gear switch controlling the defective gear. If solenoid fails to close when using emergency gear switch, throw a jumper across the solenoid or close it manually. If defective gear does not move within ten seconds, return emergency gear switch to neutral and proceed as follows: Set landing gear transfer switch to normal and bus selector switch to EMERGENCY.

4. Operate normal gear switch and emergency gear switch simultaneously (for defective gear), to the down position. If defective gear does not move within ten seconds, return both gear switches to NEUTRAL and proceed as follows: Move landing gear transfer switch and bus selector switch to EMERGENCY.

5. Place the emergency gear switch on the defective gear to the UP position for approximately 10 seconds. Then return switch to the DOWN position. If defective gear does not move within 10 seconds, return emergency gear switch to NEUTRAL and proceed as follows: As a last resort, turn off all engine-driven generators and move bus selector switch to EMERGENCY and landing gear transfer switch to NORMAL. Move emergency gear switch on defective gear to DOWN position. When gear is "down and locked," return emergency gear switch to NEUTRAL. Turn on all operating engine generators and watch closely for movement of defective gear. If gear does not move, ship may be landed safely with generators on. If defective gear starts to retract, set wing flaps at 25°, set props at 2400, and service main and emergency hydraulic systems, if necessary. Then turn all engine generators off. Lower defective gear again with emergency gear switch. Land with generators off and bus selector switch on EMERGENCY. Stop the ship with as few brake applications as possible. Cut all engines, switches, and putt-putt while still on runway. Have ship towed to the line. Whether landing was made with generators on or off, ship should be jacked up for a retraction test before any switches are turned on and before any motors are replaced.

Note:

If nose gear alone fails to extend, check nose gear motor fuse (100 amps) in nose wheel well.

Emergency Manual Landing Gear Operation

A manual system for the extension and retraction of the landing gear is installed in the new production airplanes. The system is composed of a hand crank for each main gear and a crank for the nose gear, torque tubes, and gear boxes to actuate the landing gear screws. Clutches disconnect the normal motors from the screws during emergency operation. The clutches on the main gear also disconnect the manual system which does not turn during normal operation of the gears.

Note

The manual landing gear system can also be actuated by the portable wing flap motor.

MAIN GEAR

The main landing gear are each operated manually from a gear box installed just aft of the rear wing spar and above each catwalk in the rear bomb bay. The box on the righthand side actuates the left gear. A hand crank, which is inserted in the gear box during manual operation, is stowed just above the catwalk at station 520. In B-29A's, this crank is located on the rear spar bulkhead. A crank is provided for each gear. From each gear box, a torque tube projects outboard through the wing trailing edge ribs to a right angle gear box near wing station 137. From the gear box another tube projects forward to a gear box on the rear side of the front spar from which a short tube goes to the gears that actuate the landing gear screw. The clutch that disconnects the normal electric motor from the screw and engages the manual system is cable operated from the same pull handle that operates the emergency nacelle door release. A single cable runs from the handle to a quadrant mounted on the rear side of the front spar in the wheel well, then over a pulley on the clutch release lever to a tension spring. The cables actuating the nacelle door releases are operated by the quadrant. The pull handle formerly located on the Airplane Commander's control stand is now replaced with two handles, one on each side of the airplane, at bulkhead 485. The handles are within easy reach of the crew members at the hand cranks.

TO OPERATE EACH MAIN GEAR WITH THIS EMERGENCY SYSTEM:

(1) Pull the nacelle door release and clutch engagement handle. Allow the swaged ball on the cable to drop into the slot on the handle bracket which retains the cable in the extended position. This puts a spring tension on the clutch lever, which subsequently moves to mesh the clutch when the jaws are aligned. The engagement of the clutch on the manual side is simultaneous with the release of the clutch on the motor side.

(2) To raise the gear manually, insert the crank in the upper position on the gear box. Turn clockwise until the stops engage. About 30 minutes will be required to complete the 774 turns. It is necessary to use the upper position with its gear ratio of 12 to 1 to lighten the crank loads when raising the gear.

(3) To lower the gear manually, insert the crank in the lower position and turn it clockwise until the stops are engaged. The gear ratio is 6 to 1, and 387 turns are required. This takes about 12 minutes.

(4) To operate the gear by emergency auxiliary power, install the portable auxiliary flap motor in the lower position. BE SURE THE CLUTCH HAS BEEN SHIFTED. The switch directions are noted on the motor handle. Run the motor until the stops engage. A jar will occur, and the motor clutch will start slipping.

RESTRICTED

One minute is required for retracting, 40 seconds for extending. The motor is normally stowed on the center wing section and is plugged into a power receptacle. The cord on the motor has been lengthened to make it possible to reach both gear boxes from this receptacle.

(5) ALWAYS RETURN THE CLUTCH HANDLE TO THE "IN" POSITION IMMEDIATELY AFTER EMERGENCY EXTENSION OR RETRACTION IS COMPLETE. This will cause an internal spring in the clutch mechanism to release the emergency manual system and engage the normal electric motor. Since the retraction motor is series wound, it will develop excessive speed and destroy itself if run with the load removed. Therefore, it should always remain engaged except when the emergency system is actually being used.

NOSE GEAR

To operate the nose gear manually:

(1) Remove the beam from the clamp on the copilot's armor plate stanchion and rotate to a horizontal position.

(2) Secure the beam with eye bolt and wing nut to the bracket on the Airplane Commander's plate stanchion.

(3) Remove the hand crank from under the entrance hatch and insert into the square hole in the beam.

(4) Unscrew the pressure sealing plug in the floor, using the hand crank as a wrench.

(5) Insert the crank in the gear box.

(6) If the crank will not turn, open the entrance hatch and disengage the motor with the clutch lever. Moving the lever toward the right (facing forward) disengage the motor. A spring that attaches to either of two clips is provided on the handle to retain it in the engaged or released position. Normally, the motor is left engaged and is allowed to rotate as the gear is actuated. The number of turns of the crank required to raise or lower the gear is 257, and the gear ratio is 3 to 1. Extension and retraction are each accomplished in two to three minutes.

(7) ALWAYS RETURN THE CLUTCH HANDLE TO THE ENGAGED POSITION AFTER HANDCRANKING if the clutch has been released. Also remove the crank and stow the beam.

Note

Instruction decals are installed in the airplane to explain the operation of the manual retraction system. A decal is provided above each gear box at the cranking stations for the main gears. A decal is also provided on the back of the airplane commander's armor plate for instructions regarding the nose gear.

Emergency Bomb Bay Door Operation

EMERGENCY ELECTRIC OPERATION OF DOORS

1. Install portable motor (normally stowed in center wing section) in forward or aft bomb bay door socket (center of starboard catwalk) and connect plug in outlet just above socket. Motor switch neutral.

2. Landing gear transfer switch or bus selector switch on EMERGENCY. If bus selector switch is used, the putt-putt must be on the line.

3. Portable motor switch (on top of motor) UP to open doors, DOWN to close doors.

Warning

This motor has no limit switch. Operation beyond the full open or full closed position burns out the motor. The engine hand crank will not operate bomb bay doors (see flaps).

EMERGENCY MECHANICAL BOMB RELEASE

1. Pull release cable by winding bombardier's hand wheel 2½ turns clockwise or by pulling emergency release handle (one on airplane commander's control stand, another on forward wall of rear pressurized compartment, near floor, on port side). The first part of this pull releases the doors, allowing them to open. The second part of the pull operates the bomb release levers, releasing bombs unarmed. Total length of pull is about 30 inches.

2. After release with wheel, re-wind system by turning wheel counterclockwise 2½ turns.

3. Close doors after emergency release by putting bomb door handle in full OPEN position and holding until retracting screw engages door mechanism. Then move handle to CLOSE.

EMERGENCY ELECTRICAL BOMB RELEASE

1. With normal electrical power, salvo release of bombs unarmed is accomplished by closing any one of three salvo switches located at the airplane commander's station, bombardier's station, and right hand sighting station in the aft pressurized compartment. With any one of the salvo switches closed, power goes directly to the bomb door "open" solenoid, salvo indicator lights, and bomb salvo relay.

2. If electrical operation is impossible, opening of the bomb doors is accomplished by actuating the emergency bomb door release situated on the airplane commander's control stand. Bombs may then be dropped singly by manually tripping the "release" lever on each bomb shackle.

PULL PILOT'S EMERGENCY BOMB RELEASE HANDLE OUT APPROXIMATELY 30 INCHES

RESTRICTED

Emergency Landing (WHEELS UP)

The B-29 can be crash-landed with a minimum of injury to the crew. Land on hard surface whenever possible in preference to sod or dirt. Do not feather props unless engine trouble requires feathering.

With wheels up, drag is reduced considerably so plan your approach to land short.

When you are positive that an emergency landing is inevitable, contact the control tower and continue to circle the field until the immediate area is cleared of all other traffic, and an ambulance, crash truck, and fire truck are ready on the flying line. If feasible, circle until the remaining fuel supply is 200 gallons an engine. If it is found inadvisable to land at your home base, proceed to the prescribed alternate and observe the same precautions.

It is the prerogative of any crew member not essential to the emergency landing operation to jump from a safe altitude over the airport if he so desires. If he decides to stay with the airplane, he must help prepare for a crash landing and then take up his prescribed crash-landing position. Crew members should stay clear of the lower turret areas—the turrets may tear loose and be forced up into the cabin.

To prepare for the crash landing, drop all bombs, auxiliary bomb bay tanks, and flares, and open all emergency escape hatches except the bomb bay doors. Then proceed in the following order:

1. Close wheel well nacelle doors, if possible.
2. Make normal approach sufficiently far back from the field and high enough to allow remaining crew members to perform the following last-minute preparations at the command of the airplane commander.
3. Lower full flaps for landing.
4. Stop putt-putt.
5. Shut off fuel boost.
6. Close fuel shut-off valves on final approach when certain of making the field. (Approximately 10 to 15 seconds of fuel, at low power, remains in the lines after closing the fuel shut-off valve.)
7. Just before contact with the ground, throttle the engines back and place mixture control in IDLE CUT-OFF, then gradually open the throttles to clear fuel from the carburetor without causing a surge of power.
8. Turn the master ignition switch OFF, then turn the individual ignition switches and battery switches OFF.
9. See that flight engineer is ready to set engine nacelle fire extinguisher selector to any engine that may catch fire after landing.
10. Warn crew members just before ground contact, then land normally by sliding airplane in on its belly.

MAKE NORMAL LANDING

108   RESTRICTED

Emergency Landing (BOTH MAIN GEAR DOWN, NOSEWHEEL PARTIALLY UP OR ALL THE WAY UP)

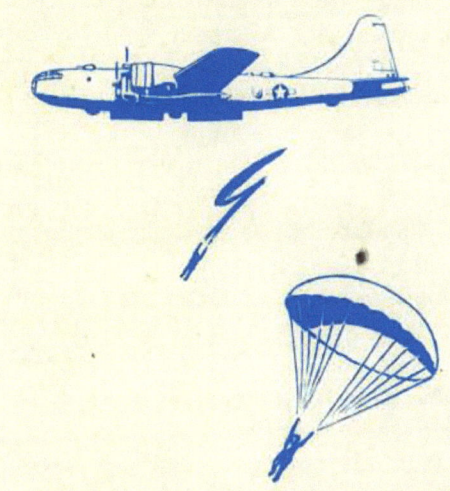

1. Check with the operations control tower and stand by in the air until an ambulance, crash, and fire truck are ready on the flying line. If it is found inadvisable to land on the home base, proceed to alternate base directed and observe the same precautions.

2. Check with the operations control tower to be sure all air traffic is clear of the proposed landing zone.

3. Drop all bombs or auxiliary bomb bay fuel tanks and flares in a safe zone.

4. Allow all crew members not essential to the landing operation, who wish it, to jump from a safe altitude over the field. Otherwise, they are to help prepare for a crash landing and take their positions.

5. Open all emergency escape hatches to avoid their jamming, with the exception of the bomb bay doors.

6. Shift disposable load and crew, if necessary, to the after compartments to shift the C.G. as far back as possible.

7. Using 45° of flaps, make a normal approach to land on runway.

8. Stop putt-putt.

9. Shut off fuel boost.

10. Close fuel shut-off valves on final approach, when certain of making the field, and just prior to throttling engines for landing. Approximately 10 to 15 seconds of fuel, at a low power setting, remains in the fuel lines and carburetor after shutting off these valves.

11. Just before contact, throttle the engines and place the mixture controls in IDLE CUT-OFF position, then gradually open the throttles to clear fuel from carburetor without causing a surge of power.

12. Turn master ignition switch OFF, then turn individual ignition switches and battery switches OFF.

13. See that the flight engineer is ready to set engine nacelle fire extinguisher selector to any engine that may catch fire after landing.

14. After the main wheels touch the ground, hold the nose of the airplane in the air as long as possible with the elevators and then lower it gently until it strikes the runway.

15. After the nose of the airplane strikes the runway, apply brakes as necessary to bring airplane to a stop.

HOLD NOSE UP AS LONG AS POSSIBLE...THEN LET IT DOWN GENTLY AND APPLY BRAKES

Emergency Landing (ONE MAIN WHEEL UP, NOSEWHEEL AND ONE MAIN WHEEL DOWN.)

1. Check with the control tower and stand by in the air until an ambulance, crash truck, and fire truck are ready on the flying line. If it is found inadvisable to land on the home base, proceed to the alternate base directed and observe the same precautions.
2. Check with control tower to be sure all air traffic is clear of the proposed landing zone.
3. Drop all bombs or auxiliary bomb bay fuel tanks and flares in a safe zone.
4. Allow all crew members not essential to the landing operation, who wish it, to jump from a safe altitude over the field. Otherwise, they are to help prepare for a crash landing and take their positions.
5. Open all emergency escape hatches to avoid their jamming, with the exception of the bomb bay doors.
6. Stop putt-putt.
7. Shut off fuel boost.
8. Close fuel shut-off valves on final approach, when certain of making the field, and just before throttling engines for landing. Approximately 10 to 15 seconds of fuel, at a low power setting, remains in fuel lines and carburetor after shutting off these valves.
9. Just before contact, throttle the engines and place the mixture controls in IDLE CUT-OFF position, then gradually open the throttles to clear fuel from carburetor without producing a surge of power.
10. Turn master ignition switch OFF, then turn individual ignition switches and battery switches OFF.
11. See that the flight engineer is ready to set engine nacelle fire extinguisher selector to any engine that may catch fire after landing.
12. With 45° of flaps, make normal landing on good wheel with the wingtip slightly low on the good-wheel side.
13. Hold the wing on bad-wheel side up as long as possible with ailerons.
14. Be prepared for an extremely sharp groundloop in the direction of the crippled wheel, when wingtip and nacelle dig into runway. Use brakes to minimize groundloop.

Emergency Landing (ONE MAIN WHEEL DOWN, NOSEWHEEL AND ONE MAIN WHEEL UP.)

Follow the foregoing procedure up to and including item No. 11, then continue as follows:

12. With 45° of flaps, make normal one-wheel landing on the good wheel.
13. Hold nose of the airplane up and hold up the wingtip on the damaged main wheel side with elevator and aileron as long as possible.

Note: Land on any two of three wheels. If neither main wheels will lower, raise all wheels and crash land.

FIRE

For fighting engine or nacelle fires, the B-29 has a CO_2 system fed by two high-pressure CO_2 bottles mounted in the nosewheel well. Lines from each bottle run to all four engine nacelles and they may be used singly or together. The flight engineer can direct the CO_2 charge to the desired engine by turning the selector knob on his instrument panel, and pulling the CO_2 release handle for whichever bottle (or both) he wishes to use.

Besides the nacelle extinguisher system, each airplane has three hand extinguishers for cabin fires. One CO_2 extinguisher is on the inboard side of the flight engineer's control stand, another is in the aft pressurized compartment, aft of the auxiliary equipment panel. The third, a CO_2 extinguisher or a carbon tetrachloride extinguisher depending on the B-29 model, is by the rear entrance door.

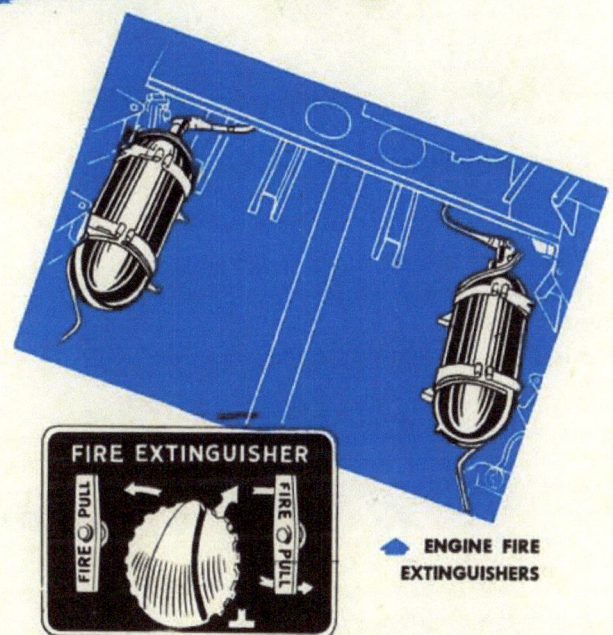

▲ ENGINE FIRE EXTINGUISHERS

▲ CONTROLS ON FLIGHT ENGINEER'S PANEL

One CO_2 type fire extinguisher is located on the side of engineer's stand

One CO_2 type fire extinguisher is located beside the rear entrance door

One CO_2 type fire extinguisher is located in the aft pressurized compartment

Cabin Fires During Flight

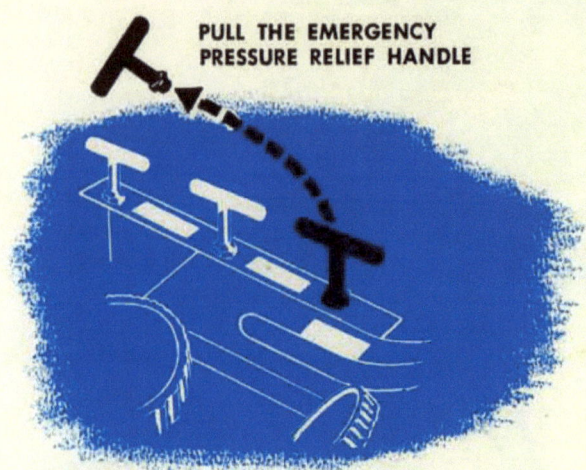

PULL THE EMERGENCY PRESSURE RELIEF HANDLE

In all cabin fires during flight, whether the origin is electrical or otherwise, immediately pull the emergency pressure relief handle if the cabin is pressurized. If the fire is in a rear compartment, use the portable carbon tetrachloride extinguisher first, and if necessary, the CO_2 extinguisher. If the fire is in the forward pressurized compartment, use the CO_2 extinguisher mounted beside the flight engineer's control stand.

If the cabin fire is caused by an electrical short circuit, the procedure is the same, except that the flight engineer must turn all electrical power off with the battery control and generator switches.

If the cabin becomes excessively smoky or gaseous after using the fire extinguishers, open the bomb bay doors for ventilation.

If the fire is extremely bad, and there is danger of an explosion from fuel tanks, sound the alarm bell so the crew can prepare to abandon the airplane. Under no conditions should any crew member abandon the airplane before the order is given by the airplane commander.

Nacelle or Engine Fire on the Ground

If the fire is known to be a torching turbo, put it out by increasing throttle setting momentarily. For other engine or nacelle fires on the ground, the following procedure should be used:

1. Move mixture control to IDLE CUT-OFF on all four engines.
2. Close fuel shut-off valves on all four engines.
3. Turn booster pump switches to OFF on all four engines.
4. Close throttles.
5. Open cowl flaps.
6. Set nacelle fire extinguisher to proper engine and pull release control handle. Before pulling second release handle, the flight engineer checks with the side gunners on the condition of the fire.
7. Turn all ignition switches OFF.
8. Turn battery switch OFF.
9. Stop putt-putt.
10. Send crew members for additional ground fire-fighting equipment.

Nacelle Fire in Flight

Crew member spotting the fire uses CALL position on jackbox and says, "Fire on No..... engine." (If possible crew member identifies the fire as to type and location.) From this point, at the airplane commander's discretion, the following procedure should be used:

1. Airplane commander closes throttle, feathers propeller, and says to flight engineer, "Use engine fire procedure."
2. Flight engineer puts mixture on feathered engine in IDLE CUT-OFF and shuts off boost pump and fuel valve as airplane commander increases airspeed in an attempt to blow out the fire, and alerts crew.
3. Sets cowl flaps to not more than 10°.
4. Sets nacelle fire extinguisher to proper engine, pulls first one, and then the other fire extinguisher control handle, if necessary.
5. Flight engineer closes cabin air valves and radio operator closes forward pressure door. If smoke has entered the cabin, copilot opens his window. In case of excessive smoke or fire in the cabin, follow cabin fire procedure.
6. If fire is out of control, open the bomb bay doors, and abandon the airplane.
7. If an engine catches fire during takeoff, airplane commander, if unable to put out the fire, makes emergency landing if necessary, following crash landing procedure.

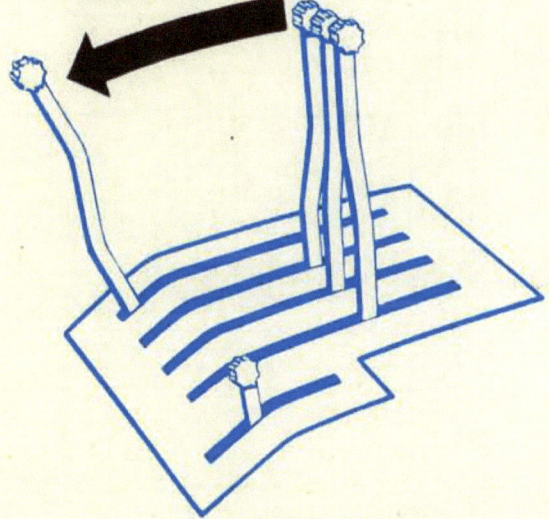

Bailout

For bailout, follow the procedures recommended on page 153.

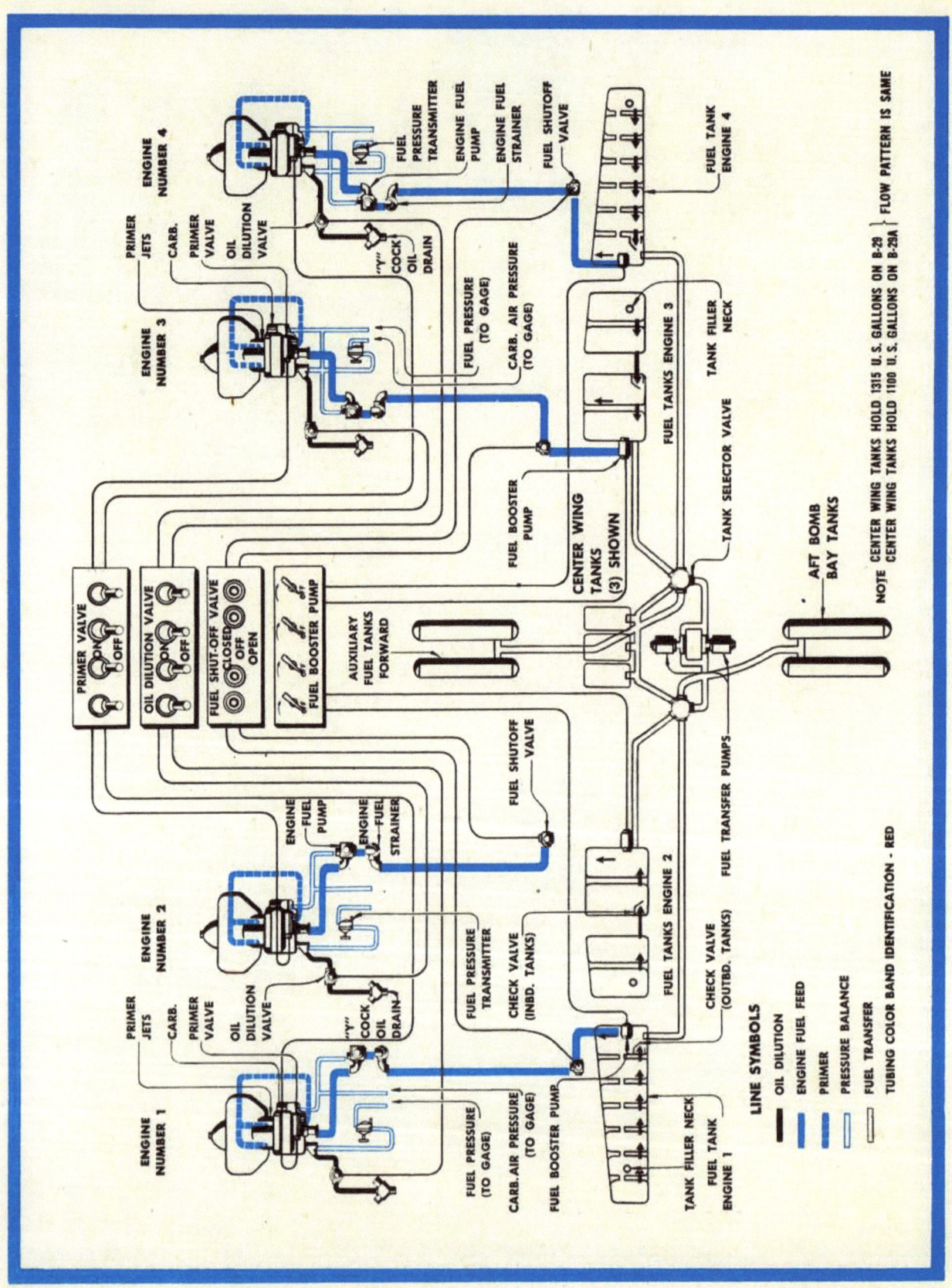

FUEL SYSTEM

The fuel system on a B-29 is similar to that on the B-17. Fuel is supplied from two inboard and two outboard self-sealing wing tanks and seven auxiliary tanks. Each inboard wing tank has a capacity of 1436.5 gallons. The outboard wing tanks each hold 1367.5 gallons. Two to four bomb bay tanks, holding 640 gallons, may be incorporated to increase the fuel supply, and the wing center section tank holds 1315 gallons (1100 in B-29A).

Each engine receives its fuel supply from a system separate from the other three engines, thereby eliminating the possibility of failure of all four engines in case of fuel-line trouble.

Fuel pressure maintained through conventional engine-driven fuel pumps. If one of these fails, there is an electrically driven fuel-boost pump at the outlet of each gasoline tank. These supply pressure up to 18 psi.

You must use fuel boost on takeoff and landing as an added safety precaution against engine failure resulting from mechanical trouble developing in the normal engine-driven fuel pumps.

Under normal operations, if an engine-driven fuel pump fails and you use fuel boost to supply pressure, turn the turbo-supercharger control to 0 position, since fuel boost does not increase with carburetor duct pressure, and a lean mixture results, causing detonation.

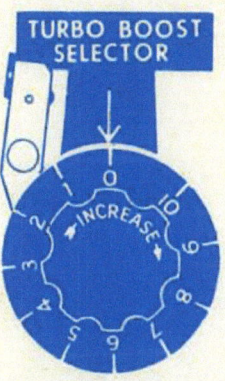

RESTRICTED

Fuel Tank Transfer

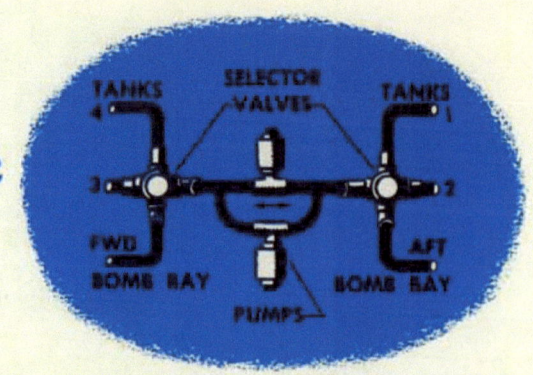

Start transferring fuel early in every flight to check the transfer system.

Fuel transfer from one tank to another is made by two reversible, electrically driven pumps located under the midwing section between the forward and aft bomb bays and controlled by toggle switches on the engineer's stand. Fuel transfer with both pumps is at the rate of 1500 gallons an hour at sea level. This rate decreases as the altitude increases. At 30,000 feet it is cut to 500 gallons an hour.

Levers on the flight engineer's stand control selection of tanks for transfer and the transfer is made by operating toggle switches which actuate the electric pump motors. Both selector levers must be set to the desired tanks. If both tanks appear on the same lever it indicates that two transfers are necessary.

Fuel may be transferred between rear bomb bay tanks and front bomb bay tanks; between rear bomb bay tanks and tank 3 or 4; between front tanks and tank 1 or 2; and across center line of airplane from engines 1 or 2 to either 3 or 4. Fuel may be transferred between wing center section tank and any other tank. Each tank selector quadrant has a position marked WING CENTER SECTION TANK.

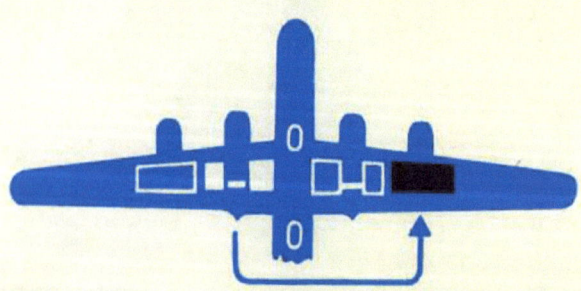

DESIRED TRANSFER—NO. 2 TANK TO ENG. NO. 4 TANK

DESIRED TRANSFER—NO. 4 TANK TO ENG. NO. 1 TANK

DESIRED TRANSFER—NO. 2 TANK TO NO. 1 TANK
A, From Eng. No. 2 Tank to Eng. No. 3 Tank
B, From Eng. No. 3 Tank to Eng. No. 1 Tank

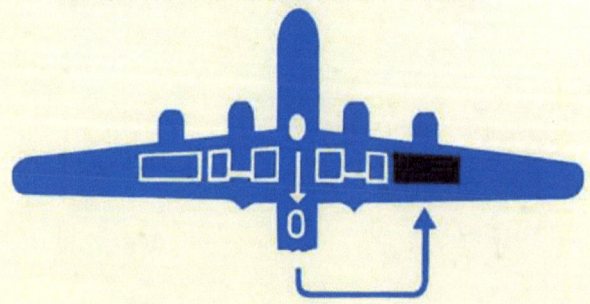

DESIRED TRANSFER—FWD. BOMB BAY TANK TO NO. 4 TANK
A, From Forward Bomb Bay Tanks to Aft Bomb Bay
B, From Aft Bomb Bay Tank to Eng. No. 4 Tank

Oil System

Besides engine lubrication, the oil system on the B-29 also serves to operate the propeller governor and propeller feathering.

Each engine receives its oil supply from an 80-gallon self-sealing tank located in the nacelle. On some airplanes a 100-gallon reserve oil tank is located on the port side of the center wing section near the oil transfer pump and the oil transfer selector valve. An oil cooler, incorporated in the oil "out" line between the oil tank and the engine, is operated automatically, or manually by the flight engineer, if so desired.

Oil dilution, when low ground temperatures are anticipated, is accomplished by operating four switches on the flight engineer's switch panel. These switches control four solenoid valves which, in turn, control the dilution of the oil.

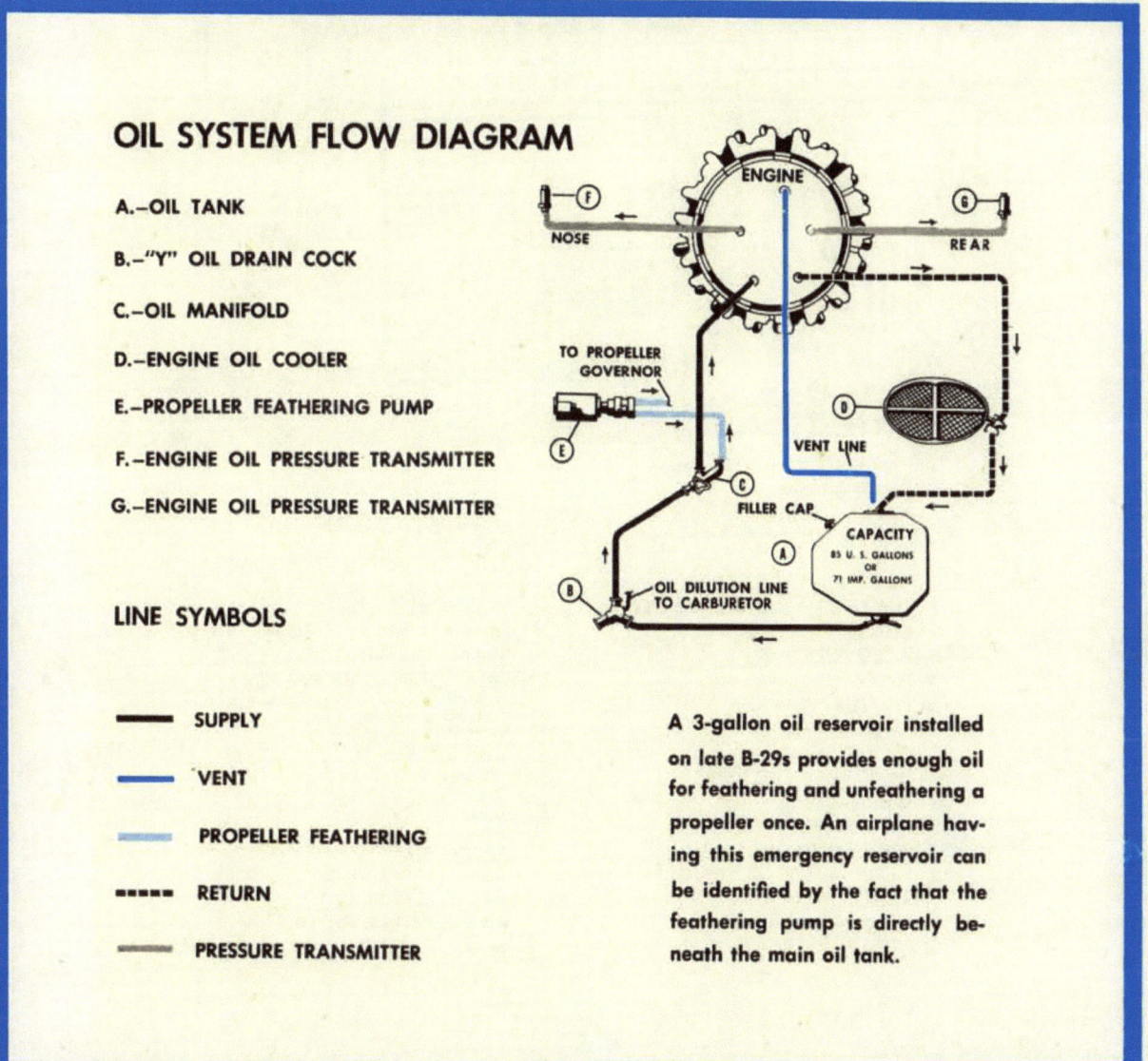

OIL SYSTEM FLOW DIAGRAM

A.—OIL TANK
B.—"Y" OIL DRAIN COCK
C.—OIL MANIFOLD
D.—ENGINE OIL COOLER
E.—PROPELLER FEATHERING PUMP
F.—ENGINE OIL PRESSURE TRANSMITTER
G.—ENGINE OIL PRESSURE TRANSMITTER

LINE SYMBOLS

— SUPPLY
— VENT
— PROPELLER FEATHERING
----- RETURN
— PRESSURE TRANSMITTER

A 3-gallon oil reservoir installed on late B-29s provides enough oil for feathering and unfeathering a propeller once. An airplane having this emergency reservoir can be identified by the fact that the feathering pump is directly beneath the main oil tank.

RESTRICTED

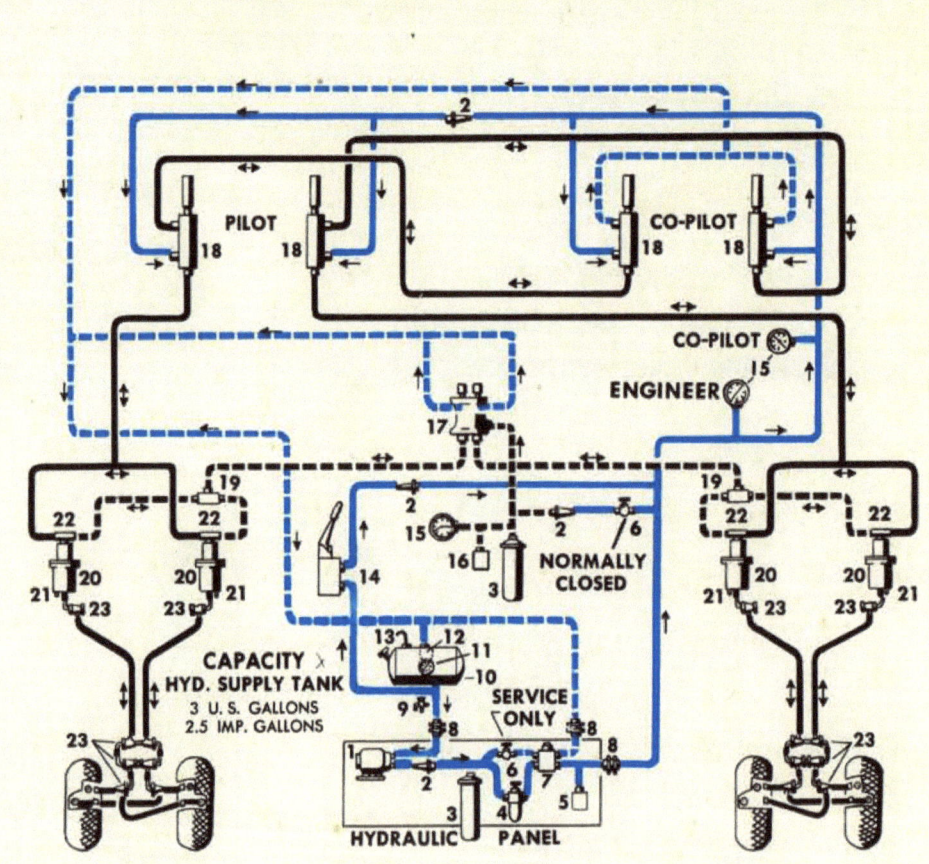

HYDRAULIC SYSTEM FLOW DIAGRAM

1—ELECTRICALLY DRIVEN PUMP
2—CHECK VALVE
3—ACCUMULATOR
4—FILTER
5—PRESSURE SWITCH
6—SHUTOFF VALVE
7—RELIEF VALVE
8—DISCONNECT FITTING
9—DRAIN COCK
10—SUPPLY TANK
11—LEVEL GAGE
12—FILTER (INSIDE OF TANK)
13—VENT
14—HAND PUMP
15—PRESSURE GAGE
16—WARNING SWITCH
17—EMERG. BRAKE METERING VALVE
18—BRAKE METERING VALVE
19—SAFETY LOCKOUT VALVE
20—BRAKE RETURN BOOST VALVE
21—BOOSTER RELIEF VALVE
22—SHUTTLE VALVE
23—SWIVEL FITTING

Symbols

— PRESSURE LINE
— BRAKE LINE
— RETURN LINE
— EMERGENCY LINE
— SUCTION LINE

RESTRICTED

HYDRAULIC SYSTEM

The B-29 hydraulic system has one exclusive function; it transmits force to actuate the brake mechanism. The system is divided into two units—one for normal use and one for emergency use. The emergency system receives pressure from the normal system, but is isolated by a check valve and shut-off valve to prevent reverse flow. A hand pump is provided on the floor at the left of the copilot's seat permits building up the pressure when the electrically driven pump does not operate. The emergency system must be recharged after 5 to 7 applications of the brakes.

The electric hydraulic pump cuts in when the main hydraulic pressure falls below 800 psi, and cuts out when the main hydraulic pressure reaches 1000 psi. If the main pressure drops below 800 psi, an amber warning light on the copilot's panel goes on. The hydraulic pump runs continuously at pressures below 800 psi, unless the pressure falls below 200 psi, when it cuts out to prevent overheating if the hydraulic fluid is lost.

When the emergency pressure falls below 900 psi, the amber warning light on the flight engineer's panel goes on. To service: switch the emergency system filler valve (on flight engineer's panel) to OPEN, press the momentary contact toggle switch (on engineer's stand) until the pressure builds up to 1075 psi. The momentary contact switch operates the pump, regardless of pressure in either system. The pressure relief valve opens at 1075 psi and reaches its full-open position at 1200 psi.

The capacity of the hydraulic tank is 3 gallons, plus a ½ gallon expansion space. *Note*: Tank gage should read approximately 2 gallons when parking brakes are set.

The hydraulic panel, at the rear of the forward pressurized compartment under the floor, contains an electric pump, a floating piston-type accumulator, a filter, a pressure switch, a relief valve, and a shut-off valve.

Don't set your parking brakes if the brakes are hot, as the brakes cannot cool properly with parking brakes on.

Air pressure preload in both normal and emergency accumulators is 400 psi.

When using the emergency brakes, a steady application of pressure is mandatory. Do not pump your brakes.

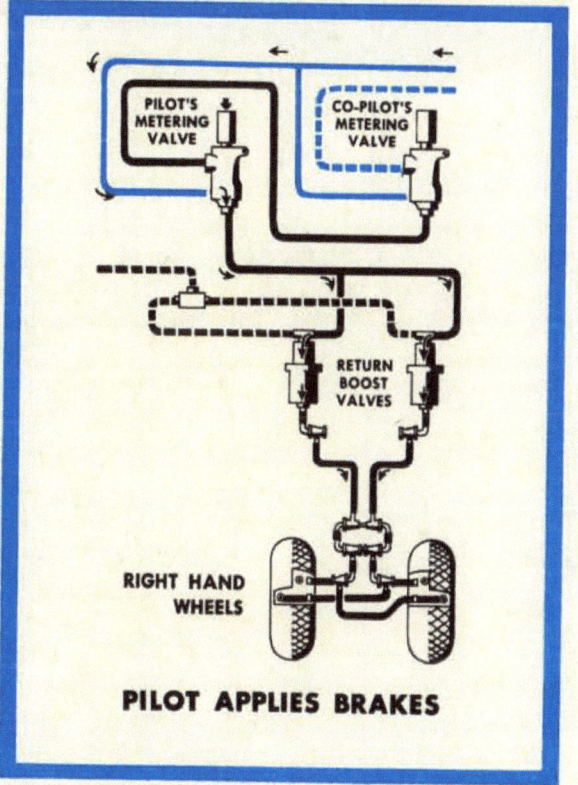

PILOT APPLIES BRAKES

ELECTRICAL SYSTEM

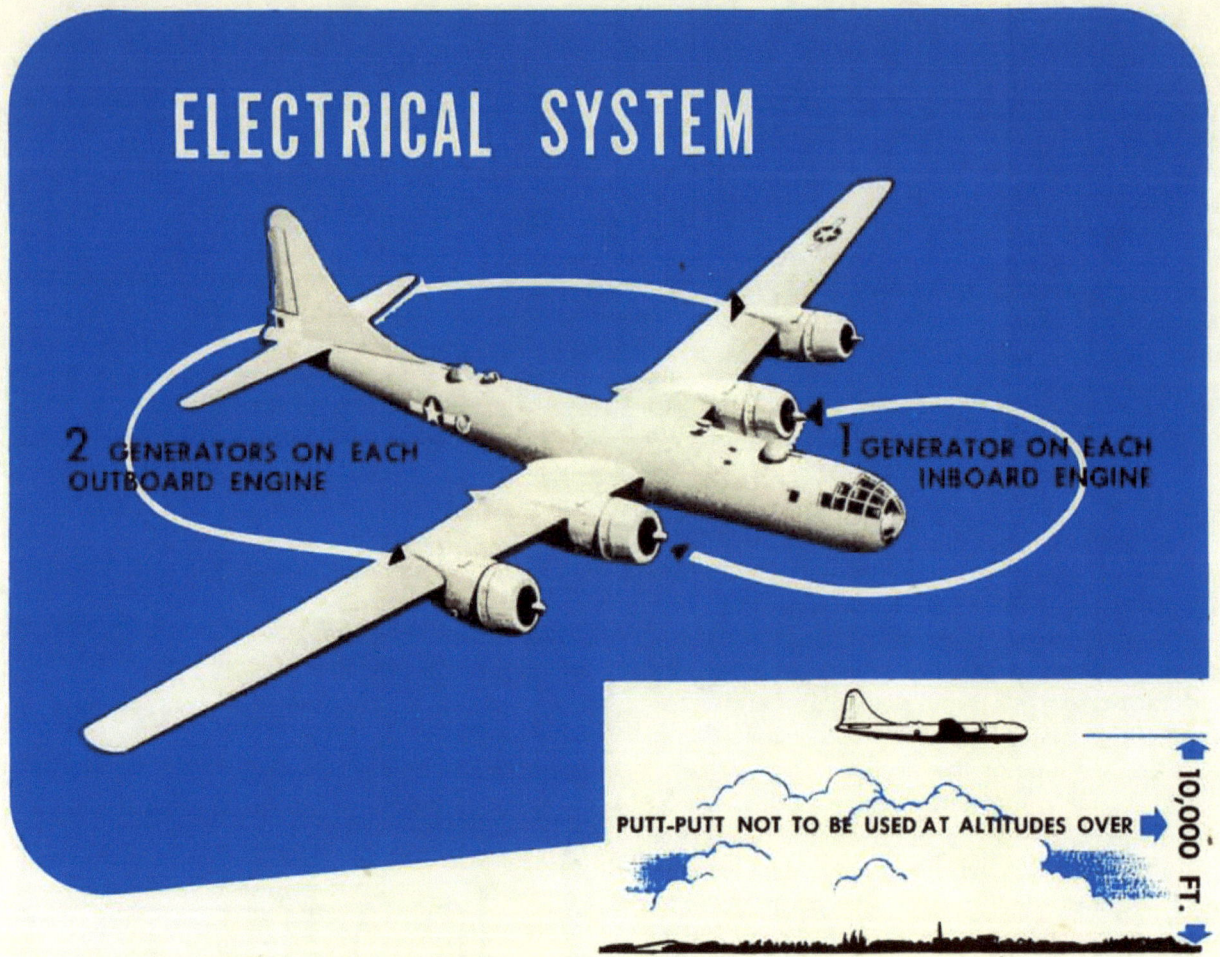

2 GENERATORS ON EACH OUTBOARD ENGINE

1 GENERATOR ON EACH INBOARD ENGINE

PUTT-PUTT NOT TO BE USED AT ALTITUDES OVER 10,000 FT.

Six 28.5-volt engine-driven generators on the B-29 furnish 300 amperes each for a total of 1800 amperes. These generators are mounted two on each outboard engine and one on each inboard engine. The engines must be turning at least 1375 rpm for the generators to put out rated current.

The putt-putt drives a 28-volt 200-ampere generator. However, it cannot be used at altitudes greater than 10,000 feet. This, plus the battery, provides an additional source of power for ground operations and emergencies and as a safety precaution during landings and takeoffs, but should not be considered a normal source of power during flight.

All engine-driven generators must be ON from takeoff to landing unless a unit fails. A defective generator should be switched OFF.

Try not to overload the system. If you operate the flaps and gear simultaneously, snap the switches ON at least a fraction of a second apart to separate the peak loads and prevent any possibility of momentarily overloading the system. Avoid sudden reversals in direction in the operation of either gear or flaps. A sudden reversal can cause an overload of several thousand amperes more than the capacity of the system. Allow about 10 seconds for the motor to slow down before flipping a switch in the opposite direction.

If one or more of the engine-driven generators fail, reduce the over-all load on the system, if possible, to a value within the capacity of the system. This is particularly important when attempting to operate flaps and gear on a go-around. The following table shows the electrical loads imposed by the operation of the various pieces of equipment:

TABLE OF AVERAGE LOADS

AMPERES

Upper forward turret	132.5 (Battle load 275.5)
Upper aft turret	132.5 (Battle load 275.5)
Lower forward turret	84
Lower aft turret	84
Tail turret	242 (Battle load 420)
Tail ammunition booster motors (2)	40
C-1 auto pilot	6
Bomb doors (Forward and aft)	480
Landing gear (2)	460
Nose gear	155
Wheel doors (2)	280
Wing flaps	200 (350 in flight)
Hydraulic pump	110
Landing lights (2)	52
ATC radio set	35

Emergency Electrical System

Two electrical buses, or wiring systems, are available—a normal bus and an emergency bus. Through the use of the landing gear transfer switch and the bus selector switch on the battery solenoid shield, you can use either power source—the engine-driven generators or putt-putt and/or battery—with either the normal bus or the emergency bus. Or you can use them in combination.

Both normal and emergency motors are provided for the nose gear and the main gear. A portable electric motor can be used for the emergency operation of flaps or bomb bay doors (see Emergency Procedures).

The tailskid, however, can be operated only by the normal electrical system. It has no emergency motor.

TURBO-SUPERCHARGERS

Each engine on the B-29 has two turbo-superchargers which boost the manifold pressure for takeoff and provide increased air pressure at high altitudes.

Engine exhaust gas passes through the collector ring and tailstack to the nozzle box of each supercharger, expands to atmosphere through the turbine nozzle, and drives the bucket wheel at high speed.

A ramming air inlet duct supplies air to the impeller which increases its pressure and temperature. However, in order to avoid detonation at the carburetor, the air supplied to the carburetor passes through the intercooler, where the temperature is reduced. The internal engine impeller, driven by the engine crankshaft, again increases air pressures as it enters the intake manifold. High intake manifold pressure results in greater power output.

Supercharger Regulator Operation

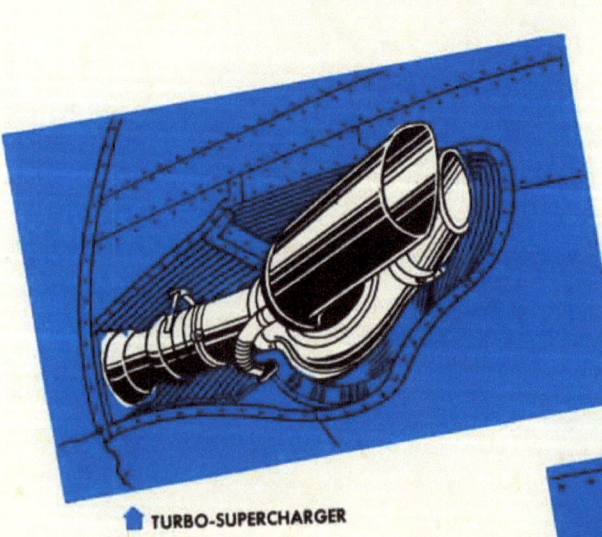

▲ TURBO-SUPERCHARGER

TURBO-SUPERCHARGER WITH FLIGHT HOOD REMOVED ▶

The amount of turbo boost is determined by the speed of the turbo bucket wheel, and the speed of the bucket wheel is determined by the pressure difference between the atmosphere and the exhaust in the tailstack, and by the amount of gas passing through the turbine nozzles. If the waste gate is opened, more exhaust gas passes to the atmosphere via the waste pipe and decreases the tailstack pressure.

Electronic Turbo-supercharger Control

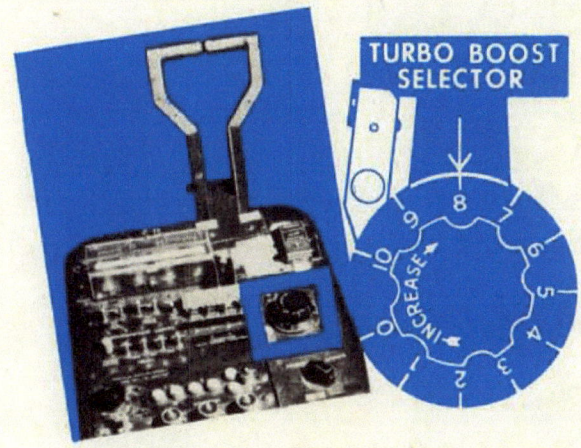

The electronic turbo-supercharger control system on B-29s consists of separate regulator systems, all simultaneously adjusted by a single **turbo selector dial** located on the pilot's aisle stand. Each system controls the induction pressure of the particular engine through a Pressuretrol unit connected directly to the carburetor air intake.

Electrical power for the entire system comes from the airplane's 115-volt, 400-cycle inverter.

Each regulator includes a turbo governor which prevents turbo overspeeding both at high altitude and during rapid throttle changes.

Both exhaust waste gates on each engine are operated by a small reversible electric motor which automatically receives power from the regulator system when a change in waste gate setting becomes necessary to maintain the desired manifold pressure.

In case of a complete failure of the airplane electrical system, or failure of the inverter, the waste gates on all engines remain in the same position as when failure occurred, and approximately the same manifold pressure that was in use at time of failure is available.

If a failure occurs in any one of the electronic regulator systems, provision is made for the waste gate motor to drive the waste gate to the open position, and no supercharger boost is available on that **particular** engine.

Upon installation of the equipment, the system is adjusted so that a selector dial setting of 8 furnishes maximum desired takeoff power. A dial setting of 10 furnishes maximum emergency power.

All engines should deliver the same power at a dial setting of 8. If it is necessary to adjust power on individual engines, use a screwdriver to turn the calibration screws located on the turbo selector dial unit.

HIGH ALTITUDE OPERATION

When flying at high altitude, you may reach a point where further turning of the selector dial fails to produce an increase in manifold pressure. This means that the overspeed portion of the turbo governor is limiting the turbo speed to safe rpm. When you encounter this condition, turn the manifold pressure selector dial counter-clockwise until it controls manifold pressure again. This prevents undue wear of the overspeed governor mechanism.

Emergency Power

You can obtain full emergency power (war power) at maximum engine rpm and full throttles by releasing the dial stop and turning the selector to setting 10. However, this setting places heavy strain on the engines and must be used only in emergencies and then only for periods not exceeding 2 minutes.

THE C-1 AUTOPILOT

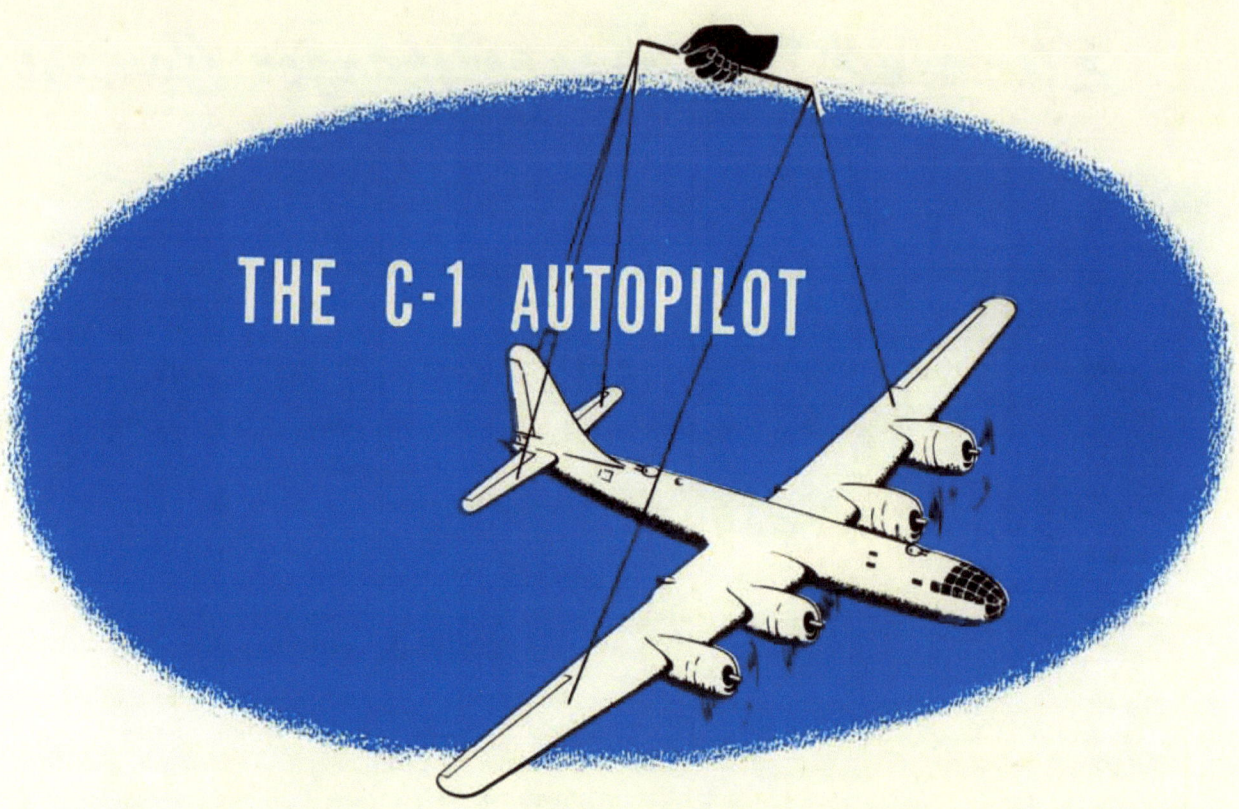

The C-1 autopilot is an electromechanical robot which automatically flies the airplane in straight and level flight, or maneuvers the airplane in response to the fingertip control of the human pilot or bombardier.

Actually, the autopilot works in much the same way as the human pilot in maintaining straight and level flight, in making corrections necessary to hold a given course and altitude, and in applying the necessary pressure on the controls to make turns, banks, etc. The difference is that the autopilot acts instantaneously and with a precision that is not humanly possible.

The precision of even the most skillful human pilot is limited by his own reaction time, i.e., the interval between his perception of a certain condition and his action to correct or control it. Reaction time itself is governed by such human fallibilities as fatigue, inability to detect errors the instant they occur, errors in judgment, and muscle coordination.

The autopilot, on the other hand, detects flight deviations the instant they occur, and just as instantaneously operates the controls to correct the deviations. Properly adjusted, the autopilot neither overcontrols nor undercontrols the airplane, but keeps it flying straight and level with all three control surfaces operating in full coordination.

The C-1 autopilot consists of various separate units electrically interconnected to operate as a system. The operation of these units is explained in detail in AN-11-60AA-1. You can get a general over-all understanding of their functions and relation to each other by studying the accompanying illustration.

Assume that the airplane in the illustration is flying straight and level and that the autopilot is operating.

Suddenly a crosswind turns the airplane away from its established heading. The gyro-operated directional stabilizer (1) detects this deviation and moves the directional panel (4) to one side or the other, depending upon the direction of the deviation.

The directional panel contains two electrical devices, the banking pot (5) and the rudder pick-up pot (6), which send signals to the aileron and rudder section of the amplifier (16) whenever the directional panel is operated. These signals are amplified and converted (by means of magnetic switches or relays) into electrical impulses which cause the aileron and rudder Servo units (15 and 18) to operate the ailerons and rudder of the airplane in the proper direction and amount to turn the airplane back to its original heading.

Similarly, if the nose of the airplane drops, the vertical flight gyro (10) detects the vertical deviation and operates the elevator pick-up pot (11) which sends an electrical signal to the elevator section of the amplifier. The signal is amplified and relayed in the form of electrical impulses to the elevator Servo unit (19) which in turn raises the elevators the proper amount to bring the airplane to level flight.

If one wing drops appreciably, the vertical flight gyro operates the aileron pick-up pot (12), the skid pot (13), and the up-elevator pot (14). The signals caused by the operation of these units are transmitted to their respective

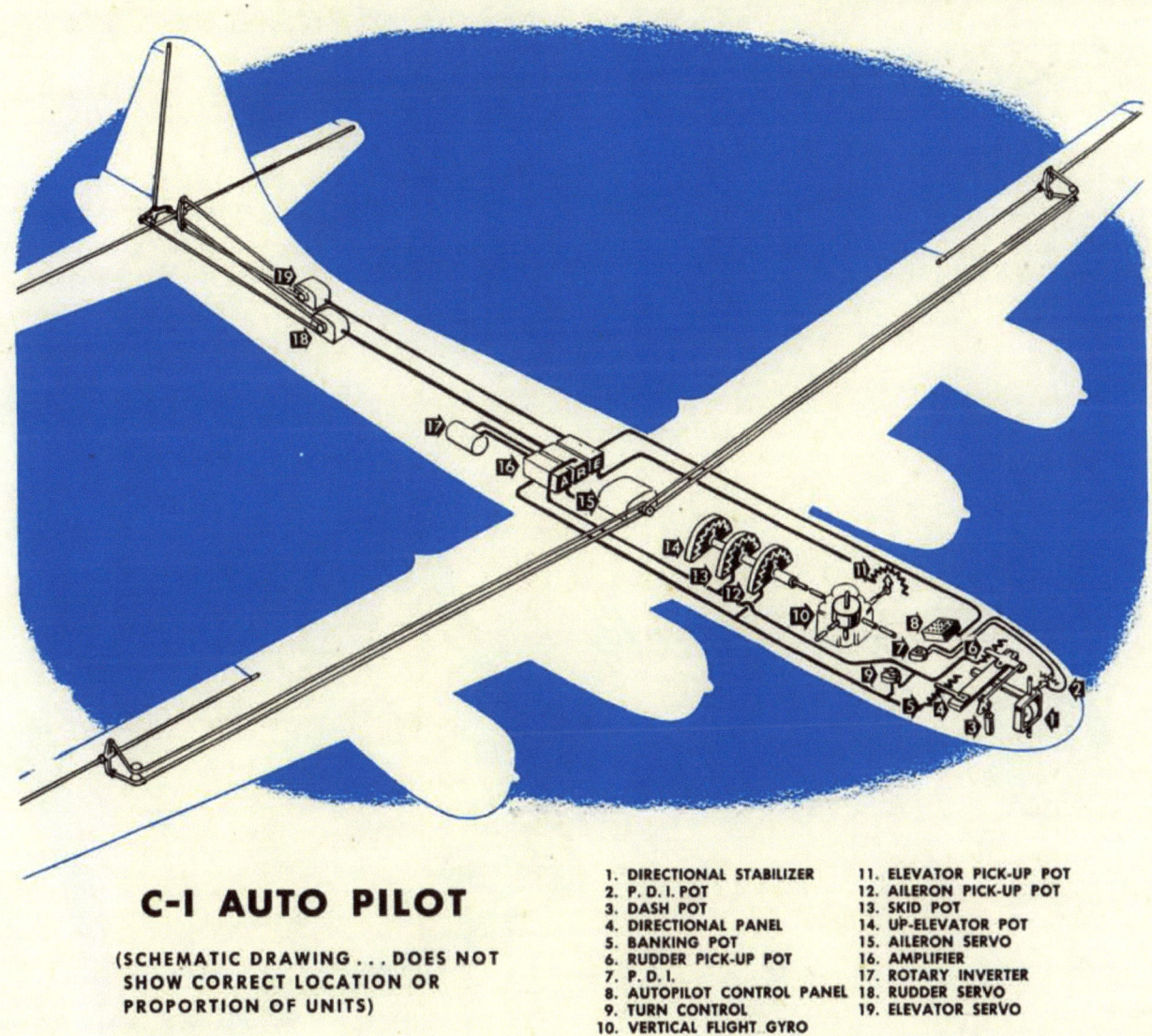

C-1 AUTO PILOT

(SCHEMATIC DRAWING...DOES NOT SHOW CORRECT LOCATION OR PROPORTION OF UNITS)

1. DIRECTIONAL STABILIZER
2. P. D. I. POT
3. DASH POT
4. DIRECTIONAL PANEL
5. BANKING POT
6. RUDDER PICK-UP POT
7. P. D. I.
8. AUTOPILOT CONTROL PANEL
9. TURN CONTROL
10. VERTICAL FLIGHT GYRO
11. ELEVATOR PICK-UP POT
12. AILERON PICK-UP POT
13. SKID POT
14. UP-ELEVATOR POT
15. AILERON SERVO
16. AMPLIFIER
17. ROTARY INVERTER
18. RUDDER SERVO
19. ELEVATOR SERVO

(aileron, rudder, and elevator) sections of the amplifier. The resulting impulses to the aileron, rudder, and elevator Servo units cause each of these units to operate its respective control surface just enough to bank and turn the airplane back to an even keel or level-flight attitude.

When the human pilot wishes to make a turn, he merely sets the turn control knob (9) at the degree of bank and in the direction of turn desired. This control sends signals, through the aileron and rudder sections of the amplifier, to the aileron and rudder Servo units which operate ailerons and rudder in the proper manner to execute a perfectly coordinated (non-slipping, non-skidding) turn. As the airplane banks, the vertical flight gyro operates the aileron, skid, and up-elevator pots (12, 13, 14). The resulting signals from the aileron and skid pots cancel the signals to the aileron and rudder Servo units to streamline these controls during the turn.

The signals from the up-elevator pot cause the elevators to rise just enough to maintain altitude. When the desired turn is completed, the pilot turns the turn control back to zero and the airplane levels off on its new course. A switch in the turn control energizes the directional arm lock on the stabilizer, which prevents the stabilizer from interfering with the turn by performing its normal direction-correcting function.

The autopilot control panel (8) provides the pilot with fingertip controls by which he can conveniently engage or disengage the system, adjust the alertness or speed of its responses to flight deviations, or trim the system for varying load and flight conditions.

The pilot direction indicator, or PDI (7), is a remote indicating device operated by the PDI pot (2). When the autopilot is used, the PDI indicates to the pilot when the system and airplane are properly trimmed. Once the autopilot is engaged, with PDI centered, the autopilot makes the corrections automatically.

The rotary inverter (17) is a motor-generator unit which converts direct current from the airplane's battery into 105-cycle alternating current for operation of the autopilot.

Before Takeoff

 1. Turn control centered.

2. Make sure that all switches on the control panel are in the OFF position.

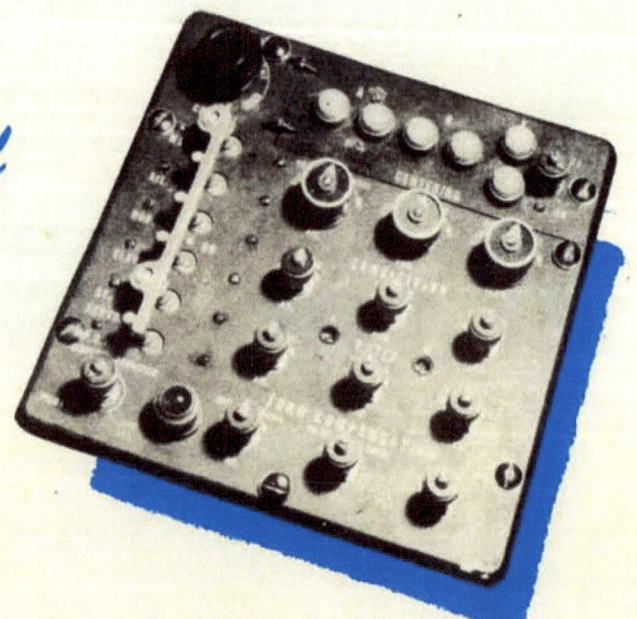

Alternate Method: The airplane commander centers PDI by turning the airplane in direction of the PDI needle. Then resume straight and level flight.

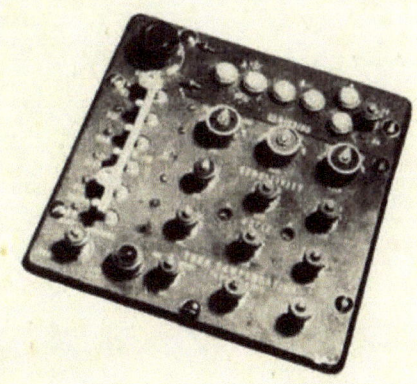

After Takeoff

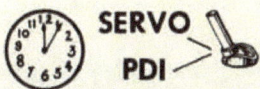

1. Turn on the master switch.

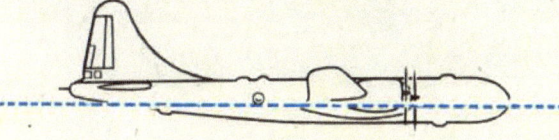

2. Ten minutes later, turn on PDI switch (and Servo switch, if separate.)

3. Ten minutes after turning on the master switch, trim the airplane for level flight at cruising speed.

5. Engage the autopilot. Put out aileron telltale lights with the aileron centering knob, then throw on the aileron engaging switch. Repeat the operation for rudder, then for elevator.

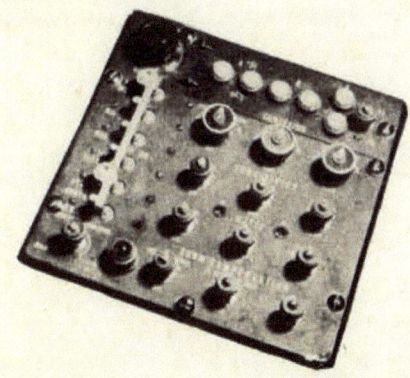

6. Make final autopilot trim corrections. If necessary, use centering knobs to level wings and center PDI.

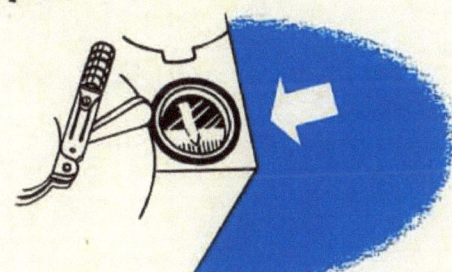

4. Have the bombardier disengage the autopilot clutch, center PDI and lock it in place by depressing the directional control lock. The PDI is held centered until the airplane commander has completed the engaging procedure. Then the autopilot clutch is re-engaged, and the directional arm lock released.

CAUTION
Never adjust mechanical trim tabs while the autopilot is engaged.

FLIGHT ADJUSTMENTS AND OPERATION

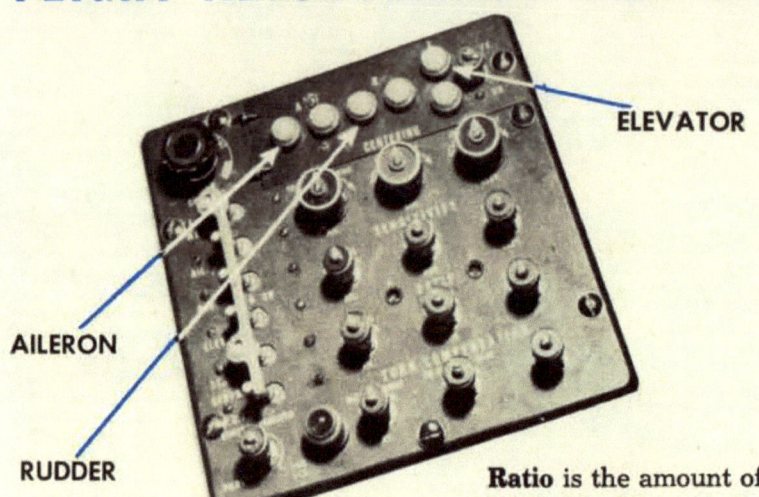

AILERON
RUDDER
ELEVATOR

After the C-1 autopilot is in operation, the pilot should carefully analyze the action of the airplane to make sure all adjustments have been made properly for smooth, accurate flight control.

When both **tell-tale lights** in any axis are extinguished, it indicates the autopilot is ready for engaging in that axis.

Before engaging, use each **centering knob** to adjust the autopilot control reference point to the straight and level flight position of the corresponding control surface. After engaging, use the centering knobs to make small attitude adjustments.

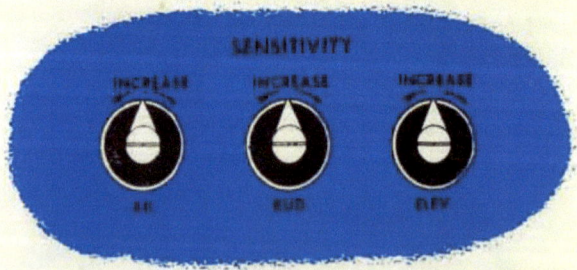

Sensitivity is comparable to a human pilot's reaction time. With sensitivity set high, the autopilot responds quickly to apply a correction for even the slightest deviation. If sensitivity is set low, flight deviations must be relatively large before the autopilot applies its corrective action.

Ratio is the amount of control surface movement applied by the autopilot in correcting a given deviation. It governs the speed of the airplane's response to corrective autopilot ac-

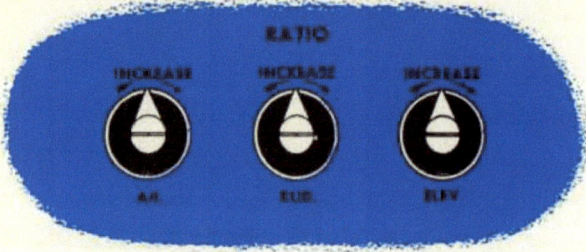

tions. Proper ratio adjustment depends on airspeed. If ratio is too high, the autopilot overcontrols the airplane and produces a ship-hunt; if ratio is too low, the autopilot undercontrols, and flight corrections are too small. After ratio adjustments have been made, centering may require readjustment.

To adjust **turn compensation**, have bombardier disengage autopilot clutch and move engaging knob to extreme right or extreme left. Airplane should bank 18° as indicated by artificial horizon. If it does not, adjust aileron compensation (bank trimmer) to attain 18° bank. Then, if turn is not coordinated, adjust rudder compensation (skid trimmer) to center inclinometer ball. Do not use aileron or rudder compensation knobs to adjust coordination of turn-control turns. Recovery from a bombardiers turn must be coordinated. If the PDI returns to center before the wings are level, decrease the rudder ratio or increase the aileron ratio, depending on the speed of the recovery. If the wings are level before the PDI is centered, increase rudder ratio or decrease aileron ratio, depending on the speed of recovery.

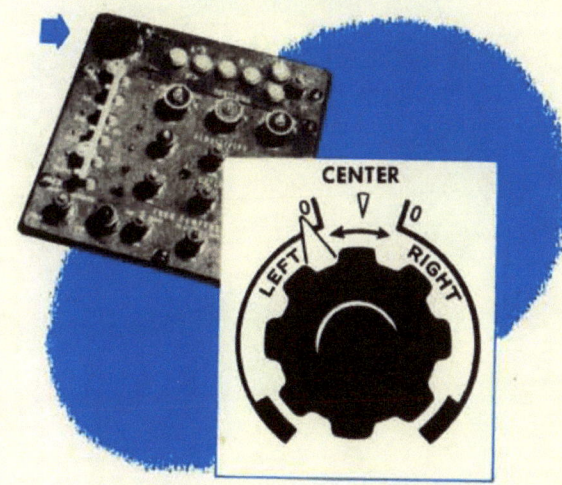

The airplane commander uses the **turn control** to turn the airplane while flying under automatic control. To adjust turn control, first make sure turn compensation adjustments have been made properly, then set turn control pointer at beginning of trip-lined area on dial.

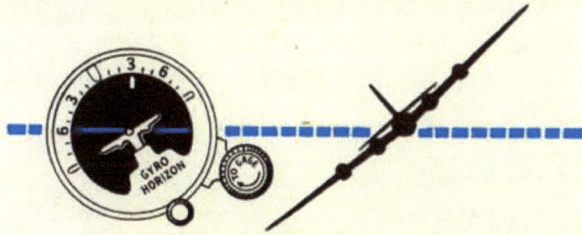

Airplane should bank 30°, as indicated by artificial horizon. If not, remove cap from aileron trimmer and adjust trimmer until a 30° bank is attained. Then, if turn is not coordinated, (inclinometer ball not centered), adjust rudder trimmer to center ball. Make final adjustments with both trimmers and replace caps. Set turn control at zero to resume straight and level flight; then re-center.

The **turn control transfer** has no effect unless the installation includes a remote turn control.

The **dashpot** on the stabilizer regulates the amount of rudder kick applied by the autopilot to correct rapid deviations in the turn axis. If

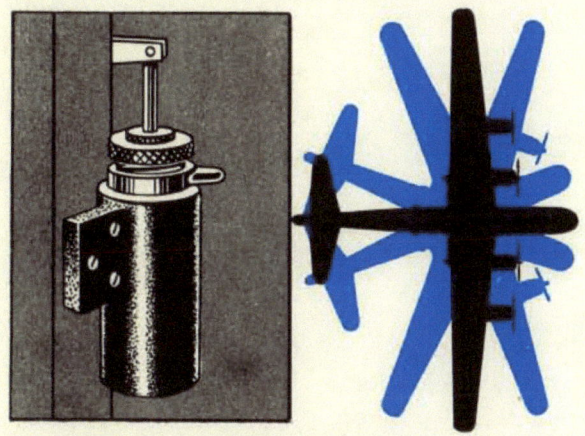

a rudder hunt develops which cannot be eliminated by adjustment of rudder ratio or sensitivity, the dashpot may require adjustment. To do this, loosen the locknut on the dashpot, turning the knurled ring up or down until hunting ceases, then tighten the locknut.

Cold-Weather Operation — When temperatures are between −12° and 0°C (10° and 32°F) autopilot units must be run for 30 minutes before engaging. If you desire accurate flight control immediately after takeoff, perform the autopilot warm-up before takeoff by turning on the master switch during the engine run-up, but make sure **autopilot is off during takeoff.** If warm-up is performed during flight, allow 30 minutes after turning on master switch before engaging. When temperatures are below −12°C (10°F) units must be preheated for 1 hour before takeoff. Use special heating covers or blankets with heating tubes.

Never operate the Turn Control without first making sure the PDI is centered

RESTRICTED

FLYING THE PDI MANUALLY

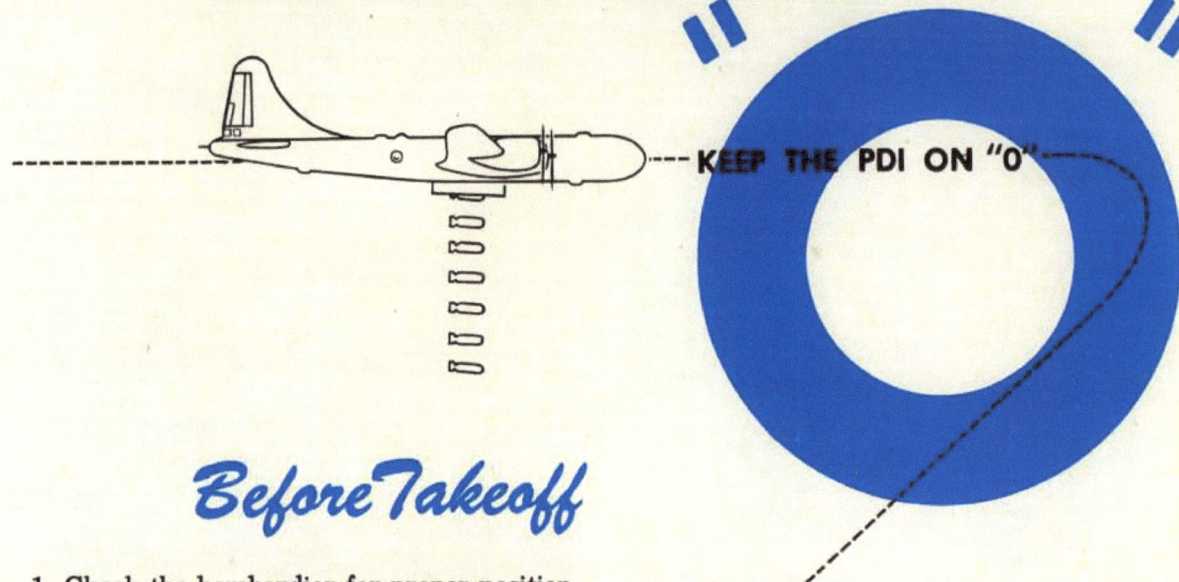

Before Takeoff

1. Check the bombardier for proper position of PDI needle for a left turn, right turn and neutral or 0 position.
2. When bombardier's PDI is left, airplane commander's PDI is right, and vice versa.

On the Bombing Run

Note: Normally bombing is done using the autopilot; however, if the autopilot is out of order the airplane commander may use the PDI.

1. To center the PDI needle, turn the plane in the direction of the needle.
2. At the beginning of the bombing run, the airplane commander can usually expect maximum PDI corrections. Avoid tendency to overcorrect by refraining from leading the needle.
3. No matter how slight the deviation of the PDI needle from 0, the needle must be immediately returned to 0.
4. Set turns must be coordinated; aileron and rudder turns, to effect more rapidly the desired degree of turn, and to avoid any excessive sliding of the bombsight lateral bubble and induced precession of the gyro.
5. Banks must never exceed 18°, to avoid tumbling of the bombsight gyro.
6. Keep PDI on 0 until bombardier calls "Bombs away."

RESTRICTED

RADIO EQUIPMENT

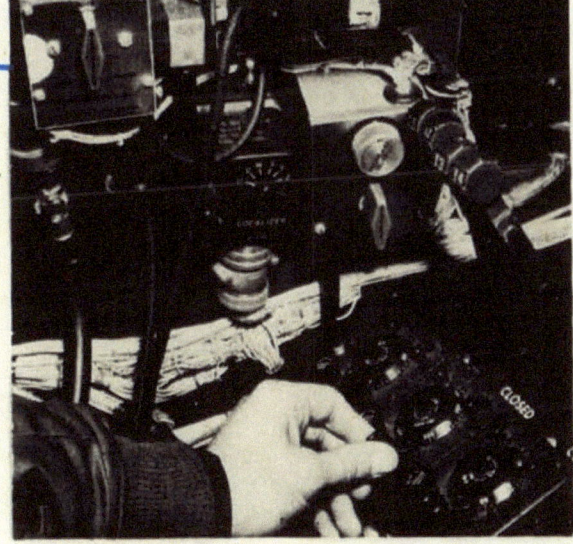

The general communications facilities in the B-29 consist of radio and interphone equipment to provide 2-way communication with ground stations and other airplanes, interphone communication between crew members, and the reception of radio range and marker beacon signals.

In addition, the B-29 also carries specialized equipment for automatic radio-direction finding, and the recognition and identification of friendly aircraft. However, since this is specialized and classified equipment, it is not covered in this manual. Special publications covering their maintenance and operation are available.

The general communications equipment consists of the following:

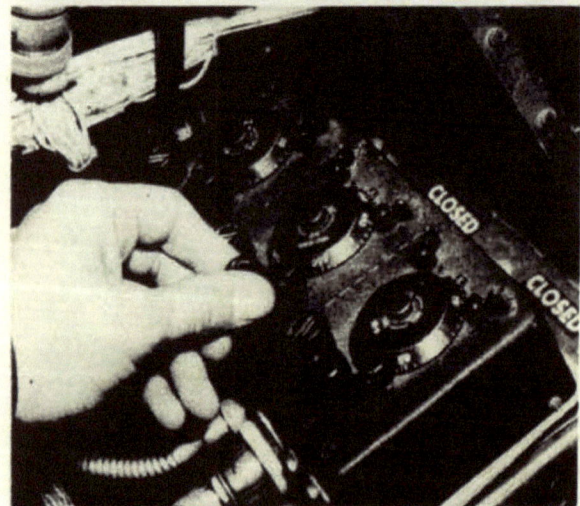

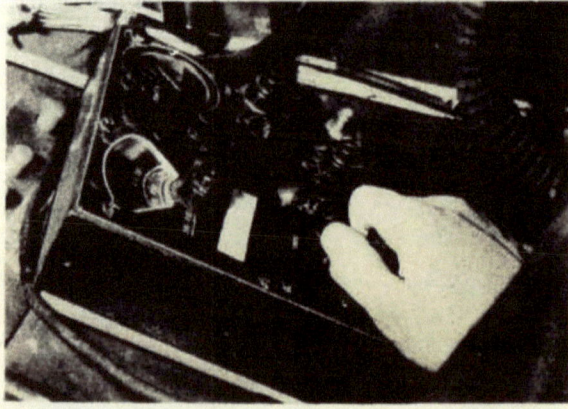

1. LIAISON RADIO SET

Receiver and transmitter for operation in the frequency ranges of 200 to 500 kilocycles (Kc) and 1500 to 12,000 Kc which are covered by seven interchangeable tuning units. Two antennas—a fixed antenna and a trailing antenna—are available for use with the liaison set. The right-hand wing skin forms the fixed antenna; a 250-foot wire wound on a motor-driven reel forms the trailing antenna. Either antenna may be selected by operating the shielded antenna transfer switch mounted on the cabin bulkhead above the radio operator's table. Your B-29 may be equipped with an eleven channel AN/ART 13 set. (See "Standard Procedures for Radio Operators.")

2. COMMAND RADIO SET

The command radio consists of two transmitters, three receivers, and auxiliary equipment. The equipment is short-range, and serves primarily for plane-to-plane communication on the following channels: Transmitters—4000 to 5300 Kc and 7000 to 9100 Kc. Receivers—190 to 500 Kc, 3000 to 6000 Kc, and 6000 to 9100 Kc. The command set antenna consists of half of the wire extending from the lead-in insulator at the radio operator's station to the top of the vertical stabilizer.

3. RADIO COMPASS

The radio compass consists of a receiver mounted in the forward bomb bay, control boxes mounted at the copilot's and radio operator's stations, a relay to switch control from one box to the other, an automatic direction-finding loop antenna mounted on the fuselage above the bomb bay, a retractable whip antenna aft of the upper forward turret, and direction indicators on the airplane commander's instrument panel and the radio operator's table. The compass operates on a frequency range from

> **Warning**
> The whip antenna should not be extended at airspeeds greater than 240 mph.

150 to 1750 Kc and may be used with the loop antenna, the whip antenna, or both.

4. MARKER BEACON RECEIVER

The marker beacon receiver operates on the ultra-high frequency of 75 megacycles (Mc). In use, it indicates signals received from instrument landing markers, fan-type markers, and cones of silence, and other ground facilities which employ 75-Mc horizontally polarized radiation. The antenna is mounted below the fuselage between the bomb bays.

5. INTERPHONE

The interphone system provides communication facilities for crew members at 11 stations — bombardier, airplane commander, copilot, flight engineer, navigator, radio operator, top gunner, side gunners, tail gunner, and crew compartment. Besides interphone facilities, the system also allows the crew limited use of the radio facilities.

6. IFF RADIO SET

The operation of this equipment is automatic and controlled by switches on top of the airplane commander's instrument panel and at the IFF control box. Two detonator switches are provided next to the airplane commander's control switch. Their purpose is to set off a detonating charge which destroys the equipment if it becomes necessary to abandon the airplane. When you push both buttons together, a small charge explodes in the receiver. There is also an automatic detonator switch which can be set to destroy the equipment when it is subjected to any severe shock. The IFF antenna is mounted on the forward bomb bay left-hand door.

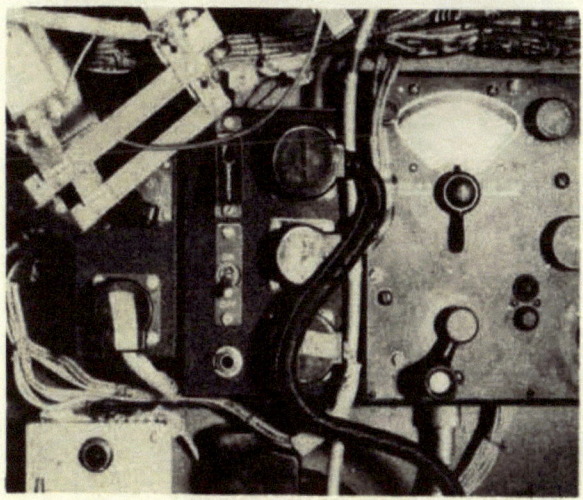

7. NAVIGATIONAL RADIO EQUIPMENT

This equipment is designed to give the airplane commander lateral guidance during landing operations. It consists of a receiver which can operate on six tuned frequencies (108-3, 108.7, 109.1, 109.5, 109.9, 110.3 Mc), a control box, antenna, and an indicator on the airplane commander's instrument panel. The antenna is mounted on the fuselage above the wing.

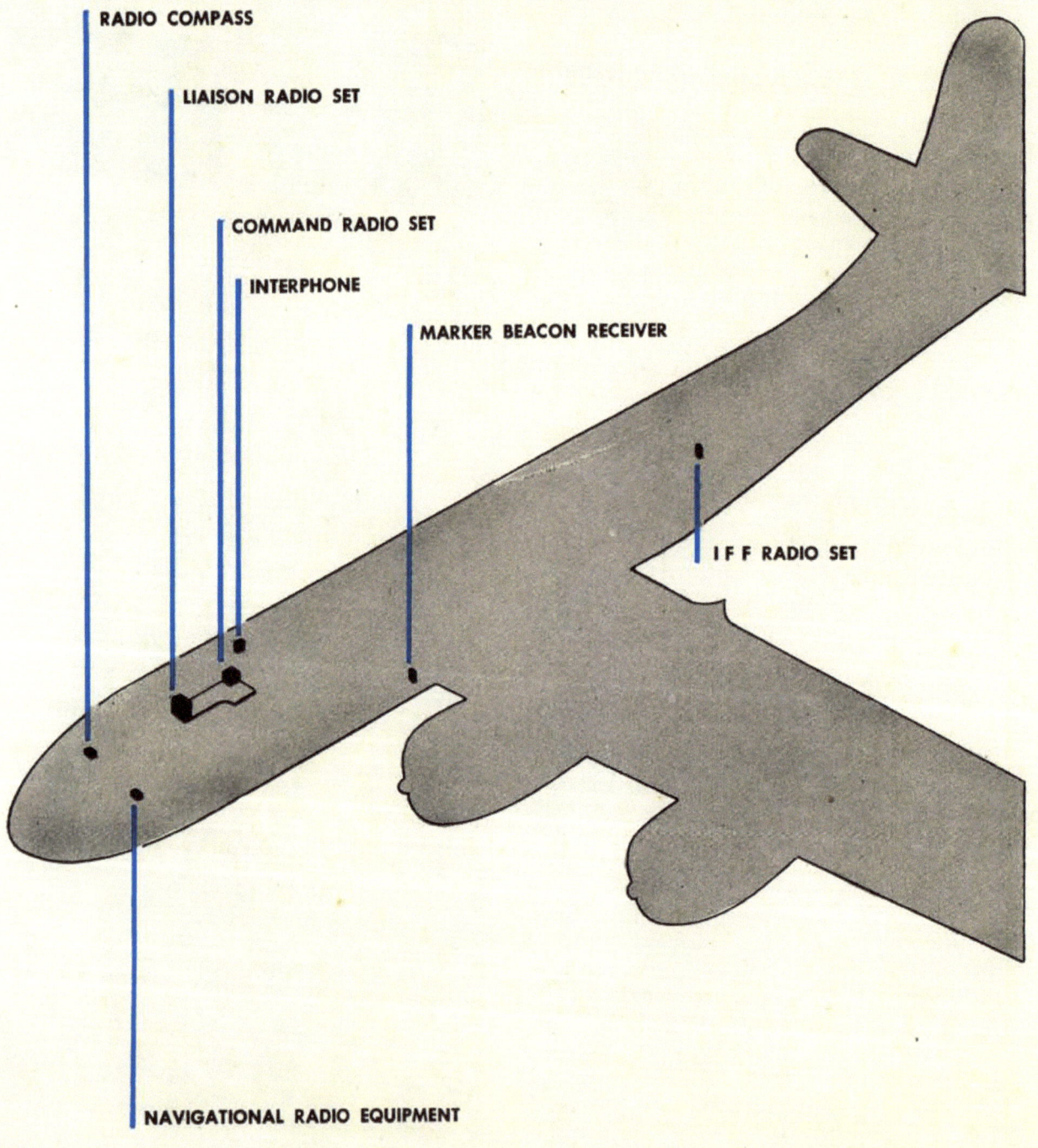

THE GYRO FLUX GATE COMPASS

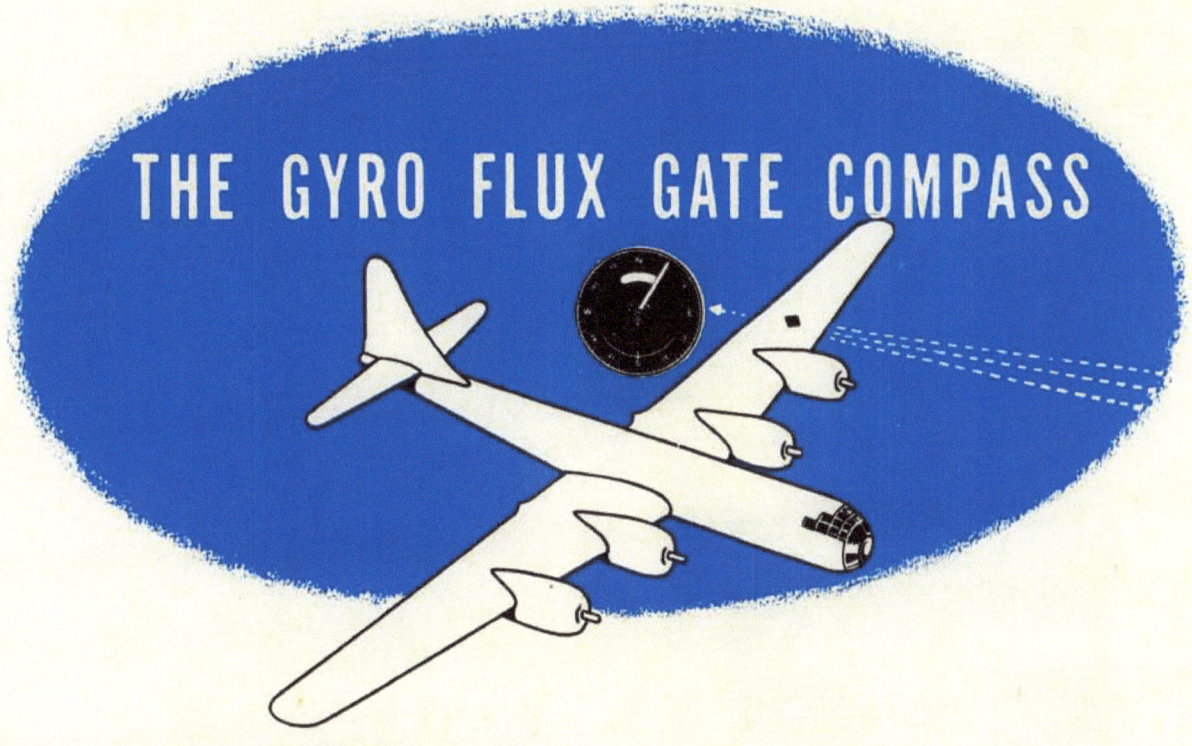

The gyro flux gate compass, remotely located in the left wing of the airplane, converts the earth's magnetic forces into electrical impulses to produce precise directional readings that can be duplicated on instruments at all desired points in the airplane.

Unlike the magnetic needle, it does not go off its reading in a dive, overshoot in a turn, hang in rough weather, or go haywire in polar regions.

DEVELOPMENT OF THE GATE

The gyro flux gate compass was developed to fill the need for an accurate compass for long-range navigation. The presence of so many magnetic materials (armor, electrical circuits, etc.) in the navigator's compartment made it almost impossible to find a desirable location for the direct-reading magnetic compass.

To eliminate this difficulty, it became necessary to place the magnetic element of the navigator's compass outside the compartment, i.e., **to use a remote indicating compass.** The unit which is remotely located is called the **transmitter**. The unit used by the navigator is the **master indicator**. For the benefit of the airplane

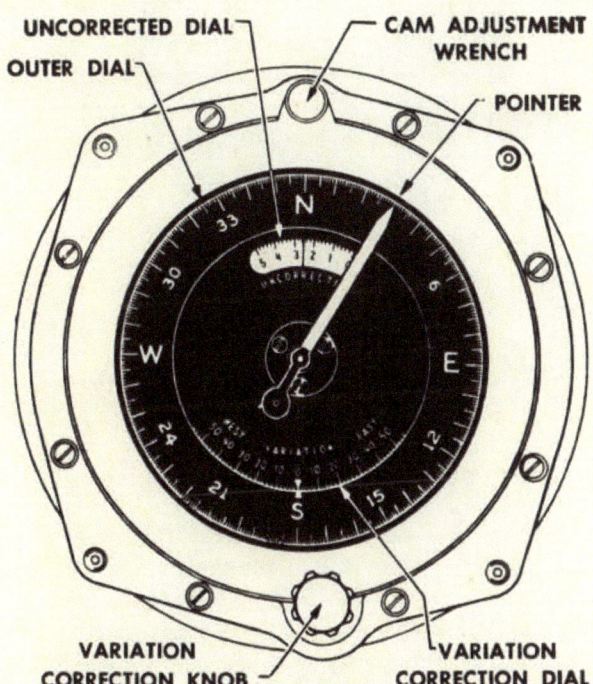

commander and such other crew members as may need compass readings, auxiliary instruments called **repeater indicators** may be installed in other parts of the airplane.

Units of the Flux Gate Compass

The gyro flux gate compass consists of three units which are analogous to the brain, heart, and muscles of the human body. The **transmitter**, located in the left wing of the airplane, is the brain of the instrument. The **amplifier** is the source of power for the compass and corresponds to the human heart. The **master indicator** does the work of turning a pointer and performs a function similar to that of the muscles in the human body.

1. THE BRAIN

Inside the remotely placed **transmitter** there is a magnetic sensitive element called the **flux gate** which picks up the direction signal by induction and transmits it to the **master indicator**. This element consists of three small coils, arranged in a triangle and held on a horizontal plane by a gyro. Each coil has a special soft iron core, and consists of a primary (or excitation) winding, and a secondary winding from which the signal is obtained.

Because each leg of the flux gate is at a different angle to the earth's magnetic field, and the induced voltage is relative to the angle, each leg produces a different voltage. When the angular relationship between the flux gate and the earth's magnetic field changes, there is a relative change in the voltages in the three legs of the secondary. These voltages are the motivating force for the gyro flux gate compass master indicator, which provides indications of the exact position of the flux gate in relation to the earth's magnetic field.

Each coil is a direction sensitive element; but one alone would provide an ambiguous reading because it could tell north from east, for instance, but not north from south. Therefore, it is necessary to employ three coils and combine their output to give the direction signal.

2. THE HEART

The amplifier furnishes the various excitation voltages at the proper frequency to the transmitter and master indicator. It amplifies the autosyn signal which controls the master indicator and serves as a junction box for the whole compass system.

Power for the amplifier comes from the airplane's inverter and is converted to usable forms for other units. The input of the amplifier is 400-cycle alternating current and various voltages may be used depending upon the source available.

3. THE MUSCLE

The master indicator is the muscle of the system because it furnishes the mechanical power to drive the pointer on the main instrument dial. The pointer is driven through a cam mechanism which automatically corrects the reading for compass deviation so that a corrected indication is obtained on all headings. The shaft of the pointer is geared to another small transmitting unit in the master indicator which can operate as many as six repeat indicators at other locations.

The amplifier, master indicators and repeaters all are unaffected by local magnetic disturbances.

How to Operate the Compass

1. Leave the toggle switch on the flux gate amplifier ON at all times so that the compass starts as soon as the airplane's inverter is turned ON.

2. Leave the caging switch in the UNCAGE position at all times except when running through the caging cycle.

3. About 5 minutes after starting engines, throw caging switch in CAGE position. Leave it there about 30 seconds and then throw to UNCAGE again.

4. With the new push-button type caging switch, depress it for a few seconds until a red signal light goes on. Then release the switch and the caging cycle is automatically completed, at which time the red light goes out.

5. Set in the local variation on the master indicator if you wish the pointer to read true heading.

6. If at any time during flight the compass indications lead you to suspect that the gyro is off vertical, run through the caging cycle when the airplane is in normal flight attitude, especially when leveling off after climb.

NOTE For further details concerning functions, operation and flight instructions, see T. O. 05-15-27.

COLD-WEATHER OPERATION OF THE B-29

The following units in the B-29 are important in cold weather operation. Give them special attention and check when cold weather operation is anticipated.

Oil dilution is so arranged that all engines may be diluted simultaneously or individually by momentary-contact switches on the flight engineer's control panel. The oil dilution line runs from the Y-drain valves to the carburetor.

Each engine fuel-tank assembly has a drain cock reached through a small access door on the underside of the wing. Drain the bomb bay tanks by removing squareheaded pipe plugs.

To facilitate the draining of the oil, drain tubes can be attached to the drain cocks to carry oil overboard. Complete oil drainage is possible through the Y-drain cocks. Oil and fuel tank vent lines are designed so that moisture drains out of them and the engine breather lines end aft of the cowl flaps in a warm area. Oil cooler shutters play a vital part in cold weather operation and operate automatically.

The operation of the intercooler shutters is important in cold weather operations.

Supercharger boost control is sometimes useful in disposing of any accumulation of carburetor ice.

All B-29's have American Bosch induction vibrators for added starting boost. They are controlled by the starter switches.

Propeller anti-icing is used on all B-29's, and is controlled by a rheostat on the flight engineer's stand.

The external electric power receptacle is located in the No. 2 nacelle wheel well in older aircraft or in the nosewheel well in newer modified models. Use the external power cart in all winter ground operation to save the battery.

All oxygen valves should be opened and closed slowly during cold weather to prevent a surge of pressure which might result in an explosion.

When operating under extreme cold weather conditions, carefully check all safety latches and emergency exit latches for freedom of action prior to takeoff. Water and moisture may enter the latches, causing them to freeze and stick.

Batteries must have special attention in cold climates. At freezing temperatures, or below, the battery should be removed if portable generators are not available for engine starting, and stored in some suitable place where the temperature is above freezing, preferable around 20°C. Battery freezing temperatures are in proportion to the specific gravity of the electrolyte. The lower the specific gravity, the higher the freezing point.

NOTE Remove all ice and snow from the airplane and control surfaces before takeoff.

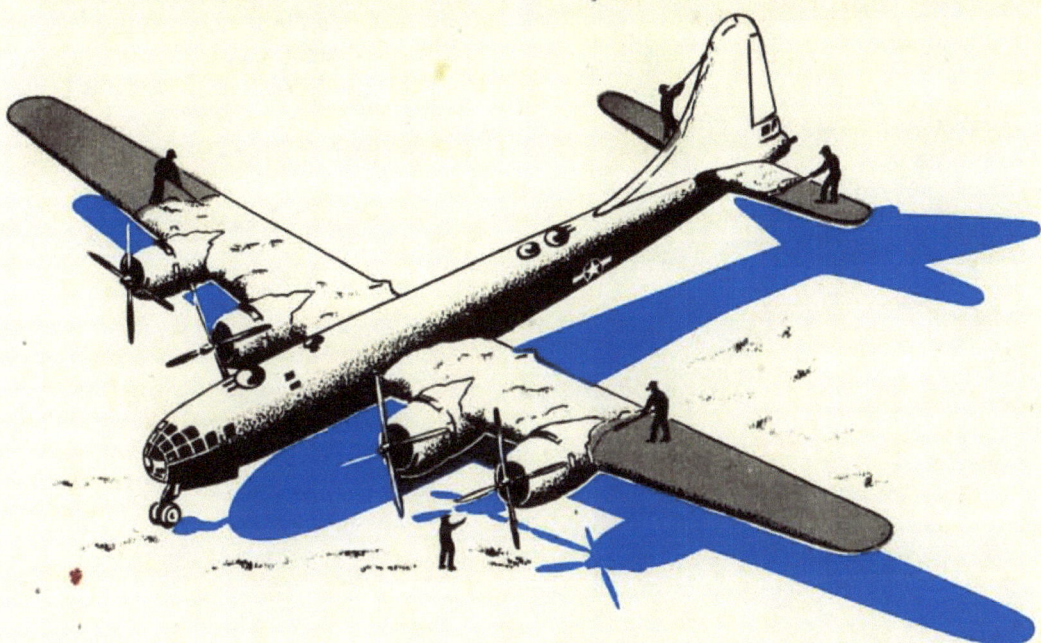

When parking an airplane on snow or ice, provide some sort of insulation under the tires to prevent them from freezing to the ground. Failure to adhere to this rule may result in tearing off large chunks of rubber when the airplane is moved.

Special Ground Procedures

Perform these more frequently than routine maintenance checks.

1.—Drain fuel tank sumps and fuel strainers frequently to avoid freezing of accumulated water.
2.—Check booster and fuel transfer motor for proper operation.
3.—Check fuel shut-off valve operation.
4.—See that fuel tank vent lines are clear.
5.—Drain oil tank sump, oil cooler, and Y valve to remove water.
6.—Check for water at engine oil sump magnetic plug.
7.—Be sure that the vent lines to engine crankcase are clear.
8.—Check engine oil outlet connections for tightness and possible slippage.
9.—Drain hydraulic system filter.
10.—Check air pressure and drain condensation from hydraulic accumulators.
11.—Operate the propeller feathering pumps long enough to place a fresh supply of oil in the lines and dome. This eliminates water in the lines.
12.—Check battery to determine if specific gravity is sufficient to avoid freezing under the expected temperatures.
13.—Use proper cold weather fluids and lubricants.
14. Check pitot head for ice and obstructions.
15.—Drain oil gage lines and refill with proper fluid.
16.—Check controls for freedom of operation. Condensation inside the wing may cause ice to form on control mechanisms. Removal of such ice is difficult. (Use heat. Chipping frequently results in damage to the airplane.)
17.—Check ice elimination equipment.
  a.—Operate the propeller anti-icing system and check for steady flow of fluid.

Communication Equipment Check

1.—Don't use a hand microphone in cold weather. Moisture collects and freezes in the small holes of the microphone mouthpiece. Use throat type microphones for all cold weather operations.
2.—Be sure that all antennae are clear of ice.
3.—In transmitters, frequency shift occurs with wide variations in temperature. Retune and check the transmitter frequently until a stable temperature is reached.

Preflight Instructions and Procedure

Before starting the engines see that all items under ground maintenance and special ground maintenance have been checked, and then proceed in the following manner:

1.—If the ground temperature is below −23°C (−10°F), preheat the engine and the accessory compartment. Use the sleeve on the engine cover and the starter meshing handle access door for warm air inlets. Preheating takes at least an hour in extremely cold weather. The engine may be started when the head temperature reaches 0°C (32°F).

2.—If the engine oil has been drained, heat it to 70° to 80°C (158° to 176°F), and put it into the tank just before starting.

3.—If the oil has been heated by the tank immersion heaters, the oil in the lines may still be congealed. Check by opening the Y drain. If oil does not flow out, heat the lines.

4.—You may have to warm up the putt-putt with a portable heater to start it.

WARNING Portable ground heaters give off carbon monoxide. Don't use them in closed occupied space.

5.—In extremely cold weather, preheat the instrument panel and the autosyn transmitters in the nacelles.

Cold Weather Starting

When the engines are warm enough to start, take off the covers and follow the normal starting procedure, except as noted below.

1. After one turn of the propeller, hold primer on about 2 to 4 seconds and release. Then prime intermittently, at 1-second intervals. When the engine fires several cylinders consecutively and starts to pick up speed, (hold the primer down) until engine speed reaches at least 800 rpm and starts to smooth out. Move mixture controls to AUTO-RICH and release primer. The engine will then keep running on the carburetor feed.

2. Watch for fuel running out of the blower case drain. This will happen if the engine dies after the mixture controls are moved to AUTO-RICH, or if you have overprimed. If fuel does run out of the blower drain, shut off the ignition, open the throttle wide, and have the engine pulled through by hand to clear out the excess fuel. A second attempt at starting may now be made.

3. If the engine doesn't start on the second try, check a top and bottom sparkplug for icing or fouling.

4. Always use external power for starting.

Engine Warmup

1. Keep the cowl flaps open. Closed flaps may cause engine damage or fire.

2. Operate the propellers several times through their full rpm range.

Precautions Before Takeoff

1. All ice, snow, or frost **must be** removed from the wings. Even a thin layer of frost can cause loss of lift and create dangerous stall characteristics.

2. Check for snow and frost just before takeoff. Don't depend on your takeoff speed to blow away snow that has blown around fuselage and wing openings during the taxi run.

3. When frost is forming rapidly, keep all possible covers on while taxiing out to takeoff position.

4. At the last possible moment, check all controls for complete freedom of movement.

5. Apply brakes slowly. The rubber expander tubes in the drums become brittle in cold weather.

RESTRICTED

Flight Instructions and Procedure

1. Keep the cowl flaps at least 7½° open during cold weather takeoff, regardless of head temperatures. Since there is no possibility of an engine cooling off too much during takeoff and rated power climb, you take a needless risk of damaging your engine by closing the flaps.

3. Carburetor icing is most likely to occur when the carburetor air temperature is below 25°C in high-humidity air. You can recognize it by roughness and loss of power if the turbos are on. If the turbos are off, the manifold pressure also drops.

3. To avoid carburetor icing, check the intercooler flaps. Under conditions likely to produce ice, they should be adjusted to maintain carburetor air temperatures (CAT) between 25°C and 38°C.

4. To prevent carburetor icing during an approach and landing, watch CAT closely, maintaining temperature limits given above.

5. Watch the outside air thermometer, and if you run into a cold front, run up the engines frequently to keep them warm and check their acceleration.

Post-Flight Instructions and Procedure

AFTER LANDING

1. Insulate the tires from snow or ice with fabric, hay, grass, green boughs, or other material to prevent the tires from freezing to the surface. Failure to take this precaution often results in large chunks of rubber being torn from the tires when the airplane moves.

2. Leave the emergency escape hatch or some other opening partly open for circulation of air and to prevent frosting of windows.

3. Dilute the oil before stopping the engines, if you expect a cold weather start.

Oil Dilution Before Leaving Airplane

1. If the oil temperatures are too high, stop engines and allow oil to cool. Restart engines and proceed with dilution when oil temperature falls below 40°C (104°F).

2. Idle engines between 1000 and 1200 rpm. (Avoid sparkplug fouling by a short acceleration period at the end of the dilution run.)

3. Recommended oil dilution periods for various outside air temperatures are as follows:

RESTRICTED

GRADE 1120 OIL

OUTSIDE AIR TEMPERATURE	DILUTION PERIOD
4°C to −7°C (39°F to 20°F)	3 minutes
−7°C to −18°C (20°F to 0°F)	4 minutes
−18°C to −29°C (0°F to −20°F)	6 minutes
−29°C to −34°C (−20°F to −29°F)	8 minutes

FLIGHT ENGINEER'S CONTROL STAND ➤

GRADE 1100 OIL

OUTSIDE AIR TEMPERATURE	DILUTION PERIOD
4°C to −12°C (39°F to 10°F)	2 minutes
−12°C to −29°C (10°F to −20°F)	4 minutes
−29°C to −46°C (−20°F to −51°F)	8 minutes
−46°C to −51°C (−51°F to −60°F)	7 minutes
−51°C to −56°C (−60°F to −67°F)	9 minutes

TIPS ON OIL DILUTION

1. If the engine has run less than 30 minutes since the last oil dilution, the oil still is partly diluted. To allow for this, shorten the dilution period shown in the chart. For example, if the engine has been running only 15 minutes, dilute the oil only half as long as the chart shows. Never dilute oil for less than ½ minute.

2. Under all conditions, release dilution switch only after engine stops.

3. Do not permit engine oil pressure to fall below 15 psi. If necessary, stop the engine, wait 15 minutes, and continue dilution.

4. If oil tank servicing is necessary, split the dilution period in half and service the oil at end of the first period.

5. If the oil temperature rises about 50°C (122°F) because of a long dilution period, it is necessary to dilute the oil in two or more periods.

6. Operation of the dilution system is indicated by a substantial fuel pressure drop. If this fuel pressure drop does not occur, investigate. The dilution solenoid may be stuck, the line may be plugged, or a restricted fitting reversed.

7. To provide diluted oil to the dome of the propeller during the last 2 minutes of dilution, move the throttle up to 1500 rpm and move the propeller rpm switches from limit light to limit light. Run the props through two cycles. Then move the throttle back to the original position. Repeat the operation. **Note:** A slight amount of oil leakage through blade packings is to be expected.

8. To provide diluted oil in the feathering lines before releasing the oil dilution switch, increase the engine speed to 1200 rpm. Depress the feathering button until the rpm drops to 1000. Then pull the button out to stop the propeller from completely feathering.

9. Oil Dilution at Engine Start—In starting the engine make a normal start without regard to the oil dilution system. After starting the engine, if a heavy viscous oil is indicated by an oil pressure that is too high, or by an oil pressure that fluctuates or falls back when the engine rpm is increased, push the dilution control momentarily several times to decrease the viscosity of the oil. Use this procedure with caution. Use it only if time and extreme temperature conditions do not permit engine warm-up in the normal manner.

10. It is safe to make immediate takeoffs, after oil dilution, without the normal warm-up, provided there has been a rise in oil temperature and oil pressure is steady and the engine is running smoothly. Cold oil, properly diluted, has the same viscosity as hot undiluted oil, and, therefore, the same ability to circulate and properly lubricate an aircraft engine.

11. High percentage of oil dilution does not harm the engine bearings if oil pressures remain normal.

12. Over-dilution may result in complete loss of oil because the scavenging system is unable to return oil to the tank at a sufficient rate. When this occurs, oil is discharged through the engine breather lines.

13. Engines which suddenly show a loss in oil pressure or throw oil out of the breather during flight should be checked to make certain that the oil dilution valve is in the closed position and fully seated. Momentarily actuating the dilution switch to turn the valve on and off may seat the valve. Satisfactory operation will be resumed after the fuel evaporates from the oil. **Note:** For any additional information, refer to T. O. 01-20EJ-1.

ICE PREVENTION AND ELIMINATION

CARBURETOR ICE

To eliminate carburetor ice—indicated by engine roughness, a drop in manifold pressure, and carburetor air temperatures below 25°C—increase power to 2400 rpm and 43.5" Hg. and close the intercoolers (controlled by four toggle switches on flight engineer's stand). This eliminates carburetor ice within a few seconds. If

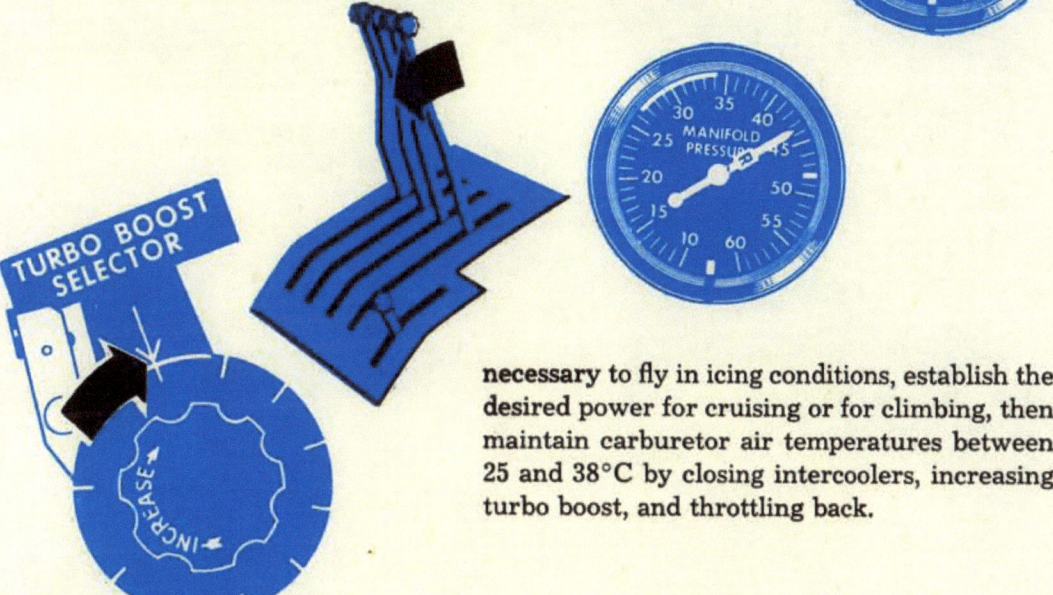

necessary to fly in icing conditions, establish the desired power for cruising or for climbing, then maintain carburetor air temperatures between 25 and 38°C by closing intercoolers, increasing turbo boost, and throttling back.

PROPELLER ICE

To prevent or eliminate prop ice, turn on anti-icer pumps (toggle switch on flight engineer's switch panel). Pumps are under floor of rear pressurized compartment—one for inboard engines and one for outboard engines. Under flight engineer's switch panel are two separate rheostats for controlling flow of anti-icer fluid.

PITOT TUBE

To prevent or eliminate pitot tube ice, turn pitot heat on (toggle switch on flight engineer's switch panel).

WING ICE

To eliminate wing ice, use de-icer toggle switch (flight engineer's switch panel) as necessary.

RESTRICTED

HIGH ALTITUDE OPERATION OF THE B-29

Pressurized Cabin

Compressed air for supercharging the fuselage compartments is supplied by the inboard turbos of the inboard engines. After compressed air passes from the impeller into the carburetor air duct, some of the compressed air is directed through the cabin air duct, through the aftercooler, and into the cabin through the cabin air valve. This happens only when the cabin air valve is open.

When the cabin air conditioning system is used, the aftercooler flap is closed to provide heat, opened to provide cooling. With the aftercooler flap closed, hot air from around the exhaust collector ring is directed through the aftercooler to heat the cabin air. With the aftercooler flap open, cool air is directed through the aftercooler, overcoming heat of compression and reducing the temperature of the cabin air.

MAINTAINS PRESSURE EQUAL TO THAT AT 8000 FEET FROM 8000 TO 30,000 FEET

Air is released from the cabin by two automatic regulators in the rear pressurized compartment, which maintain the following cabin pressures:

0 to 8000 feet—Pressure differential of 1".
8000 to 30,000 feet—Cabin altitude 8000 feet.
30,000 to 40,000 feet—Cabin altitude increases from 8000 feet to 12,000 feet.

30,000 FEET AND ABOVE A DIFFERENTIAL OF 13.34" HG. BETWEEN CABIN AND OUTSIDE AIR

RESTRICTED

Cabin-pressurizing controls and indicators are located at the flight engineer's station...

The job of pressurizing and depressurizing (except in emergencies) belongs to the flight engineer. He must watch outside and cabin altimeters outside and cabin rate-of-climb indicators, cabin differential pressure gage, and cabin air rate-of-flow gages.

Pressurizing Procedure

Under normal conditions, begin pressurizing at 8000 feet. Close all windows, pressure doors, and the cabin pressure relief valve (under left side of flight engineer's seat). Open the cabin air valves on the engineer's control stand. **Note:** Be sure that knurled knobs on top of cabin pressure regulators, at forward end of rear pressure compartment, are unscrewed, as these regulators do not operate if knobs are screwed down. When leveling out for cruising, the airplane commander sets up the predetermined power. If cabin air flow is then too low with the cabin air valves full open, the airplane commander increases the turbo boost slightly and retards throttles to the desired manifold pressure.

The cabin air flow desired is the minimum flow which maintains the cabin altitude but never more than 1000 cubic feet per minute and not more than 600 cubic feet per minute at altitudes above 33,000 feet.

For maximum engine efficiency, set the turbos to the lowest point which maintains the desired cabin air flow. If the cabin pressure regulators are not working properly, screw down the knurled knobs on the cabin pressure regulators and then regulate the cabin pressure with the cabin air valves and cabin pressure relief valve.

When operating above 30,000 feet, the flight engineer should not allow the cabin pressure differential to exceed 13.34" Hg. Close the cabin air valves enough to prevent higher differentials.

On all pressurized flights above 8000 feet, the airplane commander orders the crew members to have their oxygen masks ready for instant use. Masks should always be attached to the left side of the helmet. If the cabin is suddenly depressurized, crew members can use oxygen immediately and prevent suffering from oxygen lack. A sudden increase in cabin altitude is not harmful unless flying above 30,000 feet, in which case some crew members may experience a temporary painful reaction from the bends.

If power is set for range or maximum endurance cruising, it may be necessary to run the inboard engines at 200 rpm higher than the outboard engines, to provide the additional boost necessary to supercharge the cabin. In this case, transfer fuel to the inboard engines since they use more fuel. Set the outboard engines at the rpm which maintains the proper airspeed.

When pressurizing at high altitudes, open the cabin air valves slowly, adjusting these valves to a 1000-foot-per-minute rate of descent. Differential pressure may sometimes seal up a leak, suddenly, during pressurizing procedure. This may push the cabin rate-of-descent far beyond 1000 feet per minute (FPM). So while pressurizing, until the cabin altitude is stabilized, watch the cabin rate of descent closely and be prepared to adjust the cabin air valves if the rate of descent changes quickly.

Depressurizing Procedure

The cabin may be depressurized by closing the flight engineer's cabin air valves and opening the cabin pressure relief valve, if necessary. In emergencies, the cabin can be quickly depressurized by pulling either of the two emergency cabin pressure release handles (one on the airplane commander's control stand, and the other on the starboard sidewall of the rear pressure compartment near forward bulkhead).

Always depressurize when expecting enemy action, when ship is on fire, or when preparing to abandon ship.

RESTRICTED

OXYGEN SYSTEM

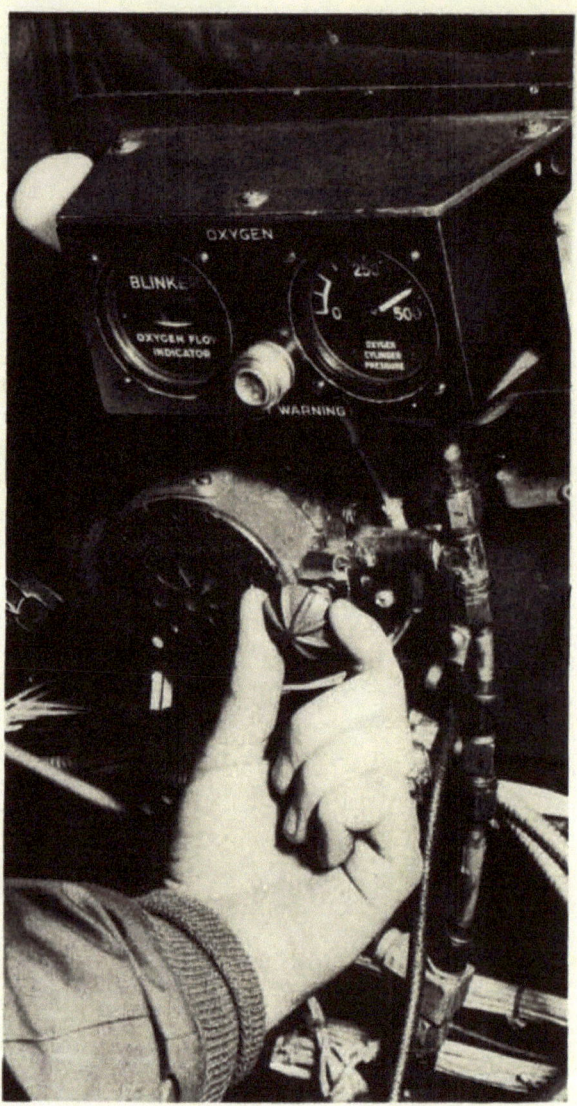

The B-29 demand oxygen system is supplied by 18 type C-1 low-pressure, shatterproof oxygen cylinders.

There are 14 oxygen stations, each station consisting of the following equipment—A-14 demand mask, A-12 demand regulator, pressure gage, flow indicator, low-pressure supply cylinders, and filler and distribution manifolding. Two types of demand regulators are used in the B-29—the Airco and the Pioneer. You may find either one on your plane. They look slightly different but the principle of operation is the same for both.

The length of time that the oxygen supply lasts varies with the individual requirements of your crew, their activity, the temperature, and the equipment. For this reason it is difficult to abide by any hard and fast rule. In general, however, with 400 psi pressure and the automix ON, there is more than 10 hours' supply of oxygen for a crew of 11 men flying at 15,000 feet. Both types of regulators are least economical at altitudes between 20,000 and 30,000 feet.

For more detailed information for the operation of your oxygen equipment, particularly that at your own station, see "Personal Equipment—A Manual for B-29 Crews."

There is safety in altitude if you know your oxygen...

see your *Personal Equipment Officer*

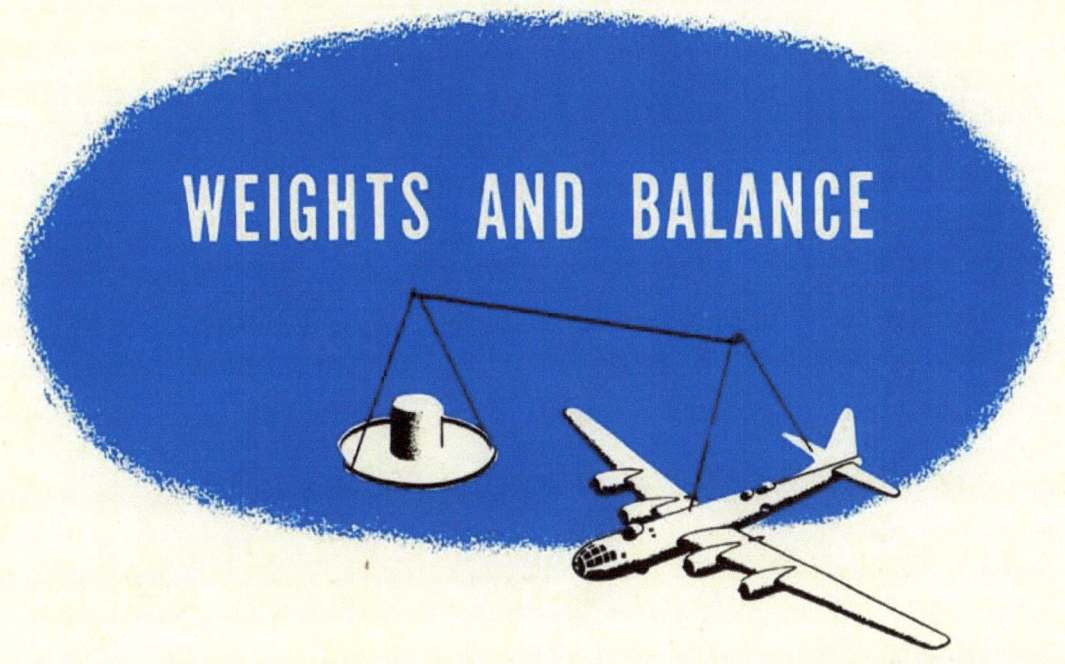

WEIGHTS AND BALANCE

The balance of any airplane is just as important as its total weight. On the B-29, it is even more important. Pay particular attention to the location of the center of gravity and impress your flight engineer with its importance. At any time during any flight he must be able to supply you with complete weight and balance information. Never take off and never land without first consulting the Form F. Have your copilot check it also.

A relatively small difference in the location of the center of gravity can make a considerable difference in the flying characteristics of the B-29. For best operation, the center of gravity should be well within the allowable range of limits, as near 25% MAC as possible. If it is not, you will find it difficult to get on the step, with the result that the airplane will mush through the air.

Read and understand the weight and balance information in T. O. AN 01-1B-40. Check your flight engineer on his understanding of weight and balance.

All loads in all 12 compartments of the airplane not part of the basic airplane must be calculated with the load computer.

Here is a sample computation; follow it through:

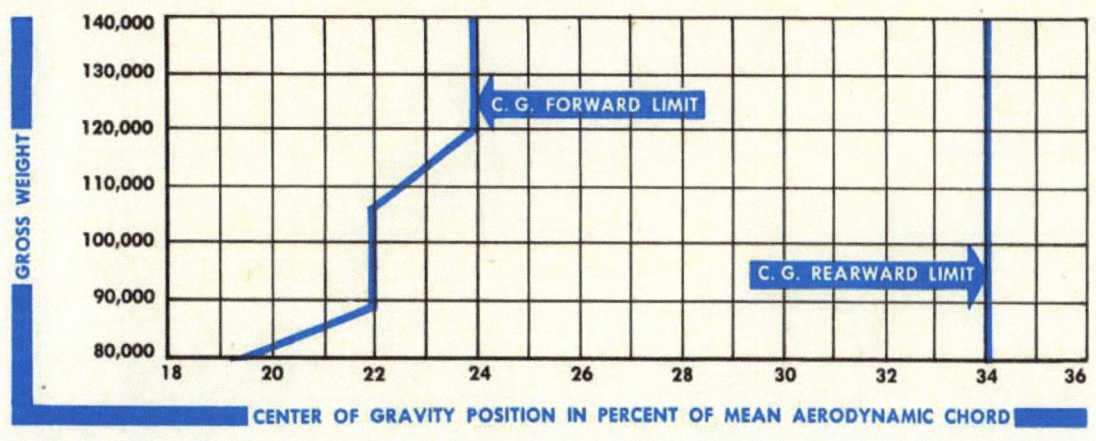

RESTRICTED

WEIGHT and BALANCE CLEARANCE — FORM F

DATE	5/12/44	MISSION	TACTICAL
AIRPLANE	B-29	FROM	SALINA, KANSAS
SERIAL NO.	41-36965	TO	ELGIN FIELD, FLORIDA

COMPARTMENT	ITEM	WEIGHT	INDEX OR MOMENT	COMPARTMENT	ITEM	WEIGHT	INDEX OR MOMENT
Y	Basic Airplane	78,800	69.7	Y	Totals Brought Forward	80,800	56.1
A (STRUCTURAL CAPACITY) ___ lb.	Crew 1 / Cargo / TOTAL	200	56.6	Q (STRUCTURAL CAPACITY) ___ lb.	Crew / Cargo / TOTAL		
B (STRUCTURAL CAPACITY) ___ lb.	Crew 3 / Cargo / TOTAL	600	48.5	R (STRUCTURAL CAPACITY) ___ lb.	Crew / Cargo / TOTAL		
C (STRUCTURAL CAPACITY) ___ lb.	Crew 2 / Cargo / TOTAL	400	44.3	S (STRUCTURAL CAPACITY) ___ lb.	Crew / Cargo / TOTAL		
D (STRUCTURAL CAPACITY) ___ lb.	Crew / Cargo / TOTAL			T (STRUCTURAL CAPACITY) ___ lb.	Crew / Cargo / TOTAL		

Minimum Landing Gross Weight

		Rd.	Cal.	Weight	Index
AMMUNITION (By Compartment)	C	1200	50	360	52.4
	G	600	50	180	54.1
	J	600	50	180	57.3
	L	600	50	180	62.7
	L	200	20M	180	66.9

COMPARTMENT	ITEM	WEIGHT	INDEX
E	Crew / Cargo / TOTAL		
F	Crew / Cargo / TOTAL		
G	Crew 3 / Cargo / TOTAL	600	50.6
H	Crew / Cargo / TOTAL		
I	Crew / Cargo / TOTAL		

BOMBS		Weight	Index
Forward		6,000	31.9
Aft		6,000	55.9
External			

COMPARTMENT	ITEM	WEIGHT	INDEX
J	Crew / Cargo / TOTAL		

OIL (U.S. 7.5 & Imp. 9 lb./gal.)

	Gals	Weight	Index
Inbd Tank	170	1275	52.5
Outbd	170	1275	50.2

FUEL (U.S. 6 & Imp. 7.2 lb./gal.)

	Gals	Weight	Index
Inbd	2900	17400	43.6
Outd	2700	16200	43.8

COMPARTMENT	ITEM	WEIGHT	INDEX
K	Crew / Cargo / TOTAL		
L	Crew 1 / Cargo / TOTAL	200	56.1
M	Crew / Cargo / TOTAL		

Bomb Bay:

	WEIGHT	INDEX
TOTAL WT. & INDEX (Uncorrected)	128,705	43.8
Corrections (If required)		
TAKE-OFF WEIGHT & INDEX	128,705	43.8

LIMITS
Recommended Max. Take-off Gross Weight — 135,000 LB.
Recommended Max. Landing Gross Weight — ___ LB.

COMPARTMENT	ITEM	WEIGHT	INDEX
N	Crew / Cargo / TOTAL		
O	Crew / Cargo / TOTAL		
P	Crew / Cargo / TOTAL		
TOTALS TO BE CARRIED FORWARD		80,800	56.1

COMPUTED BY *J+ W. D. Bailey*
APPROVED BY *J+ R. X. Muhlestead*
PILOT *William J. Bohnaker*

RESTRICTED

REVISED 1 MARCH 1945

BAILOUT

As airplane commander you must decide whether or not bailout is necessary. Give the crew the warning when an emergency first appears. If it develops that you can handle the emergency safely without bailout, you can cancel the preparation order later.

Bailout signals are as follows:

Prepare to Bail Out: Three short rings on the alarm bell. Also warn the crew by interphone and obtain acknowledgment from each crew member.

Bail Out of the Airplane: One long sustained ring.

Climb to a safe altitude for bailout, if necessary.

Teach your crew **not to leave the airplane until ordered to bail out!** Each crew member must know when, where, and how he is to leave the airplane. The only way to make sure that abandonment will be carried out safely and properly is to go through often repeated bailout drills on the ground. Don't forget to include simulating the destruction of designated instruments by specific crew members.

The illustration below shows the exit and the escape hatch used by each crew member. Have each crew member learn his part and practice the coordinated procedure with the whole crew.

It will be the responsibility of the airplane commander to formulate a bailout sequence for his particular crew and drill them until the procedure becomes automatic.

The forward bomb bay is an alternate exit for the men in the forward compartment. The center gunners use the rear exit door as an alternate exit. The radar operator's (optional gunner's) alternate exit is the aft bomb bay. The tail gunner uses the hatch in his compartment as alternate exit. Over water, he gets his individual life raft from the unpressurized section and goes out the rear exit door.

When bailout warning is given over water, each man removes the individual life raft pack from its position near his station, and snaps it onto his parachute harness. He opens the corner of raft pack cover, pulls out end of lanyard, runs it **under his parachute harness** and snaps it onto the ring of his life vest waist strap. Crew members should check each other to see that all straps and packs are secure and properly adjusted.

Raft packs for airplane commander and co-pilot are located behind the armor plate just back of respective seats. Flight engineer's raft is strapped to cabin roof between front upper hatch and aisle dome light. Rafts for navigator, radio operator, and bombardier are stowed on floor between lower forward turret and wheel well step. Right, left, and top gunners' rafts are fastened to the floor in the left forward section of their compartment. Radar operator's (optional gunner's) raft is strapped to left wall just aft of and level with rear ditching hatch. Tail gunner's raft is strapped to right wall just aft of rear bottom turret.

To bail out, face direction of flight when possible and roll out from a crouching position.

Note: If you find that any part of this procedure cannot be applied to your particular airplane because of differences of stowage of equipment, loading, or any other reason, change the drill. With the help of your Personal Equipment Officer, work out a bailout drill which you know you can use safely in your own airplane.

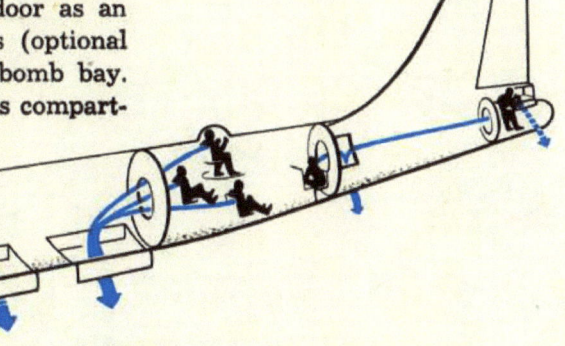

CRASH LANDINGS

CRASH LAND OR BAIL OUT?

The airplane commander decides whether crash landing or bailout is preferable. Sometimes the circumstances of the emergency dictate the procedure to be followed. When there is a choice, however, consider the following advantages of crash landings:

1. The crew can remain together for mutual support.

2. Searchers can spot the outline of the airplane more easily than they can see individual signals.

3. The airplane provides fuel, shelter, equipment and tools.

If possible make the decision to crash land early enough to give the crew time for adequate preparation. The airplane commander should notify crew to start preparation by appropriate alarm signal and by ordering "prepare for crash landing" over interphone.

DRILL

Successful crash landings, like successful ditchings, depend on the crew's familiarity with the proper procedures. Frequent dry-run drills are essential.

Don't relax your braced position until the airplane has come to a complete rest.

Get out of the plane in quick but orderly manner, using hatches and exit sequence learned in drill. Use hand axes if necessary.

PROCEDURE AFTER LANDING

Usually the question of staying with the plane or leaving it will be answered for you in pre-mission briefings.

If you leave the airplane be sure to take with you all the equipment you might need on your way back to a base. All first-aid, signaling and sustenance kits, any extra rations and everything else which might contribute to safety and comfort should be packed along with you.

For further information on forced landings and survival after forced landings consult your PIF and your AAF Survival Manual.

CRASH LANDING POSITIONS

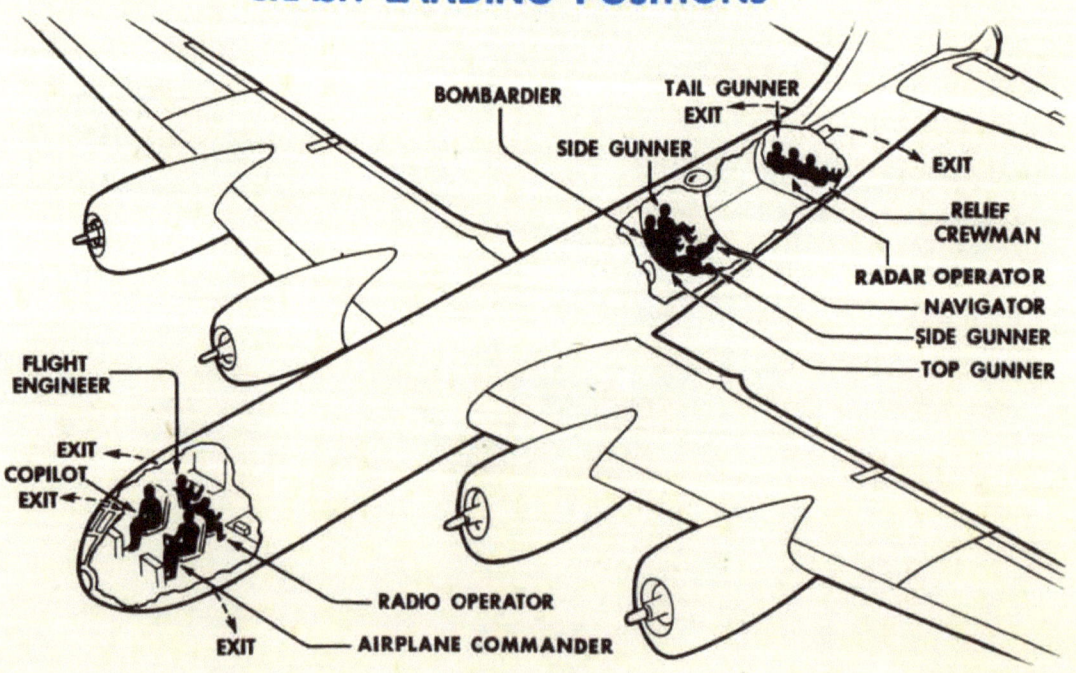

DITCHING PROCEDURE

B-29's WITH FOUR-GUN TURRET

General

For the time being, ditching procedures for B-29's with 2-gun turrets will be left to the discretion of the theatre commander. Until further evidence is accumulated, no ditching procedure will be based on pressure bulkhead door reinforcements or reinforced bomb bay doors, although mention of these modifications may be made where applicable.

Crew Procedure

The crew positions outlined below have been worked out to place most of the crew members in the forward pressurized compartment. They take into account the order in which those crew members come forward and the last minute duties they must perform. However, only ditching drills by an assembled crew will determine how the individual crew member's stature or build may affect these positions. Furthermore, in combat, injuries may cause some crew positions to be interchanged. A man with an injured leg could not hold himself in some of the positions described here and he might have to change positions with another member of the crew. The important things to remember are:

1. Seven crew positions in the forward compartment are outlined below. Fill them according to the stature and build, and possible injuries of each crew member.

2. Practice taking these positions quickly, not necessarily in the order outlined.

3. See that your back and head are supported so you will not bounce around when the airplane hits.

4. Remove parachute harness, winter flying boots, and flak suit; loosen shirt collar. Keep flak helmet on only if you can rest it against something.

5. Use cushions and parachutes for padding. Pull out canopy if desired but leave shroud lines in pack.

6. Jettison all unnecessary items which may tear loose and crash forward like projectiles when the airplane hits. This includes the bombsight, which usually tears itself from the stabilizer and crashes through the front glass, and the camera in the rear unpressurized compartment.

7. After the ditching, the bombardier and men from the four crew stations on the right side of the airplane go to the right wing; the upper gunner, tail gunner, and the men who ordinarily fly on the left side go to the left wing.

8. In case of fire, crew members will not inflate life vest until after swimming clear of fire.

9. Jettison all flak suits before ditching.

1. AIRPLANE COMMANDER

a. Give copilot warning: "PREPARE FOR DITCHING IN .... MINUTES." Give standard ditching signal on alarm bell, six short rings. Turn IFF emergency switch on. Remove parachute harness, flak suit and helmet, and winter flying boots. Fasten safety belt and loosen shirt collar.

b. Advise any nearby aircraft of distress by radio, and then turn to interphone.

c. Give copilot order: "OPEN EMERGENCY EXITS AND THROW OUT EQUIPMENT." If possible, give this order while still above 5,000 feet.

d. Give copilot order: "STATIONS FOR DITCHING. IMPACT IN .... SECONDS." If possible, give this order above 2,000 feet. Open window, brace feet on rudder pedals, knees flexed. About five seconds before impact, give copilot order: "BRACE FOR IMPACT."

e. Exit through left window. Inflate life vest when on window ledge. Climb atop cabin, thence to left wing. Secure left life raft or pull outside release handle, if necessary.

2. COPILOT

a. Relay airplane commander's order over interphone: "PREPARE FOR DITCHING IN

.... MINUTES." Receive acknowledgments. Tell the airplane commander: "CREW NOTIFIED."

b. Remove parachute harness, flak suit and helmet, and winter flying boots. Fasten belt and loosen shirt collar.

c. Stand by on interphone to relay airplane commander's orders.

d. Relay order: "OPEN EMERGENCY EXITS AND THROW OUT EXCESS EQUIPMENT." Check on crew's progress.

e. Relay order: "STATIONS FOR DITCHING. IMPACT IN .... SECONDS." Open side window, brace feet on rudder bar with knees flexed. When airplane commander gives order: "BRACE FOR IMPACT," sound one long ring on alarm bell.

f. Exit through right window. Inflate life vest on window ledge. Climb atop cabin, thence to right wing. Secure right life raft or pull outside raft release handle, if necessary.

3. BOMBARDIER

a. Acknowledge in turn: "BOMBARDIER DITCHING."

b. Remove parachute harness, winter flying boots, and flak suit. Loosen shirt collar and keep flak helmet on.

c. Destroy bombing data and remove bombsight. Pass bombsight back to rear or forward pressure compartment to be jettisoned through bomb bay doors.

d. Open bomb bay doors and jettison bombs. If bomb bay tanks are empty, retain them for their flotation value and the reinforcement they offer the bomb bay doors. When all loose equipment is jettisoned, close bomb bay doors.

e. Take sitting position on floor with back against copilot's armor plate. Squeeze in with the flight engineer and brace right foot across the aisle. Protect head with arm or pillow.

f. Exit through engineer's emergency hatch. Inflate life vest and proceed to right wing.

4. FLIGHT ENGINEER

a. Acknowledge in turn: "FLIGHT ENGINEER DITCHING."

b. Remove parachute harness, flak suit and winter flying boots. Keep flak helmet on and loosen shirt collar.

c. Open front emergency hatch and acknowledge to copilot: "FRONT HATCH OPEN." Pass it back together with any other loose equipment to be jettisoned through front bomb bay.

d. Get the emergency signal kit and tie its line to your arm.

e. Take regular position facing aft and keeping to your left, head and shoulders braced

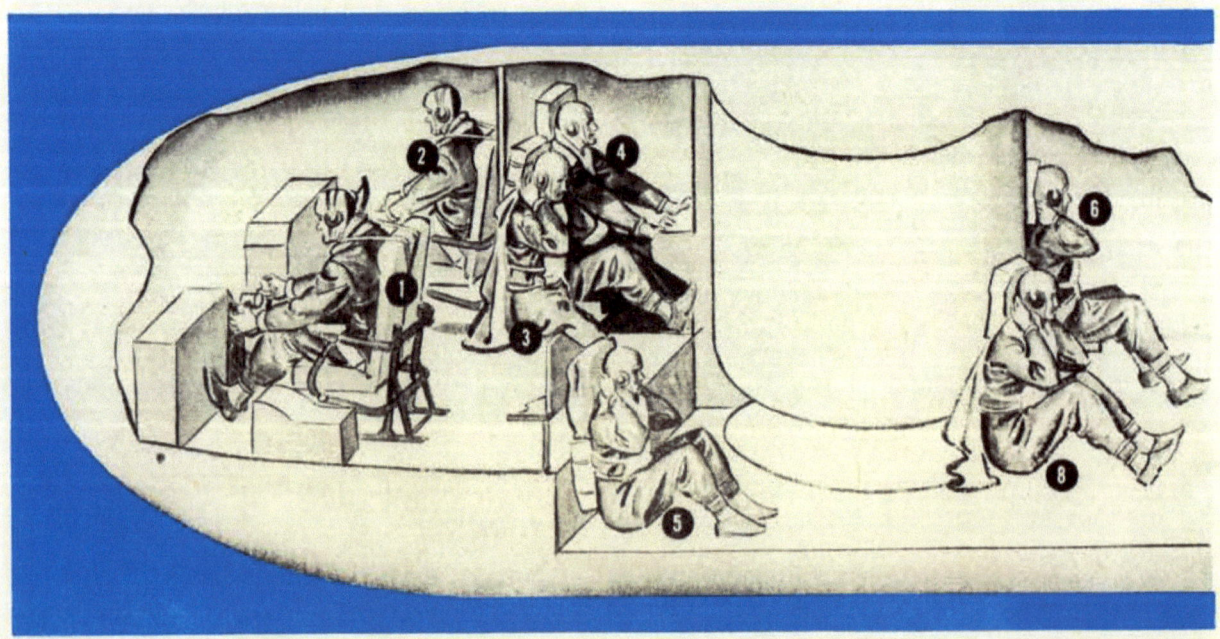

against copilot's armor plate, safety belt fastened, hands braced against control stand.

f. Carrying signal kit, exit immediately through front emergency exit.

g. Inflate life vest on window ledge. Climb atop cabin and proceed to right wing.

h. Assist bombardier and copilot in securing life rafts.

5. NAVIGATOR

a. Acknowledge in turn: "NAVIGATOR DITCHING."

b. Remove parachute harness, winter flying boots, and flak suit. Keep flak helmet on and loosen shirt collar.

c. Calculate position, course, altitude, and ground speed for radio operator to transmit.

d. Give airplane commander surface wind strength and direction. Destroy classified documents.

e. Gather maps and navigation equipment into waterproof bag or tuck inside clothing.

f. Jettison all drift signal flares through release tube.

g. Check astrodome to be sure it has been removed.

h. Fold navigator's table upward and slide seat full rear. Sit on floor facing aft with back against structure below navigator's table. Use parachute or cushions to pad back. Rest head against structure.

i. When airplane comes to rest, exit through astrodome.

j. Inflate life vest, and proceed to left wing with navigation equipment.

6. RADIO OPERATOR

a. Acknowledge in turn "RADIO OPERATOR DITCHING."

b. Remove parachute harness, flak suit, and winter flying boots. Keep flak helmet on and loosen shirt collar.

c. Transmit position, course, altitude, and ground speed as received from navigator on DF. Relay fix or bearings obtained to navigator.

d. Give DF contact all data. Don't wait too long for answer.

e. Destroy classified material.

f. Continue to send emergency signals. On command from copilot to take ditching position, screw down transmitter key.

g. Remain at radio operator's seat with safety belt fastened, resting cushioned back and head against upper turret well.

h. After airplane comes to rest, exit through astrodome.

i. Inflate life vest and proceed to right wing.

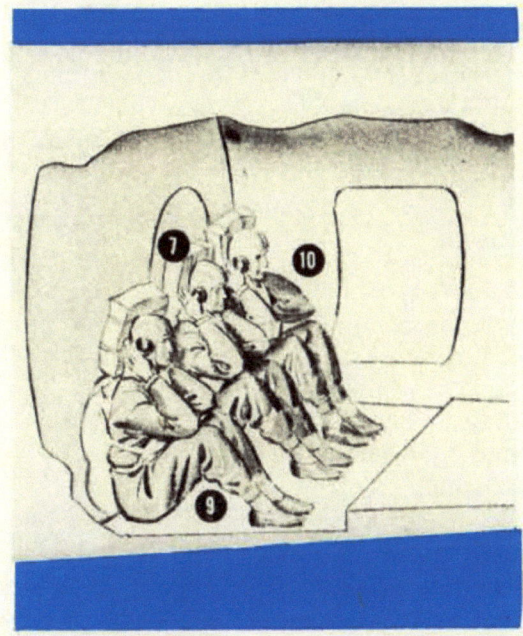
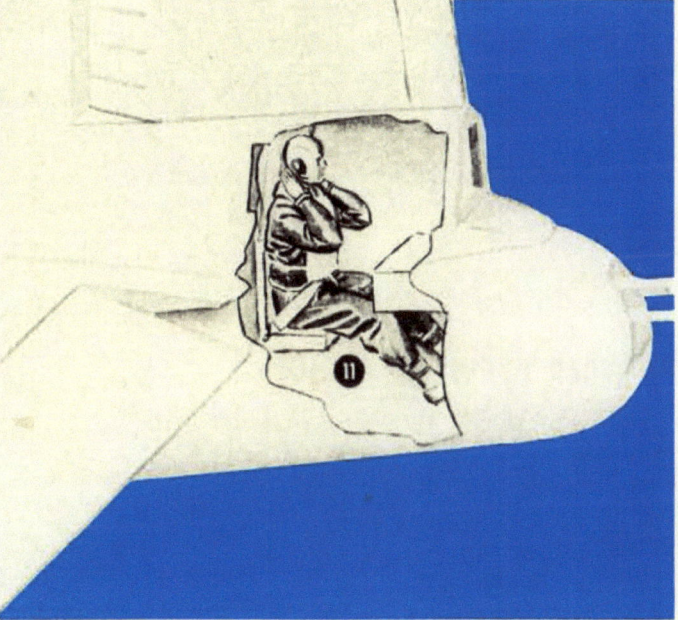

7. RIGHT GUNNER

a. Acknowledge in turn: "RIGHT GUNNER DITCHING."

b. Remove parachute harness, flak suit, and winter flying boots. Keep flak helmet on and loosen shirt collar.

c. Sit in rear unpressurized compartment between top gunner and radar operator, facing aft with back and head against bulkhead, cushioned with parachute, and with hands clasped behind head.

d. When airplane comes to rest, exit through rear escape hatch. Inflate life vest and proceed atop fuselage to right wing.

8. LEFT GUNNER

a. Acknowledge in turn: "LEFT GUNNER DITCHING."

b. Remove parachute harness, flak suit, and winter flying boots. Keep flak helmet on and loosen shirt collar.

c. Shoot out all ammunition in lower rear turret.

d. Close pressure door to bomb bay and reinforce, if possible. Proceed forward through tunnel to front pressurized compartment.

e. Grasp leather thong below astrodome and pull sealing strip away. If astrodome does not fall free, jerk sharply on center stud. A sharp jerk is better than a steady pull.

f. Take sitting position on lower turret well with cushioned back and head against upper turret well. Brace feet against bulkhead and protect head with hands.

g. When the airplane comes to rest, stand up and pull both life raft release handles at tunnel entrance.

h. Exit through astrodome. Inflate life vest and proceed along fuselage to left wing.

9. RADAR OPERATOR

a. Acknowledge in turn: "RADAR OPERATOR DITCHING."

b. Remove parachute harness, flak suit, and winter flying boots. Keep flak helmet on and loosen shirt collar.

c. Destroy or jettison radar equipment if near enemy territory.

d. Remain at position as long as pertinent information concerning altitude and other matters may be relayed to airplane commander.

e. Just before taking ditching position, pull IFF detonator plug.

f. Proceed to rear unpressurized compartment and close door carefully, being sure it is securely latched. Remain on interphone, if possible.

g. Take position with back and head against bulkhead, cushioned with parachute, and with hands clasped behind head.

h. When airplane comes to rest, exit through rear escape hatch. Inflate life vest and proceed atop fuselage to left wing.

10. TOP GUNNER

a. Acknowledge in turn: "TOP GUNNER DITCHING."

b. Shoot out all ammunition from rear upper turret. Check gunners to see that lower rear and tail turret ammunition has been shot away.

c. Remove parachute harness, flak suit, and winter flying boots. Keep flak helmet on and loosen shirt collar.

d. Be sure pressure door to bomb bay is closed and reinforced, if possible.

e. Sit in rear unpressurized compartment facing aft, back against right side of bulkhead, hands clasped behind head.

f. After airplane comes to rest, throw out extra emergency gear and exit through aft hatch. Inflate life vest and proceed to left wing.

11. TAIL GUNNER

a. Acknowledge in turn: "TAIL GUNNER DITCHING."

b. Remove parachute harness, flak suit, and winter flying boots. Keep flak helmet on and loosen shirt collar.

c. Shoot out ammunition in tail guns.

d. Under most conditions, it is desirable to ditch in the tail gunner's compartment. Jettison escape hatch; remain in seat, safety belt fastened, back and head cushioned, knees flexed. When airplane comes to rest, tail may be low in water or under water. Dive out escape hatch and make way forward to left wing.

Determine direction of approach well in advance. Touch down parallel to lines of crests and troughs in winds up to 35 mph. Ditch into wind only if wind is over 35 mph or if there are no swells. Use flaps in proportion to power available to obtain minimum safe forward speed with minimum rate of descent. In every case try to ditch while power is still available. Touch down in a normal landing attitude. Severe deceleration and several impacts may be expected so warn your crew not to move until the airplane has come to rest.

WIND VELOCITIES

Few white caps	10 to 20 mph	Streaks of foam	30 to 40 mph
Many white caps	20 to 30 mph	Spray from crests	40 to 50 mph

Notes:

1. If crew includes an additional man (ROM observer or aerial observer) he will assume sitting position in rear unpressurized compartment, back braced against top gunner's knees. He exits first through rear escape hatch.

2. On newer models, astrodome can be released and dropped into tunnel by pulling on leather thong. On older models, break out astrodome with axe if there is time enough. If astrodome cannot be removed, left gunner and radio operator exit respectively through pilot's window and flight engineer's escape hatch.

For general ditching information see Pilot's Information File

Weather Flying

THUNDERSTORMS

The first rule in flying weather is "STAY OUT OF THUNDERSTORMS." If it is impossible to avoid flying through a line of thunderstorm, enter it at right angles to shorten the period of time in it and follow these procedures:

1. Pitot heater on.
2. Set intercoolers to maintain CAT 25° to 38°C to prevent carburetor ice.
3. Set propellers at 2300—mixtures auto-rich, so you can "jockey" throttles through a greater range without exceeding engine limitations.
4. Maintain a constant airspeed of between 180 and 190 MPH indicated.
5. Turn all cockpit lights up to maximum brilliancy to prevent being blinded by an electrical discharge. In connection with this, it is a good idea for the man not actually flying to shield his eyes with his hands. This is just an added precaution in case the man flying is temporarily blinded by a bolt of lightning.
6. Keep the wings level, the airspeed constant, and ride with the up and down drafts.

PRECIPITATION STATIC

When flying through a precipitation static area not associated with thunderstorms, the static in the radio and the chances of a static discharge may be minimized by doing the following:

1. Slow down your airplane 20 to 25 mph.
2. Decrease propeller rpm as much as possible (probably 200 to 300 rpm decrease will be possible depending on gross weight).
3. Climb or descend two or three thousand feet, depending on the type of weather and the terrain. This change of altitude and resultant change in temperature will often get you out of the static area.

Instrument Approach

An instrument approach in the B-29 differs little from an instrument approach in other airplanes. Just remember these points:

1. When making an instrument approach and heading inbound toward the cone, set half flaps, 2400, and turbos on No. "8." Lower gear just short of cone.
2. Because the airplane is relatively unstable with flaps down, it is recommended that 25° flaps be set when starting to let down toward the cone, before beam bracketing becomes difficult and before changes in altitude become critical. It is also recommended that full flaps be saved until after you have broken through and are lined up with the runway on final approach.
3. When making an instrument takeoff, the attitude of the airplane is very important. If the ship is held in the proper attitude for takeoff, and immediately after takeoff, airspeed will build up steadily. Don't pull the nose too high on takeoff. Climb at a minimum airspeed of 160 MPH to 500 ft. above the terrain. Then, before continuing the climb, level off until reaching climbing airspeed (195 to 205, depending on weight), and until all CHT fall below 248°C.
4. Recommended instrument flying speeds:

T.O. 115-130 IAS
Climb 195 IAS
Let down (½ flaps) 150 IAS (Minimum)

MANIFOLD PRESSURE SURGE AT HIGH ALTITUDE

To eliminate manifold pressure surge at high altitude, use the following procedure:

1. Advance rpm and manifold pressure on outboard engines (keeping power settings related) until throttles are full open or until surge is eliminated. Reduce manifold pressure and rpm on inboard engines to balance power for best maximum range cruising airspeed or until it is impossible to maintain pressurization.
2. In the event that the above procedure fails to eliminate power surges in manifold pressure, advance rpm (approximately 50 to 100 rpm) on affected engines until surge is eliminated. A balanced power condition between opposite sides of the airplane must be maintained.

Caution

Step 2 will give unrelated power settings which are undesirable. Related power settings must be restored as soon as possible to insure economy in fuel consumption.

PROCEDURE FOR STARTING FUEL INJECTION ENGINES

BENDIX—Starting

1. Master ignition switch ON.
2. Set throttles at 800-1000 rpm.
3. Fire extinguishers—set selector to engine being started.
4. Move mixture control to Auto Rich.
5. Fuel boost to HIGH (22 psi).
6. Energize starter.
7. Mesh starter.
8. When prop has turned one revolution, turn ignition switch ON.
9. Fuel boost OFF after engine is operating smoothly.

WARNING: If this procedure does not start engine after 30 seconds of meshing, let starter cool for one minute, then repeat procedure.

BENDIX—Stopping

Stopping instructions are the same as for carburetor engines.

BOSCH—Starting

Same as for Bendix, except that throttle is set at full open position. When engine fires, bring throttle to proper idling rpm.

BOSCH—Stopping

Same as for carburetor engines, except that throttle is moved to closed position.

RESTRICTED

STANDARD B-29 PILOT'S QUESTIONNAIRE

General Specification and Structure

1. The wing span of the B-29 is approximately (a) 107 feet, (b) 141 feet, (c) 103 feet.

2. The over-all length is approximately (a) 99 feet, (b) 110 feet, (c) 74 feet.

3. The maximum height is approximately (a) 16 feet, (b) 51 feet, (c) 29½ ft.

4. The wing airfoil section is a:

    (a) Standard Boeing design similar to B-17.

    (b) High-lift, high-speed Davis airfoil.

    (c) Boeing 117.

5. Starting from the nose, name all the different compartments in the fuselage.

RESTRICTED

6. Locate the exits from all the crew compartments.

    (a) In flight.

    (b) After crash landing.

7. Name the crew compartments which are accessible and those which are not accessible when cabins are pressurized.

8. The landing gear is not completely retractable inasmuch as the tail-skid is always extended. **True** or **False**?

Wing Flaps

9. The following type of flaps are used on the B-29:

    (a) Split trailing edge flaps.

    (b) Fowler flaps.

    (c) Hinged, slotted flaps.

10. What are the flap settings for:

    (a) Takeoff?

    (b) Downwind leg?

    (c) Final approach?

11. What is the maximum flap angle?

12. What is the maximum airspeed not to be exceeded with: (a) 45° flaps? (b) 25° flaps?

    (a)

    (b)

13. Explain in detail how you would put the flaps down, using the emergency system.

14. What is the minimum speed at which the flaps are retracted after takeoff?

Auxiliary Power Plant

15. Where is the auxiliary power plant located?

16. What is the voltage and amperage output of the auxiliary power plant generator?

17. Is the auxiliary power plant supercharged?

18. What type of fuel and oil must be used?

19. Describe normal starting procedure.

Landing Gear

20. In what ways can the landing gear be extended or retracted?

21. What is the direct function of the landing gear transfer switch?

22. What is the direct function of the bus selector switch on the battery solenoid shield?

23. Locate the emergency landing gear motor switches.

24. How can the landing gear and doors be retracted after an emergency operation?

25. What means has been provided for determining whether the landing gear has been extended? Day? Night?

26. Explain in detail the correct procedure in case landing gear fails to retract on normal system after takeoff.

27. What part of the landing gear mechanism causes the down and locked lights to burn.

28. Are 3-point (tailskid contact) landings normally expected on this plane?

29. What provision is made for emergency extension of the tailskid?

30. In your preflight inspection, how would you check the nose gear and main gear shock struts for proper extension?

31. How long is required to extend the landing gear on the normal system? On the emergency system?

Engine and Accessories

32. What type of engine is installed on the B-29?

33. Propeller rotation when viewed from the rear is in which direction?

34. What type of carburetor is used on the B-29?

35. Describe the type of starter that is used on the B-29?

36. What type of propeller is used?

37. What is the main difference between the propeller governor controls used on the B-29 and on the B-17?

38. What are the normal cowl flap positions for:
Ground Operations ....
Takeoff ....
Climb ....
Cruise ....

39. What is the maximum cylinder head temperature for the following:
Takeoff (max 5 min) ....
Climb (max 1 hour) ....
Auto Lean operation..................

40. Is a cowl flap position indicator provided?

41. What accessories are affected by failure of an inboard engine?

42. What accessories are affected by failure of an outboard engine?

Turbo-Supercharger, Induction and Exhaust System

43. How many turbos are used per engine on the B-29?

44. What type of turbo supercharger control is used?

45. What is the purpose of the exhaust supercharger?

46. What is the purpose of the supercharger pressuretrol?

47. How are the supercharger pressuretrols controlled by the pilot?

48. How many pressuretrols are used?

49. How are the cowl flaps and the intercooler flaps operated?

Oil System

50. What is the oil tank capacity on the B-29?

51. What are minimum and maximum limits for oil pressure?

52. What are minimum and maximum limits for oil temperature?

53. What is the minimum oil temperature to be reached before run-up?

54. What must be done to engine oil if emergency takeoff is necessary? (Before engine is completely warmed up?)

55. What means are used to control the engine oil cooler?

Fuel System

56. What is the fuel capacity for each engine?
Outboards:
Inboards:

57. What is the fuel capacity of the bomb bay tanks?

58. How are the tanks vented?

59. What is the function of the tank safety switches and where are they located?

60. The engine priming system injects fuel into what part of the engine?

61. What is the normal fuel consumption per engine at:
2200 Hp (takeoff)
2000 Hp (climb)
1170 Hp (cruise)

62. What position should the mixture control be set at for the following conditions:

Starting......................
Takeoff......................
Climb above 2200 rpm and 35"................
Cruise above 2200 rpm and 35"................
Cruise below 2200 rpm and 35"................

63. How are the fuel boost pumps operated?

64. How should the engine be primed?

65. Describe the procedure necessary to transfer fuel from number one fuel tank to number two fuel tank.

66. With fuel pressure at 17 lbs. and oil pressure at 40 lbs., how is it that fuel is injected into the oil system for dilution?

67. What is the hourly capacity of the fuel transfer system using both pumps?

Electrical System

68. How many generators are used on the B-29, and where are they located?

69. Where is the external power plug located?

70. What units are supplied with electrical power by the emergency bus?

71. In what two ways can the emergency bus be energized?

72. Can the normal bus and the emergency bus be energized at the same time?

73. What is the source of power for each bus if each bus is used separately?

74. How many amperes are required to operate:

    (a) Wing flaps?

    (b) Bomb bay doors?

    (c) Landing gear (normal system)?

75. How many inverters are used on the B-29 to supply the AC system?

76. What instruments and pieces of equipment use AC from these inverters?

77. When the landing gear is not fully extended, under what conditions does it support the weight of the airplane?

78. If none of the landing gear would retract using the normal procedure, what would be the first thing to check and where?

79. What might make the warning horn blow

    (a) steadily

    (b) intermittently

80. If the main wheels retract, but the nosewheel does not, using the normal procedure, what should be checked first?

81. Explain in detail how you would open the bomb doors if the normal system failed.

82. Can the hydraulic pump be operated by the emergency bus?

83. Which of the door and gear motors are fused?

84. Name seven electric pumps which use 24 volt DC current.

85. Is the cowl flap operation automatic or manual?

86. If the propeller governors fail to operate, what should be checked first?

87. Do the fluorescent lights use AC or DC?

88. Name the five different systems of exterior lights.

89. Locate all fuse panels and indicate which are accessible in flight.

De-Icer and Vacuum Systems

90. When would you need all four vacuum pumps?

91. What does each pump do?

92. What should the vacuum pressure reading be?

93. Locate the anti-icer pumps and describe the function of each.

Cabin Heating and Supercharger System

94. What is the purpose of this system?

95. What provides pressure for the cabin?

96. Explain in detail how you would pressurize the cabin and how you can control the pressure manually.

97. In what ways can the cabin pressure be released?

98. Starting from sea-level, give the altitudes maintained in the cabin.

99. What check should you make on the cabin pressure regulators before pressurizing?

100. In case of failure of the cabin pressure regulator, what means are provided for keeping an excessive pressure from building up in the cabin? Where is this unit located?

101. How is the cabin heated?

102. Where is the cabin thermostat located?

Oxygen System

103. What type oxygen system is used?

104. What should the pressure gage read when the system is full?

105. How many oxygen systems are provided?

106. How many oxygen bottles are installed?

107. How many individual outlets (regulator panels) are provided?

108. Of what do these regulator panels consist?

109. What is the minimum pressure on which the system will operate?

110. Name the controls that may be used in the operation of the demand type regulator, and the difference of operation of the controls.

111. How long will one stationary cylinder last one man?

112. How long will the portable oxygen cylinder last a man?

113. Where are portable oxygen bottles located?

114. If a crew member is suffering from oxygen lack, in what position should his emergency valve be?

115. What precaution must be taken if the emergency valve is used?

Hydraulic System

116. What are the normal operating pressures of the normal and emergency systems?

117. Where is the hydraulic panel located?

118. How can the pressure of the normal and emergency systems be bled?

119. How is the emergency system serviced?

120. Is it safe to use normal brakes while servicing the emergency system?

121. Approximately how many brake applications may be made with the emergency system?

122. How many expander tubes per wheel?

123. After diligent application of brakes, it is proper to set the parking brakes. **True** or **False**? Why?

124. What power unit supplies the hydraulic pressure?

125. How is the proper hydraulic pressure maintained?

126. If you were using normal brakes on your landing roll and you broke an expander tube, what would you do?

Power Plant Performance

127. Give the following information:

T.O. Hp

Rated Hp

128. What is the proper engine rpm and mp for:

	MP	RPM
T.O.	....	....
Mil. Power	....	....
Rated Power	....	....
Auto Lean operation	....	....

129. Which should be reduced first, mp or rpm?

130. What causes detonation, how do you know when it occurs, and what would you do about it?

131. If all four engines were running hot (above 248°C) in a climb, what would you do and why?

132. Give stopping procedure.

133. Give procedure for checking prop governor system during engine warm-up.

134. What should be the intercooler flap position on T.O.?

135. In what order should the engines be started?

136. What are the minimum and maximum limits for carburetor air temperature
- (a) Under conditions likely to produce ice?
- (b) Under conditions unlikely to produce ice?

Radio Equipment

137. Name the radio sets that this plane is equipped with and what crew member has control of each.

138. Give the location of the jackboxes.

139. What switches must you turn on to operate the interphone system?

140. Give the five positions on the jack box.

141. If the interphone system fails, what is one of the first things to check, and where is it located?

RESTRICTED

Emergency Procedure

142. Why should airplane commander's, copilot's and flight engineer's escape windows and hatches be opened before an emergency landing?

143. What three emergency systems are provided for the airplane commander to communicate with the crew?

144. How is cabin pressure released in an emergency?

145. Why should airplane commander's, copilot's, and flight engineer's windows and upper escape hatch not be used as emergency exits during flight?

146. Why should lower turret areas be avoided by crew members during a crash landing?

147. Where should the crew members, with the exception of the airplane commander and copiiot, station themselves for a crash landing on land?

148. What is location of life rafts?

149. How are life rafts released?

150. What is the proper procedure in case of engine fire in flight?

Cockpit Controls

151. Give the location of the following

    a. Emergency landing gear door release.

    b. Emergency brake control.

    c. Engine fire extinguisher control.

RESTRICTED

d. Emergency hydraulic pressure gage.
e. Hydraulic servicing valve.
f. Hydraulic pressure gage.
g. Airplane commander's over-ride control (early models).
h. Airplane commander's bomb release handle.
i. Landing gear power transfer switch.
j. Surface control lock.
k. Emergency cabin pressure release.
l. Propeller anti-icer controls.
m. Surface de-icer valve.
n. Vacuum pump selector.
o. Warning horns.
p. Generator switches.
q. Position light switches.
r. Suction gage.
s. Prop feathering buttons.
t. Intercooler flap controls.
u. Engine primer controls.
v. Hydraulic hand pump.
w. Fuel shut-off valve switches.
x. Booster pump switches.
y. Landing gear switch (normal).
z. Landing light switch.
aa. Recognition light switches.
bb. Autopilot switches.

PERSONAL EQUIPMENT FOR B-29 CREWS

The success of the mission depends on. . . .

If there was ever an overworked phrase in the Army Air Forces, that's it!

According to the tactical experts, the success of the mission depends on holding the formation. The technical specialists say it depends on the performance of the individual airplane. The armament boys swear that the outcome of the show hinges on fire power. The depot group tells you that supply makes or breaks the mission. And the docs say "physical condition"; the altitude lads say "proper use of oxygen"; A-2 says "combat intelligence"; and so on and on. . . .

Therefore, following precedent, this publication adds with all the authority of bold face type: **"The success of the mission depends on the proper knowledge and use of personal and emergency equipment!"**

Because it's true!

They are completely right, from the tactical experts down to the administrative clerk who believes his paper forms win battles.

The success of the mission actually does depend on every one of these things and a great many more. Ignorance or neglect of any essential detail may mean inefficient individual performance, aborted missions, casualties.

About the Equipment

The personal and emergency equipment described in this booklet was developed and provided for you because you can't do your assigned job without it.

Some of it—oxygen equipment, altitude clothing, life vests, among other things—helps protect you against forces of nature which you have challenged by operating out of man's natural element.

Other equipment—including flak suits, flak helmets, and first-aid kits—helps protect you against the forces of the enemy.

Much of the equipment is already long familiar to you, and you are inclined to take it for granted. For example, your heavy awkward parachute or your uncomfortable life vest may seem like a highly overrated nuisance—if you've never had to use it.

It is obvious that none of this stuff is a Little Daisy, Sure-Fire, Never-Fail, Good Luck Charm that will shield you from all harm like a magic cloak. But it offers considerable aid and protection if you exercise intelligence and care in the use of it. The amount of good it will do you—or to put it more plainly—your chance of coming back safely, is directly proportionate to your knowledge of equipment and procedures.

This booklet is an attempt to collect, sort out, and simplify equipment information for your personal use.

The Personal Equipment Officer

Combat experiences showed long ago that the importance of personal and emergency equipment to overall Air Force success is so great as to require the full-time attention of a specially trained officer.

This Personal Equipment Officer, as he is now known, is responsible for supervising the care and upkeep of this equipment, and for instructing you in its proper use.

His activities do not relieve engineering and supply sections of any of their usual functions, although he works in close coordination with these sections as well as with the Flight Surgeon.

Your Responsibility

The fact that Tables of Organization designate officers to handle personal equipment does not mean that you can consider yourself relieved of your responsibility. The PEO can instruct you, and can inspect and care for the material between missions, but he can't use it for you.

If, in the middle of a flight you suddenly discover that you neglected to learn a vital procedure or forgot to check some faulty equipment, the PEO won't be available to help you!

The Personal Equipment Officer provides regular instruction in emergency procedures and use of equipment, and he will gladly give you any additional information you need. Study his exhibits of equipment; learn how to work unfamiliar gadgets, like the signaling mirror, or the emergency radio.

Use this manual as a reference, and learn the check lists prescribed. Then, practice emergency procedures frequently.

It pays off—just ask the man who's been in combat!

To the Pilot

The ultimate responsiblity for emergency equipment and procedures is yours, along with responsibility for all other operations during flight.

Don't take it for granted that all your crew members are well versed in emergency matters. Check each man and see that he knows what he's supposed to know; the safety of every man on the airplane depends on it.

Before each flight, assemble the crew and inspect the equipment of each man to see that he has with him everything required on the flight. The Personal Equipment Officer will furnish you with a check list like the one reproduced on the following page. The required items of equipment for the mission will be noted in the left column. You check off these items as each man exhibits them for your inspection. Only by using the check list can you be sure that nothing is overlooked.

The Responsibility is Yours

TAKE NOTHING FOR GRANTED

RESTRICTED

COMBAT CREW PERSONAL EQUIPMENT CHECKLIST

Time_____

Date_____

Airplane Model and No._____

Pilot's Name_____

Item	Pilot	Copilot	Engineer	Bombardier	Navigator	Radio Operator	Upper Gunner	Right Gunner	Left Gunner	Radar Operator	Tail Gunner
( ) Jacket, electrically heated											
( ) Trousers, electrically heated											
( ) Gloves, electrically heated											
( ) Shoes, electrically heated											
( ) Jacket, intermediate											
( ) Trousers, intermediate											
( ) Jacket, winter flying											
( ) Trousers, winter flying											
( ) Gloves, summer or winter											
( ) Gloves, rayon insert											
( ) Mittens											
( ) Shoes, flying											
( ) Helmet, flying											
( ) Headset											
( ) Oxygen mask											
( ) Microphone											
( ) Bailout cylinder											
( ) Parachute—proper type											
( ) Parachute first-aid kit											
( ) Parachute emergency kit											
( ) Life vest											
( ) Flak suit											
( ) Flak helmet											
( ) Goggles											
( ) Sun glasses											
( ) Pistol, cartridges, clips											
( )											

Note: Only checked (√) items are required for this mission.

RESTRICTED

OXYGEN

Your airplane was designed to operate just as well at high altitude as at low altitude.

Your body wasn't!

All organisms require oxygen to support life. At ground level you get plenty of oxygen from the surrounding air, which is packed down by the weight of the air above it.

As you go up there is less air above you. Therefore, the air you breathe becomes thinner, and your body is less able to get the required amount of oxygen out of it. At 10,000 feet your body is getting barely sufficient oxygen, and you begin to lose efficiency. Somewhere above that altitude—varying with the individual—you'll become unconscious, and then, unless you get some extra oxygen quick . . . that's all, brother!

Your airplane has an oxygen system to meet the requirements of your body and allow you to function normally.

The equipment provided is excellent, simple to operate, and safe for flights up to extremely high altitudes. **But it is not safe unless you understand it thoroughly and follow the rules regarding its use strictly.** You can't take shortcuts with oxygen and live to tell about it!

The lack of oxygen, known as anoxia, gives no warning. If it hits you, you won't know it until your mates revive you from unconsciousness, if they can. Therefore, you must check the condition and operation of your equipment with extreme care, and continue to check it regularly as often as possible during flight.

Pressurized Cabin

In a pressurized cabin you can increase the air pressure so that you are breathing air of a simulated lower altitude. As long as the cabin altitude is below 10,000 feet, you're OK. **But remember, when the cabin altitude goes above 10,000 feet, you need oxygen.**

You may worry about what happens to you if all the pressure in the cabin is suddenly lost—as a result of enemy gunfire, for example. Forget it. More than 150 experiments under extreme conditions have proved conclusively that this sudden loss of pressure causes no ill effects on the body.

You don't lose consciousness. You don't hear any noise. Your ears clear automatically. Air from your lungs rushes out your nose and mouth, an unusual but not painful sensation. A split second later you are fully alert, fully capable of putting on your oxygen mask and carrying on your duties.

Observe the following precautions, however:

1. Keep your oxygen mask handy, preferably attached to one side of your helmet. You must get it on right away if pressure is lost.

2. Stay out of the tunnel as much as possible. If pressure is lost suddenly while you are in there, you may be shot out like a cork.

3. Don't stay too close to scanning blisters except when your duties require it. If one disintegrates you can be blown out of the airplane.

YOUR OXYGEN SYSTEM IS A DEMAND SYSTEM, CONSISTING OF:

- **DEMAND MASK**
- **DEMAND REGULATOR**
- **PRESSURE GAGE**
- **FLOW INDICATOR**
- **LOW PRESSURE SUPPLY CYLINDERS**
- **FILLER AND DISTRIBUTION MANIFOLDING**

OXYGEN SYSTEM

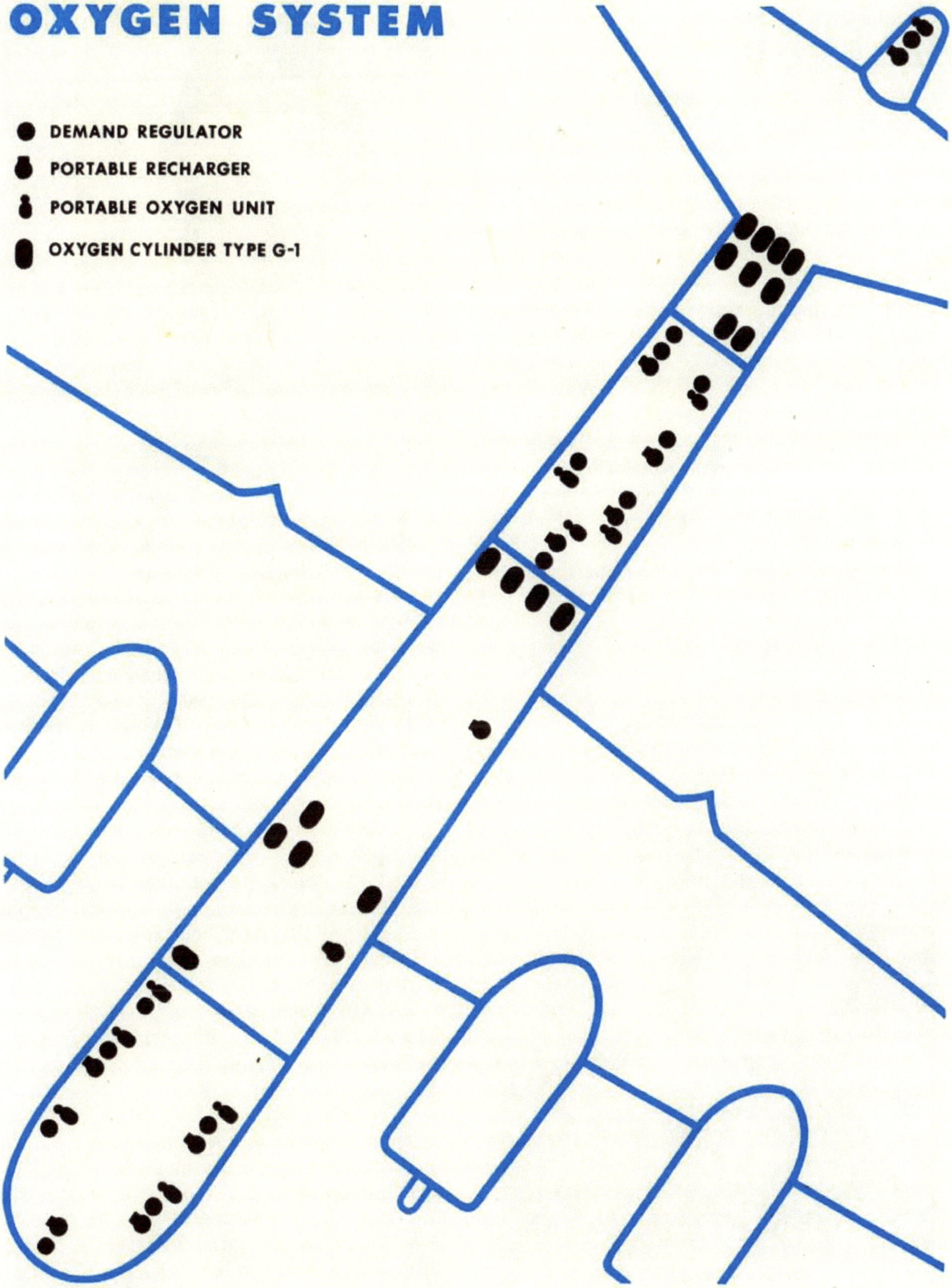

- ● DEMAND REGULATOR
- ● PORTABLE RECHARGER
- ● PORTABLE OXYGEN UNIT
- ● OXYGEN CYLINDER TYPE G-1

RESTRICTED
OXYGEN
Mask

Your oxygen mask is an item of personal issue. Take care of it. It's as important as your life.

Before you use the mask in flight, have it fitted carefully by your Personal Equipment Officer, or his qualified assistants. They will see that you have the right size, that it fits perfectly, and that the studs to hold it are properly fixed to your helmet.

Then bring it in for re-checking whenever necessary. The straps will stretch slightly after a period of use. It's a good idea to have the fit re-checked regularly whether you think it needs it or not.

Note: Shave every day. Even a short stubble can affect your mask fit.

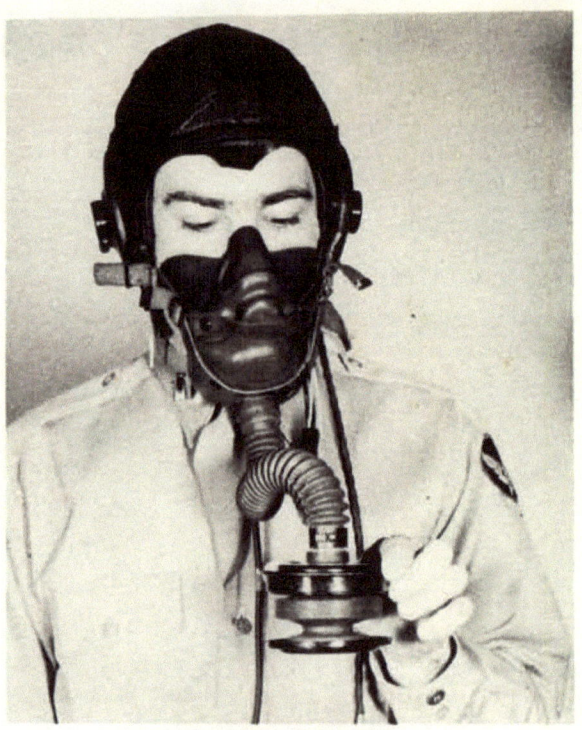

Mechanical leak detector

A-14 Demand Oxygen Mask.

Draw the mask before each mission. Return it to the supply room afterward. Equipment personnel will check it for repair and cleaning. But don't assume that this procedure relieves you of the responsibility of your own regular inspection and care of the mask.

Before each mission, make the following checks on your mask:

1. Look the mask and helmet over carefully for worn spots or worn straps, loose studs, or evidence of deterioration in facepiece and hose.

2. Put the helmet and mask on carefully. Slip the edges of the facepiece under the helmet.

3. Test for leak. Use one of the following testing procedures:

Mechanical leak detector. With mask in place, inhale and hold breath. Plug the mask hose into the leak detector firmly and release the bottom plate of the detector. If the plate descends in 10 seconds or less the mask leaks. Refit and retest.

Suction test. Hold your thumb over the end of the hose and breathe in gently. The mask should collapse on your face, with no air entering. Don't inhale strongly, because a sharp, deep breath may deform the mask to cause a false seal or a new leak.

Sniff test. Use an inhaler filled with oil of peppermint. Plug the mask into the regulator hose. Turn Auto-Mix to "OFF" ("100% OXYGEN") position and take several breaths of pure oxygen. Then, with your eyes closed, hold inhaler at various spots around the mask edge. If you can smell the oil, there is a leak.

4. Clip the end of the regulator hose to your jacket in such a position that you can move your head around fully without twisting or kinking the mask hose or pulling on the quick-

Gentle suction test for mask fit.

Sniff test for mask fit.

Clip hose in position to allow full head movement.

disconnect. Get the Personal Equipment section to sew a tab on your jacket at the proper spot.

5. See that the gasket is properly seated on the male end of the quick-disconnect fitting between mask and regulator hoses. Plug in the fitting and test the pull. If the fitting comes apart easily, it may slip out unnoticed during flight. You can adjust the old-type male fitting by spreading the prongs with a spreader tool or knife blade. This is a temporary adjustment only; have the fitting replaced as soon as possible. The new ring-type fitting, shown in the picture, provides a better fit. If you find a loose fitting with the ring-type quick-disconnect, it may be necessary to replace the female end.

General Tips

Watch carefully for freezing in the mask from the water vapor in your breath at extremely low temperatures. If you detect freezing, squeeze the mask.

Don't let anyone else wear your mask except in emergencies.

Keep it in the kit between flights, and keep it clean.

Report anything wrong with the functioning or condition of the mask when you turn it in after the flight.

OXYGEN REGULATOR

A demand regulator is mounted at each station in the plane.

There are several types of demand regulators (sometimes called "diluter-demand regulators"). You may find any one of these types in your plane. They look slightly different, but the principle of operation is the same in all.

A demand regulator is one that furnishes oxygen on demand, or only when you inhale. No oxygen comes out when you exhale.

Use of Auto-Mix

The regulator has an Auto-Mix mechanism controlled by a lever on the side of the cover. On older regulators, the lever positions are labeled "ON" and "OFF." On new regulators, the markings are "NORMAL OXYGEN" and "100% OXYGEN." **The lever should be in the "ON" ("NORMAL OXYGEN") position at all times** except in certain emergencies. When the lever is in the "ON" ("NORMAL OXYGEN") position, oxygen furnished below 30,000 feet altitude is mixed with air. The dilution is controlled automatically by an aneroid to furnish the correct amount of oxygen which your body requires for a given altitude. Above approximately 30,000 feet (33,000 feet in newest regulators) the air inlet closes and you get 100% oxygen, although the lever in the regulator is still in the "ON" ("NORMAL OXYGEN") position.

With the lever in the "OFF" ("100% OXYGEN") position, 100% oxygen is furnished at **all altitudes. This wastes oxygen.**

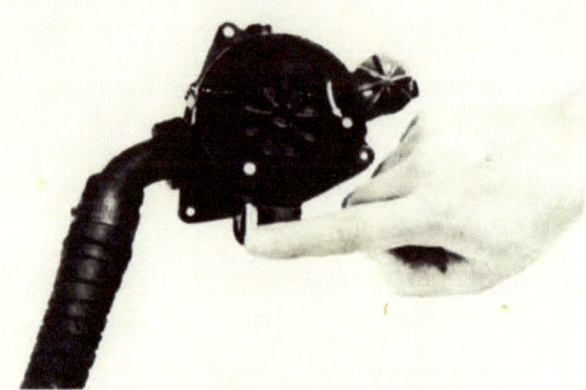

**Aro Demand Regulator. Auto-Mix "ON"
("NORMAL OXYGEN")**

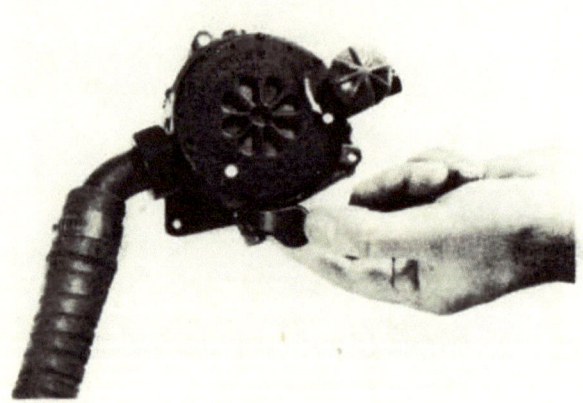

**Aro Demand Regulator. Auto-Mix "OFF"
("100% OXYGEN")**

Operation of Emergency Valve.

Never turn the lever to "OFF" ("100% OXYGEN") except in the following cases:

1. To give 100% oxygen to a wounded man below 30,000 feet.
2. If there is poison gas or carbon monoxide in the plane.

Pioneer Demand Regulator.

3. If the airplane commander prescribes breathing 100% oxygen all the way up to high altitude as a protection against the bends.

Use of Emergency Valve

To operate the emergency valve, break the safety wire and turn the red knob on the intake side of the regulator in the direction indicated.

Caution: Never pinch the mask hose or block the oxygen flow when the emergency valve is turned to "ON." This action breaks the regulator diaphragm.

Turning emergency valve to "ON" causes the oxygen flow to bypass the demand mechanism and to flow continuously into the mask. It is extremely wasteful of oxygen. Leaving the valve "ON" bleeds the entire oxygen supply to the station in a short time.

Never turn the emergency valve to "ON," except:

1. To revive a crew member.
2. In cases of excessive mask leakage.
3. Just before momentary emergency re-

Check tightness of knurled collar.

moval of your mask at high altitudes, as in vomiting. In such a case unhook one side of the mask and hold it close to your face.

Make the following checks of the regulator before each flight:

1. Check the tightness of the knurled collar. It should be so tight that movement of the regulator hose does not turn the elbow.
2. Examine the emergency valve knob. It should be closed tightly and safetied with light safety wire.

OXYGEN PANEL LOCATED AT EACH STATION

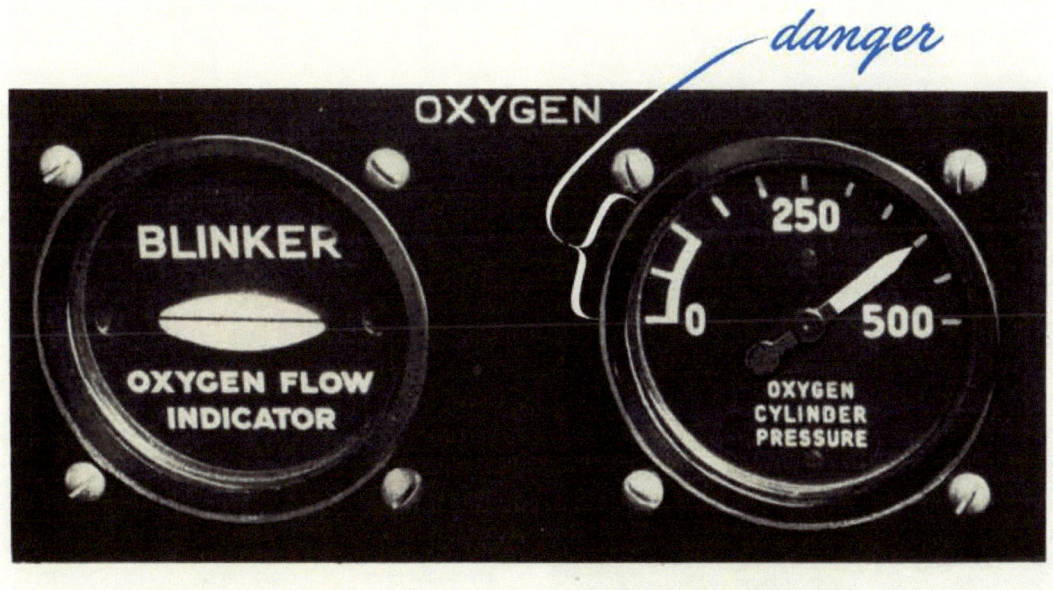

Flow indicator.   Pressure gage.

Flow Indicator

The flow indicator on the oxygen panel winks open and shut as the oxygen flows. The blinker may not operate normally at ground level with the Auto-Mix lever at "ON" ("NORMAL OXYGEN"), as the blinker operation depends on the flow of oxygen. Therefore, before the flight plug in your mask, turn the Auto-Mix lever to "OFF" ("100% OXYGEN") and see that the blinker works as you breathe.

Be sure to move the lever back to "ON" ("NORMAL OXYGEN") before flight.

The blinker does not work when the emergency valve is "ON."

Watch your flow indicator during flight. It is the only indication you have that the oxygen is flowing regularly. If it fails completely, use your portable equipment, notify the pilot, and plug in at another station if possible.

Blinker flow indicator, closed.

Blinker flow indicator, open.

Pressure Gage

Before flight, check the pressure gage on your panel. When the system on your plane is full the pressure should be between 400 and 425 psi. Check the gage also against the gages at other stations. There may be some variation between stations because of different tolerances in the gages, but if yours is more than 50 psi off the others, report it to the airplane commander.

When you are on oxygen, check the pressure gage frequently. When pressure gets down to 100 psi, you haven't much of your oxygen supply left. Notify the pilot immediately.

The regulator does not work properly when the pressure gets below 50 psi. If you can't get downstairs at that time, use your portable equipment until you can descend.

WALK-AROUND EQUIPMENT

Type A-6 walk-around bottle

Before each flight, check to see that your walk-around bottle is within easy reach. Look at the gage. If the pressure is more than 50 psi under the pressure of the airplane system, recharge the bottle.

Suck on the outlet of the bottle to see that it gives an easy flow of oxygen. Blow into outlet gently, then hard. Once the diaphragm has expanded there should be positive and continued resistance. If there is only slight resistance, the diaphragm may be leaking. Get a new bottle.

There is a recharging hose at each station. Snap the hose fitting on the nipple of the regulator. Push it home until it clicks and locks. When the bottle has filled to the pressure of the plane system, turn the hose clamp clockwise and remove hose fitting. You can carry out this operation while your mask is plugged into the bottle you are filling.

Always use a walk-around bottle if you have to disconnect from the airplane system. Hold your breath while you are switching to the bottle. Clip the A-6 bottle to your jacket. Carry the D-2 bottle in the sling provided for it.

The duration of the walk-around oxygen supply is variable. Don't depend on it to last very long, regardless of what you have heard about the capacity. **Keep watching the gage, and recharge the bottle when it needs it.**

Always recharge walk-around equipment after use.

There are two types of walk-around assemblies in most airplanes: the new green type A-6 cylinder, which has a clip for fastening to your clothing; and the yellow type D-2 cylinder, equipped with a canvas sling and shoulder strap. (Some airplanes may still have the old green type A-4 cylinders.)

Each type of assembly is equipped with gages and regulators. Older regulators furnish 100% oxygen on demand; newer ones have an Auto-Mix mechanism.

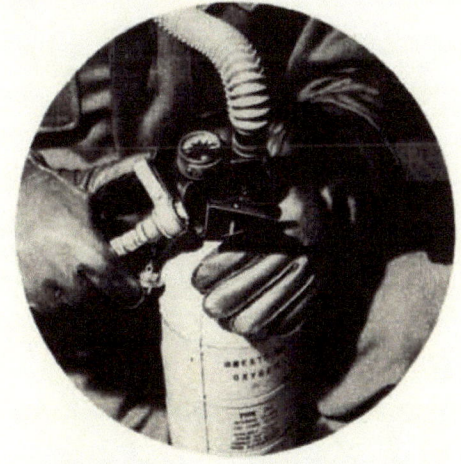

Recharging the D-2 walk-around bottle.

BAILOUT CYLINDERS

The bailout cylinder is a small high-pressure oxygen cylinder, with a gage attached, which furnishes a continuous flow of oxygen.

The cylinder comes in a heavy canvas pocket provided with tying straps. Have this pocket sewed and tied securely to the harness of your parachute. Some new flying suits have a zipper pocket to hold the bailout cylinder.

Before flight, check to see that the pressure of the cylinder is 1800 psi. Plug the bayonet connection on the hose into your mask adapter.

If you have to bail out at altitude, connect your mask to a walk-around bottle, and make your way to the proper exit. Just before jumping, pull the ripcord on the bailout cylinder, or open the valve, and disconnect your mask from the walk-around bottle. In a free fall, hold your thumb over the end of the mask tubing to prevent the venturi effect sucking oxygen out of your mask.

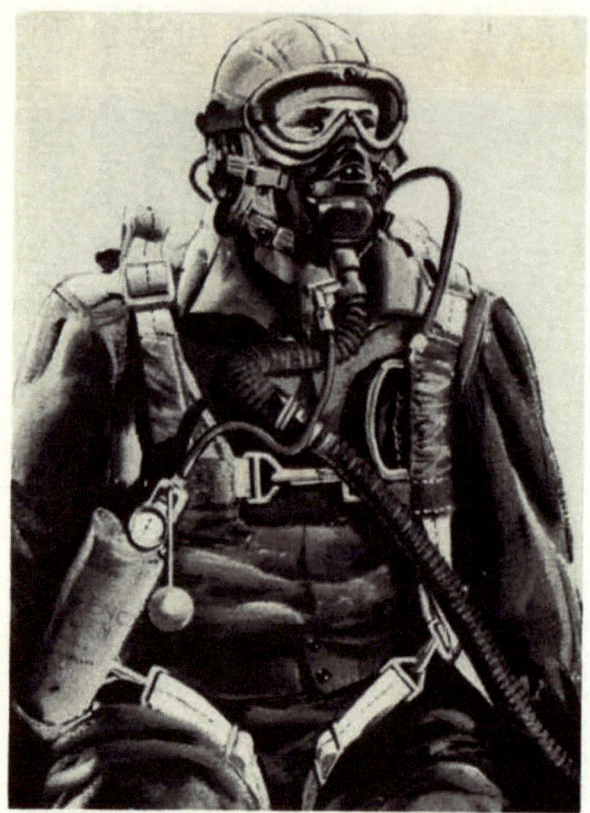

Keep bailout cylinder hose plugged into mask.

DURATION OF SUPPLY

The oxygen supply of the airplane is carried in 18 type G-1, low-pressure, non-shatterable cylinders. The entire system is filled from one filler valve, located on the outside of the fuselage, just forward of the wing root on the left side.

Each of the 13 oxygen stations is supplied from two separate distribution lines. Loss of one line or its associated cylinders still leaves each station with an alternate source of oxygen. In the event of partial destruction of the system, all stations still functioning have equal access to the remaining oxygen supply.

The duration of oxygen supply varies with the requirements of the individuals, their activity, the temperature, altitude, and charge of the system. It is impossible to make positive statements about how long your supply will last.

The duration charts on the next page, however, give you an accurate estimate of your remaining supply of oxygen at any altitude, any remaining pressure, and with any number of cylinders left intact (for A-12 regulators).

Remember that these computations are theoretical. They are based on averages and only furnish a rough guide. The experience of your own crew with your own airplane will furnish additional information for judging duration.

Both types of A-12 regulators are least economical between 20,000 and 30,000 feet. The supply lasts longer above 30,000 feet than it does between 20,000 and 30,000 feet.

The duration differs slightly according to the type of regulator used, Aro or Pioneer. The chart gives the lower duration figure in all cases.

If any cylinders have been shot out, figure only the remaining number when using duration charts.

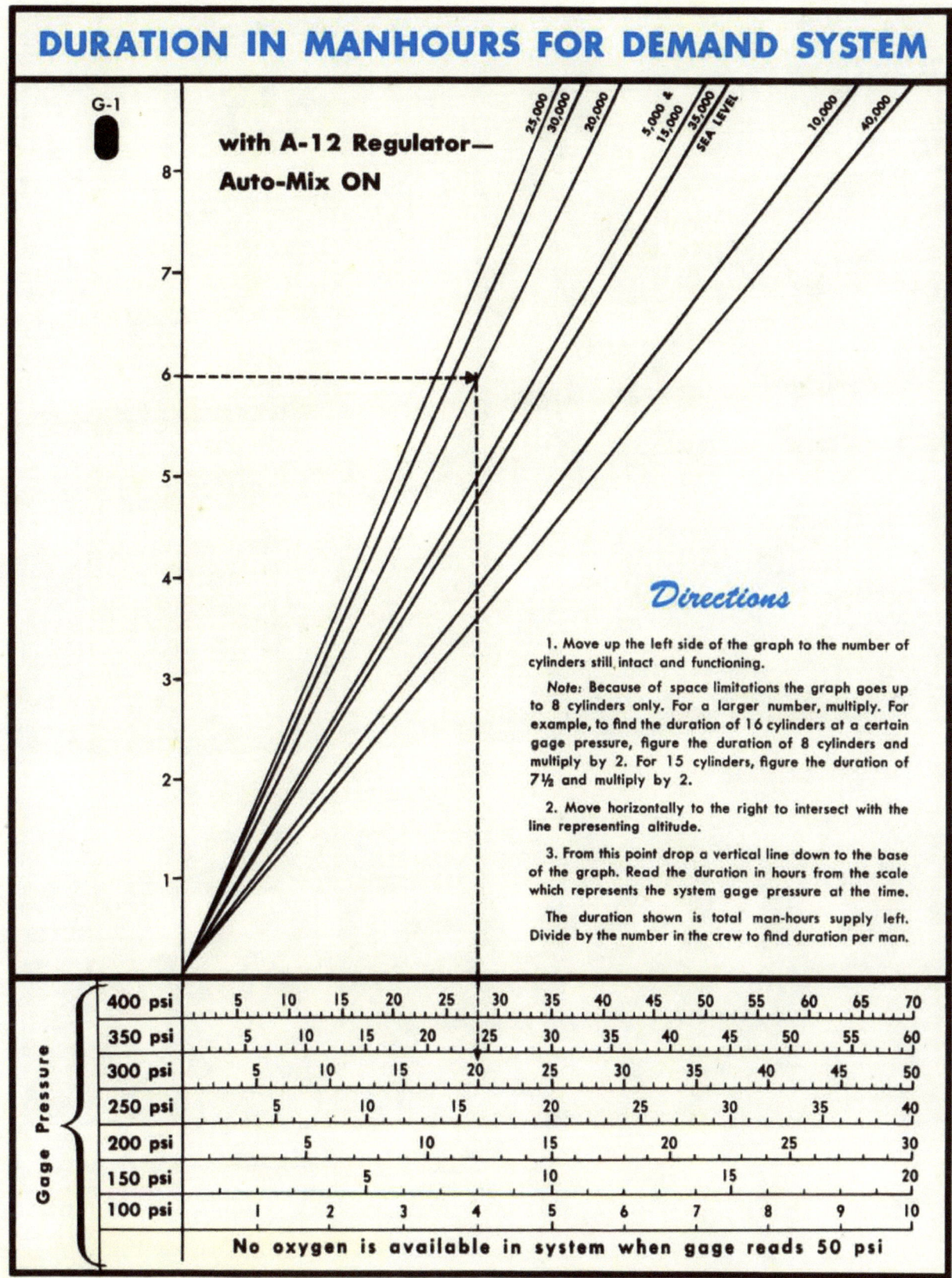

PROTECTION

 Draw all equipment needed from storage room before mission and return it afterward for drying, cleaning, and any necessary repairs. Report anything wrong when you return equipment.

COLD WEATHER CLOTHING

Protection against cold is a vital problem in high altitude flying. **At times frostbite has caused more casualties than combat.**

Most cases of frostbite occur because flyers don't appreciate the seriousness of the problem, or because they misuse the equipment furnished for their protection.

One of the difficulties is that many crew members don't know what frostbite actually is, until they experience it. The name is deceiving. It doesn't sound particularly dangerous, and to many men frostbite means the non-serious numbness which you often feel on face or hands in moderately cold weather.

Actually frostbite involves the complete freezing of body tissue. Depending on the degree of cold and time exposed, the results of frostbite range from serious incapacitating sores, to death. Loss of fingers and toes is frequent in high altitude crews who are careless about their clothing.

Adequate heating of all stations on airplanes is obviously impractical. Therefore your clothing is your main protection against frostbite. And the clothing provided really protects, if you exercise care in the use of it.

Your basic flying suit is the electrically-heated suit. When this suit is insufficient, add the intermediate flying suit over the electric apparel.

Remember to wear extra gloves also when you add extra clothing.

Most of the following precautions concerning use of cold weather clothing pertain to both heated and non-heated apparel.

Keep your clothing dry! Moisture freezes and greatly reduces the effectiveness of all clothing as protection against cold.

Before a mission, dry your skin with a towel and then dress slowly. Don't dress so early that you have to stand around for some time with heavy clothing on. The resulting perspiration will soak into the suit and freeze later.

If it's raining, wear a raincoat and galoshes over your flying equipment to the plane and let the ground crewmen take them back.

Under the type F-2 electrically-heated suit wear woolen underwear with long sleeves and legs, and a woolen shirt.

When you get the type F-3 electrically-heated suit, wear it over normal GI ground clothing for the theater in which you are operating. Wear the intermediate flying suit over the F-3.

With either electrical suit wear wool socks, electrically-heated felt liners over them, and then your flying boots.

Always wear rayon gloves under your electrically-heated gloves. Never remove your gloves in low temperatures if you can help it. With your gloves on, practice all operations which you may be required to do in flight, so that you won't have to expose your hands.

Keep your clothing clean, particularly your underwear. Soiled clothes lose their insulating qualities. And here's a tip: Wash your own clothes rather than hire a native washwoman. She'll mangle them, but literally!

Have all holes in clothing sewed up immediately. Even a small rip can admit enough cold air to be dangerous.

Don't wear tight clothing. Constriction of circulation hastens frostbite. During flight be sure to ease the restriction of tight seat belts or parachute harness often enough so that circulation of blood is not cut off.

Wear goggles at all times during the mission. They are excellent protection against cold, flash burns, and solid fragments.

Caution: When using the electric suit keep the rheostat at the lowest comfortable heat. Don't climb hot. It will mean perspiration and freezing at higher altitudes.

Note: For further dope on frostbite see FIRST AID.

RESTRICTED

Type F-2 electrical flying suit. Add a wool or silk scarf around your neck to seal the space between collar and helmet.

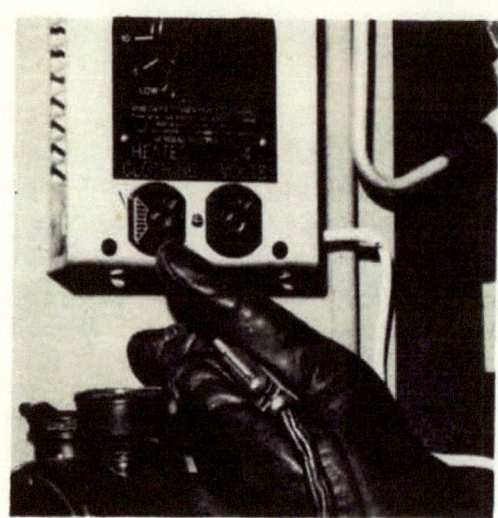

During warm-up of plane, plug electrical suit extension plug into left outlet. The left outlet works off the rheostat; the right is full current.

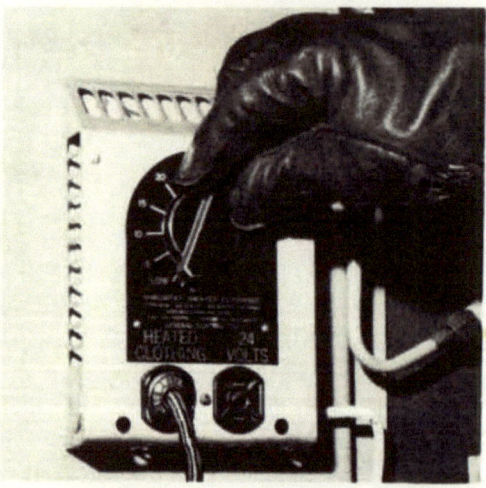

Turn up rheostat to see that suit heats; then turn it back off.

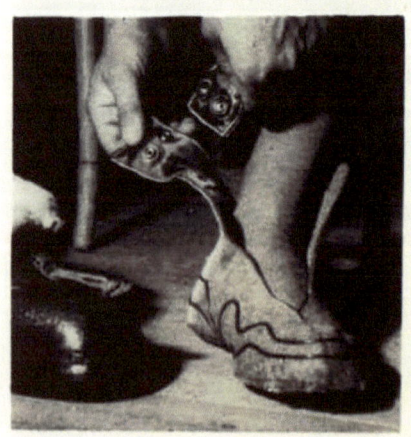
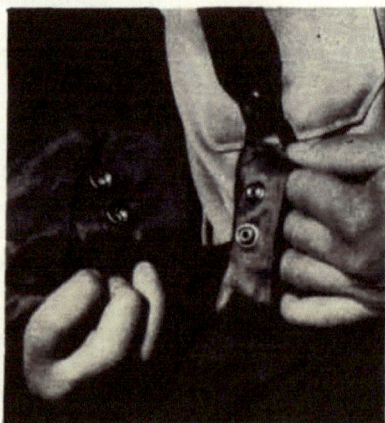
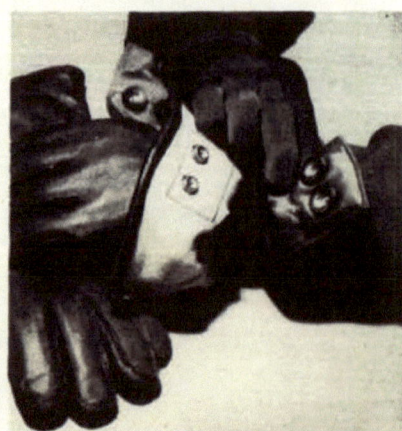

Carefully connect all circuits.

RESTRICTED

LIFE PRESERVER VEST

When the vest is first issued to you, put it on over your flying clothes and inflate it by mouth valves (don't waste a carbon dioxide cartridge doing this) to adjust the fit of the straps. With the vest inflated the waist strap should be fairly tight and the crotch and back straps snug. After adjusting the back strap, hand tack it to the waist strap. Deflate by opening mouth valves and rolling up vest.

Wear the vest at all times on flights over water.

Keep the ends of the mouth valves bent down, or cut them off flush with the retaining loop, so they won't poke you in the eye when the vest is inflated.

Wear the collar of your jacket over the collar of the life vest. And, of course, wear the life vest **under** your parachute harness.

Whenever you are wearing the life vest, tie your parachute first-aid packet to the vest strap, not to your parachute harness. When you bail out into water you lose the chute, and you might need the packet.

Before each flight inspect both CO_2 inflators. Always check the mouth inflator valves to see that they are closed. If the valves are even partly open the CO_2 goes right on through and out when you pull the cords for emergency inflation.

Notice the sea marker tab on the life vest in the illustration. When rescue planes approach, release the dye by pulling down on the tab. Stir the chemical around to color as large an area of the water as possible.

Life vests must be inspected every six

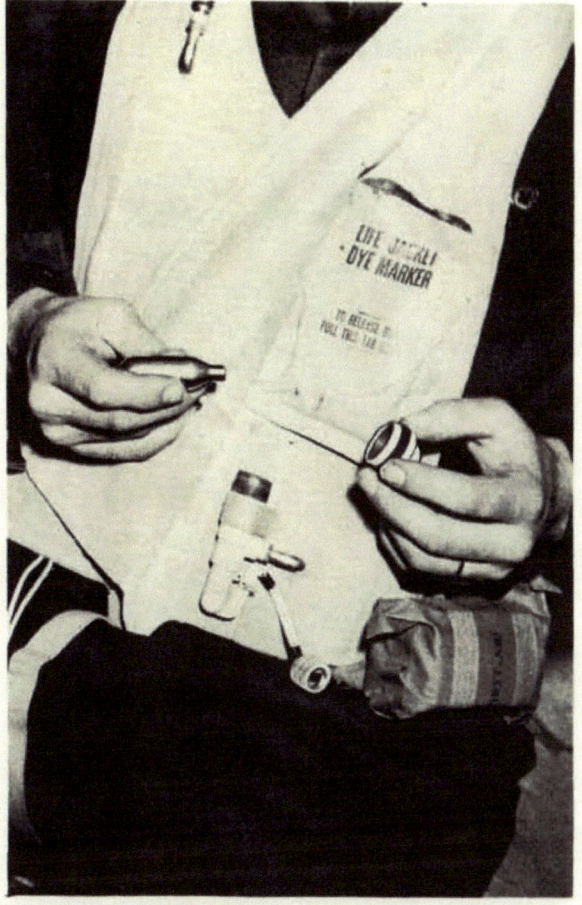

Check CO_2 inflator before flight. See that the cartridge seal is not punctured. The puncturing arm should be in a vertical position, and safetied with light wire. The cartridge goes in with small end down. Screw the cap down tight when you replace it.

months. Check the date stenciled on the vest. See that it is turned in for inspection at the proper time.

Note: See illustrations under PARACHUTES.

RESTRICTED

FLAK SUITS

Flak suits consist of armored vest and apron assemblies. They are not personal issue, but they should be delivered to the plane before the flight and picked up afterward for inspection. You couldn't carry one anyway, with everything else you're lugging. Report to the pilot if you don't find a flak suit in the plane for you.

Wear the suit when you approach the target area. It's heavy but it's guaranteed that you won't notice the weight when the fight begins to get hot.

Note: Ask your Personal Equipment Officer to have a tab sewed on your flak suit for your oxygen mask hose clip.

FLAK HELMETS

The flak helmet is personal issue. If you have worn both your flak suit and flak helmet on the mission, you have a good chance of returning the helmet to the supply room **personally** after the flight.

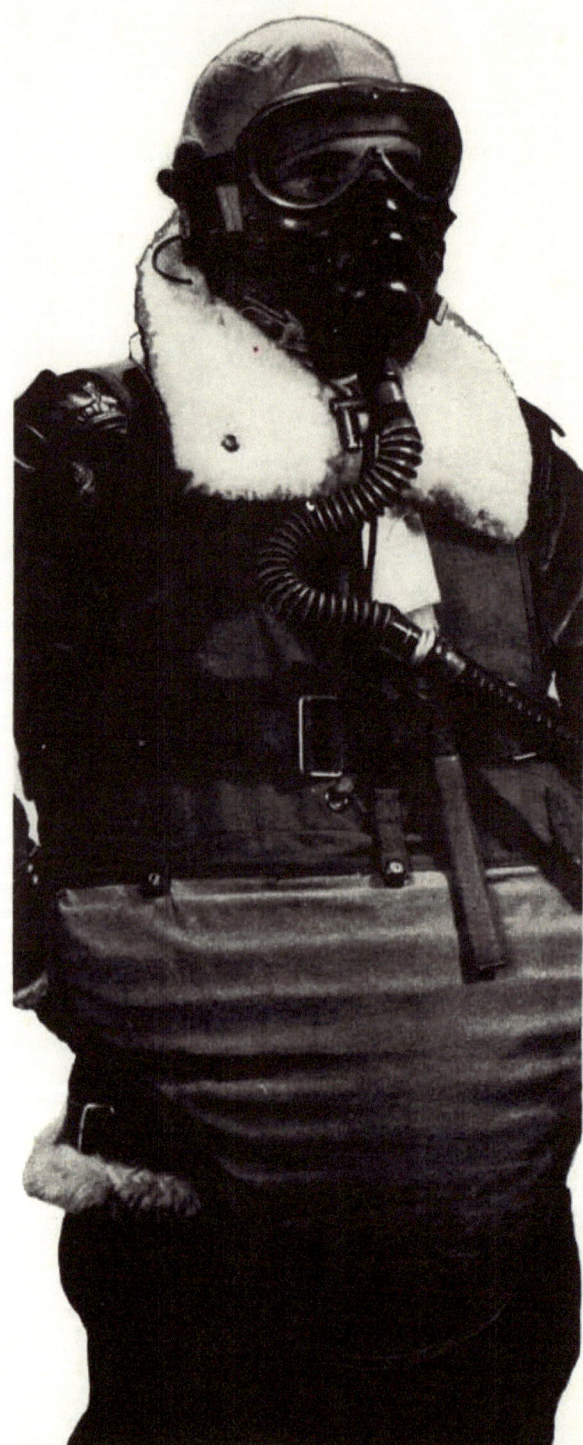

Flak Suit—Pilot's, copilot's, and tail gunner's suits have un-armored back, all others have full armor. Pulling the ripcord at the center of suit causes the whole suit to drop off.

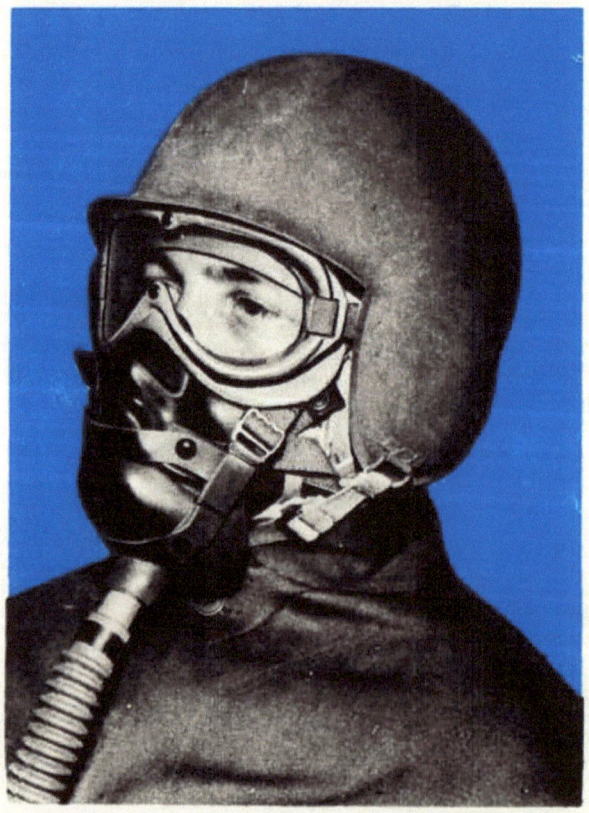

194

RESTRICTED

FIRST AID

Many a crew member is alive and flying today only because one of his buddies knew what to do for him when he was injured.

Would you have known what to do?

Prompt and efficient first aid frequently means the difference between life and death to injured men. Take advantage of every opportunity to learn first-aid procedures and to familiarize yourself with the location and use of the various first-aid kits in the airplane.

Two of your crew members have been given special training in first aid. This fact does not, however, excuse you from further preparation for emergencies. It may be the trained men who need help.

THE GENERAL OBJECTIVES OF FIRST AID ARE:
  STOP BLEEDING
  SUSTAIN BREATHING
  PREVENT SHOCK
  RELIEVE PAIN
  PREVENT INFECTION

WOUNDS

Don't touch the wound.

Press or tie a small Carlisle bandage tightly against the wound to stop bleeding. Don't touch the sterile side of the dressing.

If bleeding cannot be stopped by firm pressure, apply tourniquet above the wound. Release tourniquet every 20 minutes.

After bleeding has been controlled, sprinkle sulfa powder in wound and reapply a dressing.

Give 8 sulfa tablets by mouth.

Use morphine for pain.

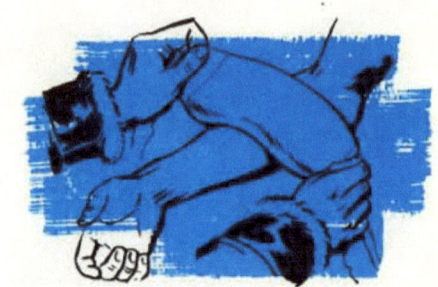

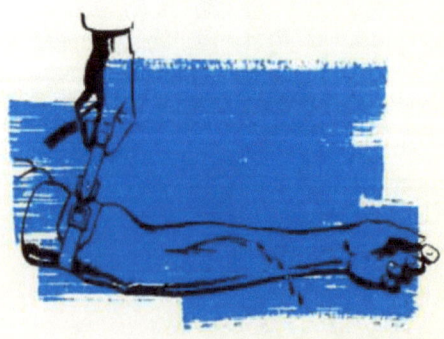

GAPING WOUNDS
CHEST AND ABDOMEN

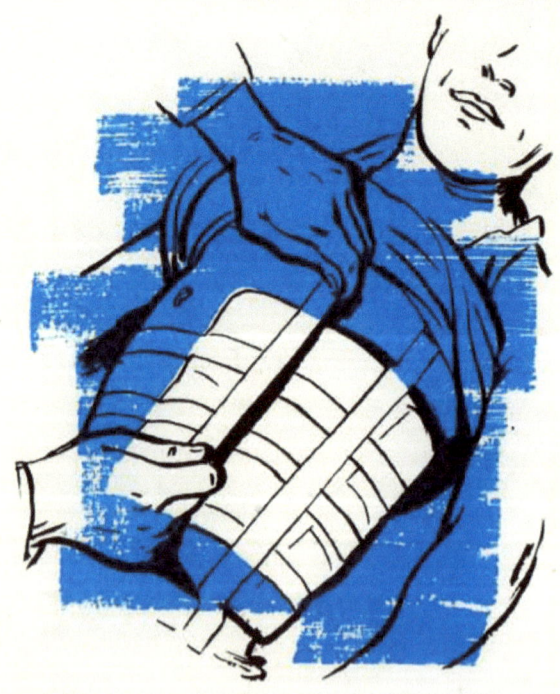

Stop bleeding by packing tightly with sterile side of large Carlisle bandage. Smear the dressing with sulfa burn ointment and tape it tightly in place with strips of adhesive tape.

Use morphine for pain.

Treat for shock.

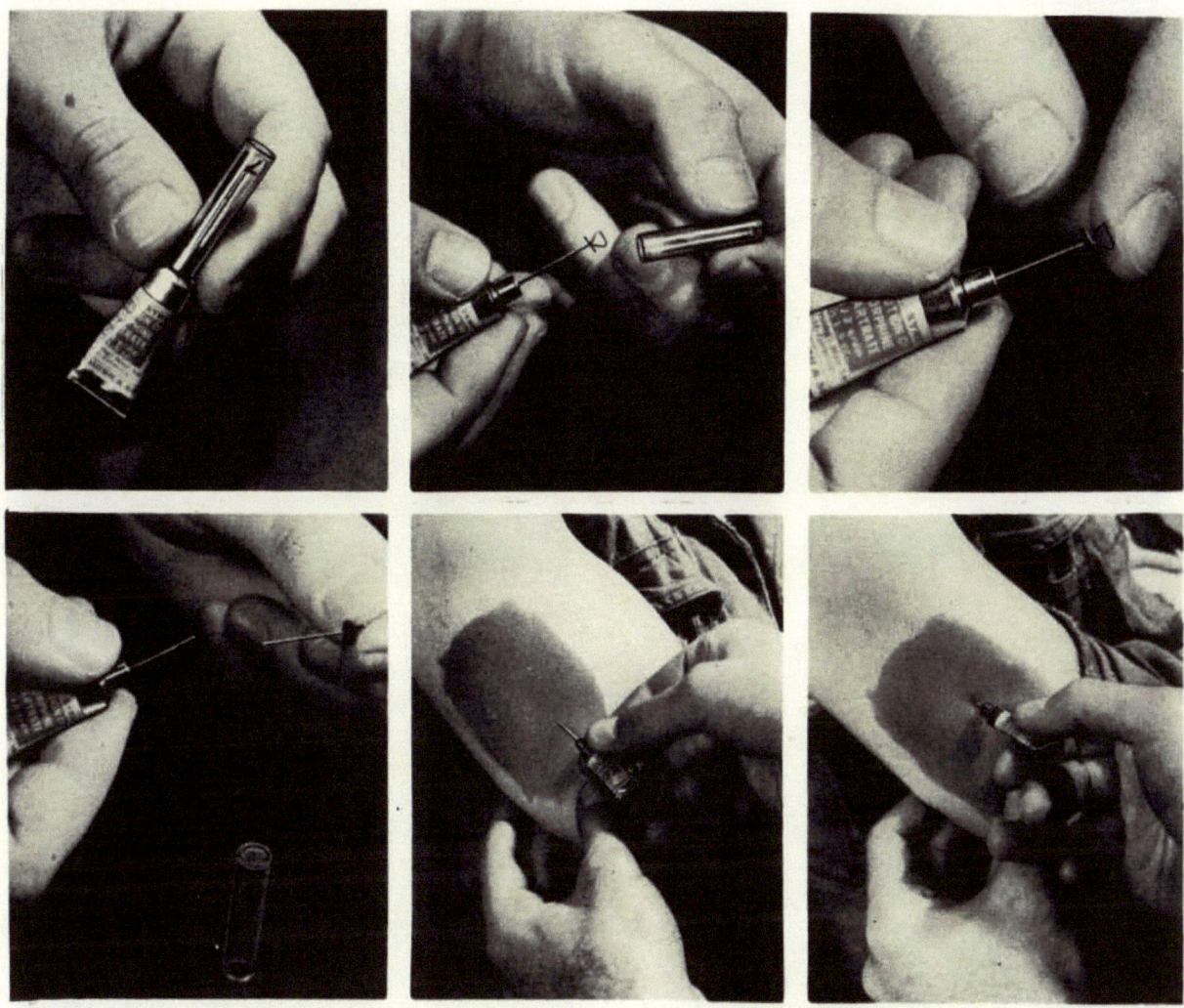

MORPHINE

Paint skin area to be injected (any handy spot) with one coat of iodine.

    Remove cover of syrette.

    Push wire loop in to break seal.

    Remove wire loop from needle.

    Hold syrette at metal collar and thrust needle into arm.

    Inject morphine by squeezing tube.

Note: Morphine is a powerful drug for the relief of pain. But it is dangerous if too much is given. The danger point is indicated by the injured man's rate of breathing; never give morphine to a man who is breathing less than 12 times per minute. It takes a while for morphine to take effect; therefore, wait at least one half hour before repeating an injection of one syrette. After that, if the pain is still severe, you can repeat the dose provided the rate of breathing is more than 12 times per minute.

Warning

Don't give morphine to an unconscious man.

Don't give morphine if the man is breathing less than 12 times per minute.

Don't repeat morphine injection for at least 30 minutes.

BURNS

Smear burn ointment on sterile side of dressing, being careful not to touch it with your hands.

Apply dressing to burned area, tying or taping it in place.

Give morphine for pain.

Treat for shock.

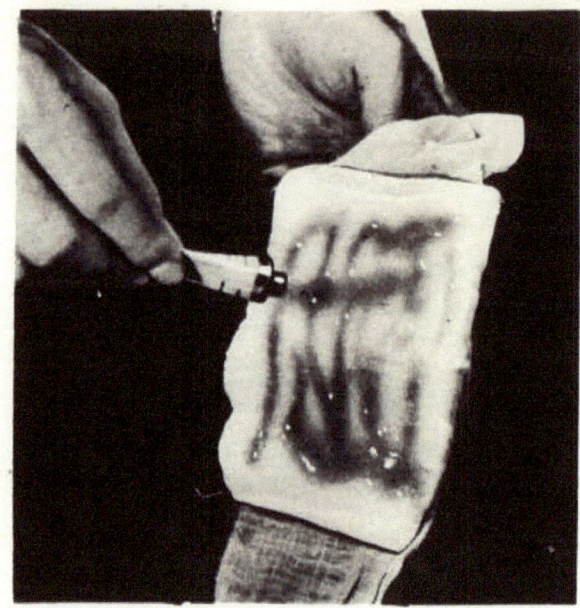

BROKEN BONES

Don't move the man if you can avoid it. Splint the broken limb.

Splinting principle is the same for breaks in lower arm, upper arm, and lower leg. For upper leg, splint the whole leg. Make a long splint by taping or tying shorter ones together, or use a carbine, an oar from the raft kit, or any other handy material.

Compound fractures are those in which a bone and the overlying skin are broken. Treat the break in the skin as you would any wound. Sprinkle sulfa powder in wound. Don't try to push bone fragments back. Apply dressing, then splint.

Give morphine.

Treat for shock.

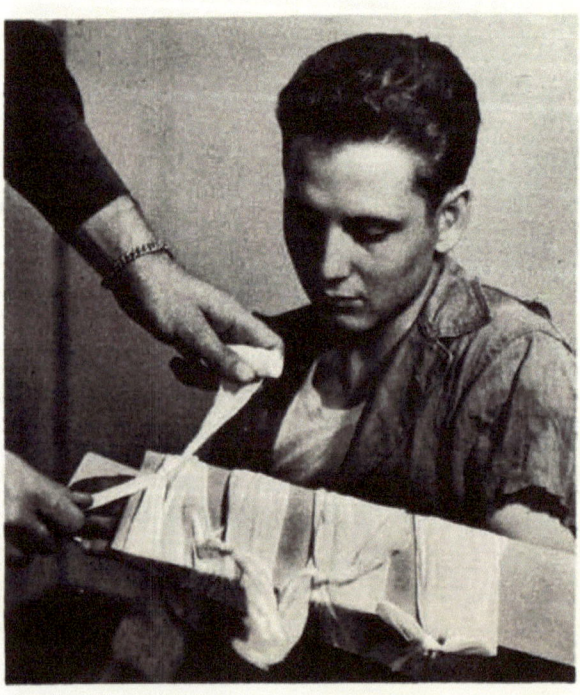

SHOCK

Shock results from serious wounds, fractures, pain, burns, excessive loss of blood.

Symptoms: Pale, cold, clammy skin. Fast, weak pulse. Shallow breathing.

What to do:

Give oxygen—Auto-Mix "OFF."

Give morphine for pain.

Elevate the man's legs: put parachutes or other equipment under buttocks and legs, except when he has a head wound.

Keep him warm.

Administer blood plasma or similar substance.

ANOXIA

You won't recognize any symptoms of anoxia in yourself, but sometimes you can spot it in other crew members.

Be suspicious of any unusual or unexpected reactions as possible anoxia effects. Errors of judgment, lack of coordination, or any uncontrolled emotional display could be the result of lack of oxygen.

Whenever you notice any of these effects, or whenever you find a man unconscious, check his oxygen immediately and see that he gets a supply.

If a man is unconscious or nearly so from anoxia, get a mask on him that works and connect it to a working regulator. Turn the Emergency Valve to "ON" until he recovers.

Note: In the case of serious wounds of any kind, see that the man gets pure oxygen—Auto-Mix "OFF"—regardless of altitude.

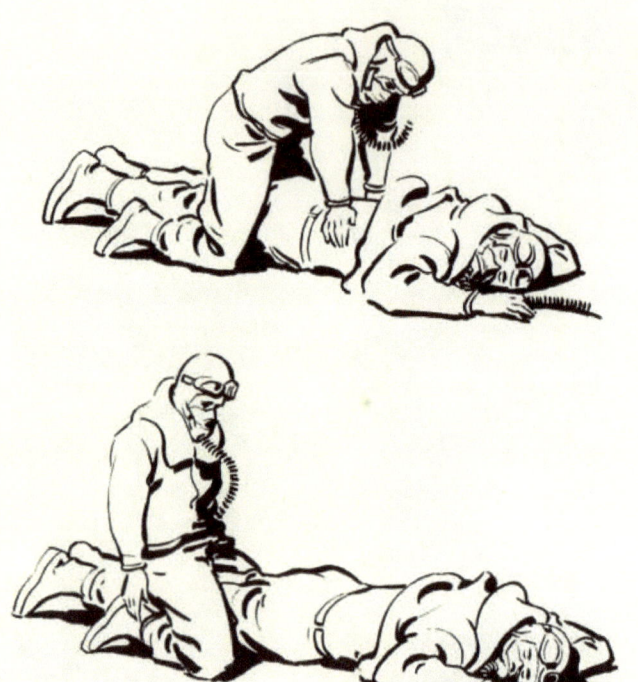

Give him artificial respiration if you can manage it in the cramped space. Keep the oxygen Emergency Valve to "ON" during artificial respiration.

FROSTBITE

Frostbite occurs in an unbelievably brief exposure of any part of the body to the extreme cold of high altitude. Don't take chances. Never unnecessarily remove gloves, mask or goggles, or any other clothing at low temperatures.

Numbness indicates the onset of frostbite. Wrinkle your face from time to time to see if it's getting numb. If you see whitening of the skin of your own hands or the face of another crew member, it may indicate frostbite.

If frostbite occurs, warm the part **gradually** by putting it inside your jacket under your armpit. Unless you are a contortionist, warm your frostbitten foot in the armpit of one of your buddies, or between his thighs.

Never warm a frozen part quickly by artificial heat. Quick warming will increase the damage to the tissue.

Warning

NEVER PUT YOUR BARE HAND ON METAL AT EXTREMELY LOW TEMPERATURES. INSTANTANEOUS FREEZING RESULTS AND YOU WON'T GET IT BACK WHOLE!

FIRST-AID KITS

NOTE: INSTRUCTIONS FOR USE OF COMPONENTS ARE INCLUDED IN EACH KIT

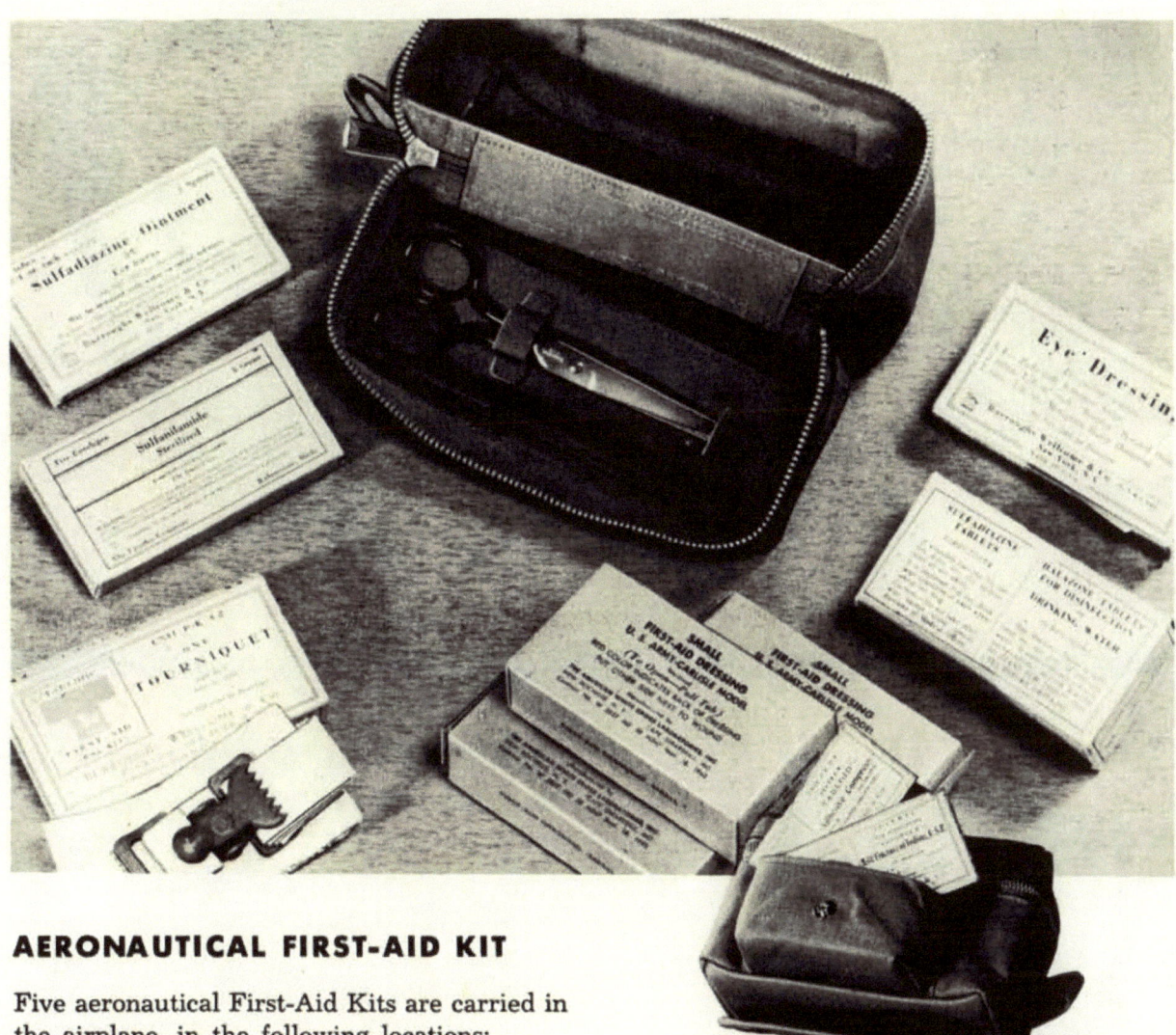

AERONAUTICAL FIRST-AID KIT

Five aeronautical First-Aid Kits are carried in the airplane, in the following locations:

1. Above the flight engineer.
2. On door of navigator's cabinet.
3. On seat pedestal of upper gun sighting station.
4. On rear compartment auxiliary panel forward of bunk area.
5. Tail gunner's compartment.

Each Aeronautical First-Aid Kit contains:

    Iodine swabs
    Adhesive gauze bandages
    Halazone tablets
    Burn-injury set
    Eye-dressing set
    Morphine syrettes
    Sulfa tablets
    Sulfa powder
    Small Carlisle first-aid dressings
    Scissors
    Tourniquet

RESTRICTED

The Arctic First-Aid Kit is located under the lower bunk in the rear unpressurized cabin.

ARCTIC FIRST-AID KIT

The Arctic First-Aid Kit contains:
- Halazone tablets
- Absorbent cotton
- Adhesive tape
- Burn ointment
- Burn-injury sets
- Iodine swabs
- Ammoniated mercury ointment
- Morphine syrettes
- Salt tablets
- Sulfa tablets
- Sulfa powder
- Adhesive gauze bandages
- Compress gauze bandages
- Aspirin tablets
- Aloin compound tablets
- Sodium bicarbonate and peppermint tablets
- Bismuth subcarbonate tablets
- Protein silver tablets
- Multivitamin capsules
- Sulfaguanidine

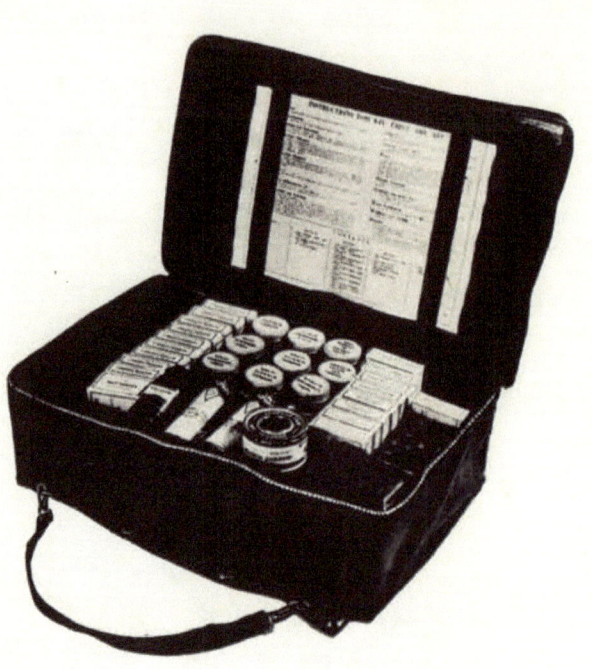

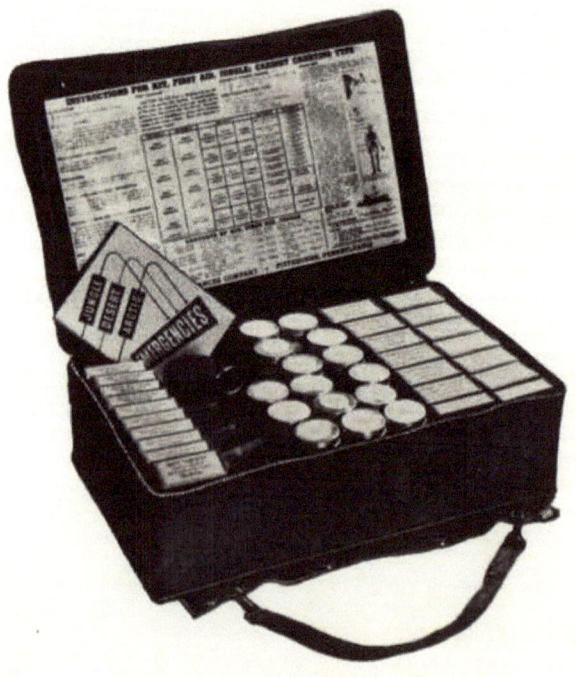

JUNGLE FIRST-AID KIT

The Jungle First-Aid Kit is located with the Arctic First-Aid Kit, under the lower bunk.

The Jungle First-Aid Kit contains:
- Halazone tablets
- Insect repellent
- Suction kit for snake bite
- Iodine swabs
- Morphine syrettes
- Salt tablets
- Sulfa tablets
- Adhesive gauze bandages
- Aspirin tablets
- Aloin compound tablets
- Atabrine tablets
- Sodium bicarbonate and peppermint tablets
- Sulfaguanidine

BATTLE SPLINT AND DRESSING KIT

Two Kits, Battle Splint and Dressing, are carried. One is located behind the copilot's seat, and the other under the bunk in the rear pressurized cabin.

Each Kit, Battle Splint and Dressing, contains:

Gauze bandages
Small Carlisle first-aid dressings
Large Carlisle first-aid dressings
Serum albumin units for treatment of shock
Basswood splints
Adhesive tape
Safety pins

BLOOD PLASMA KIT

Two Kits, Blood Plasma, are carried. One is located on the ceiling above the flight engineer's head, and the other under the lower bunk in the rear pressurized cabin.

Each Kit, Blood Plasma, contains two complete sets of apparatus for the administration of plasma or serum albumin, concentrated from plasma.

PARACHUTE FIRST-AID PACKET

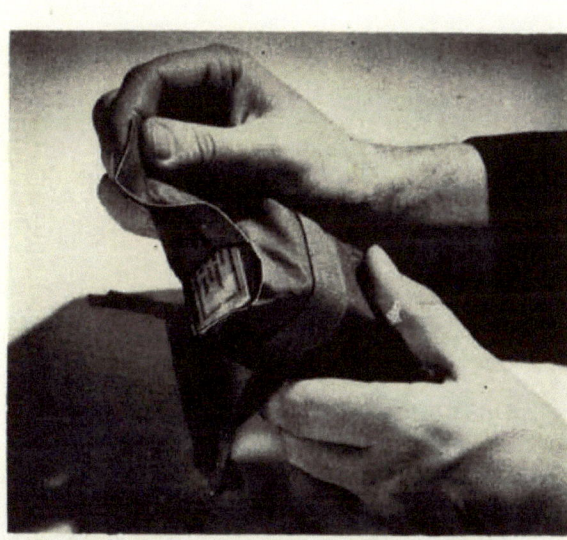

Tear cover to open.

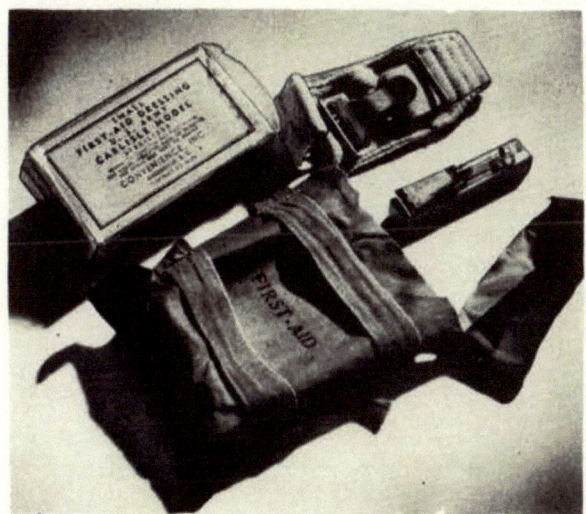

Contents of packet.

One Parachute First-Aid Packet is issued to each man. Tie the packet to the strap of the life vest when wearing the vest. If you are not going to use the life vest, tie the packet to the shoulder strap of the parachute harness, well down on the lower part of the strap. See illustrations under PARACHUTES.

The Parachute First-Aid Packet contains:
- Tourniquet
- Small Carlisle first-aid dressing
- Morphine syrette
- Sulfa tablets
- Sulfa powder

RESTRICTED

A Life Raft First-Aid Kit is included in the accessory kit of each life raft.
    Each Life Raft First-Aid Kit contains:
        Morphine syrettes
        Iodine
        Burn ointment
        Compress bandage
        Sulfa powder
        Sulfa tablets

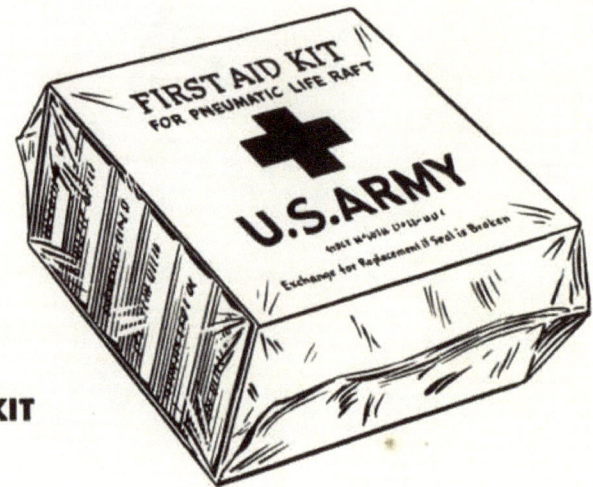

LIFE RAFT FIRST-AID KIT

PARACHUTE FIRST-AID KIT, FRYING PAN INSERT

A Parachute First-Aid Kit, Frying Pan Insert, is included in each B-4 emergency kit, attached to your parachute harness.
    Each Parachute First-Aid Kit, Frying Pan Insert, contains:
        Atabrine tablets
        Benzedrine sulfate tablets
        Halazone tablets
        Burn-injury set
        Iodine swabs
        Salt tablets
        Sulfa tablets
        Adhesive gauze bandages
        Compress gauze bandages
        Curved needle, with 120 inches carpet and button thread (for clothing repair)
        Cake soap
        Compressed tea tablets

PARACHUTES

In lots of ways, your parachute is like the Ideal Girl Friend.

Take care of her, treat her right, and she's steady, safe and dependable—you'd be a fool to go out without her!

If you ever have a falling out, she lets you down easy!

But if you've been kicking her around and treating her like dirt, don't expect her to come through just because you happen to need her!

General

Crew members are required to wear a parachute at all times during flight.

There are several different models of each of the three main types of parachutes: seat, back, and quick attachable chest-type. Become familiar with the one issued you.

If you have a quick attachable chest chute, snap the pack onto the harness before every flight to check the attachment.

You may have a standard or quick-release harness. If you have the latter, operate the quick-release mechanism a few times to become familiar with its use.

Back-type parachute. Note: If not wearing life vest, tie first-aid packet to parachute harness. When you have the bailout bottle on the right strap, put the first-aid packet on the left strap.

Quick attachable chest-type parachute.

Quick release harness.

Have your parachute harness correctly fitted and tacked by a competent parachute maintenance man. Check the harness fit each time you put it on. Shoulder and chest straps should be snug without play; the chest buckle should be 12 inches below the chin. Leg straps should be snug. In fact, the harness should be comfortably snug when you are seated and disagreeably tight when you stand up.

Pre-Flight Check

Inspect your parachute carefully before each flight. You never know when you may have to use it.

Check the date of the last inspection. The packing interval should not exceed 60 days in the United States or 30 days in tropical climates.

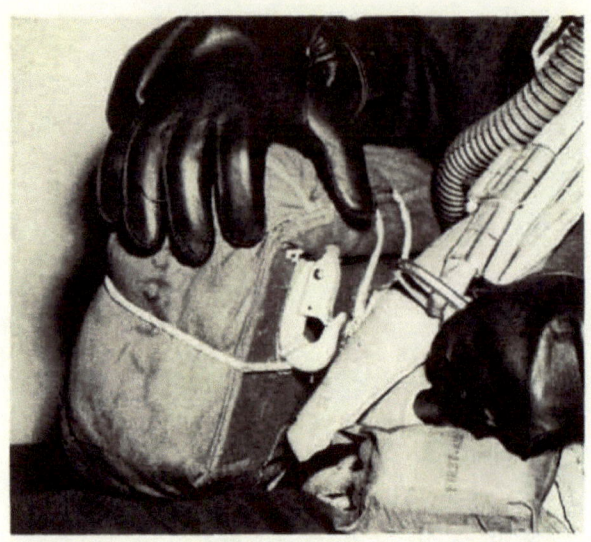

Attach chest-type chute like this, ripcord on the right-hand side.

Caution!

There are two groups of attachable chest-type parachute assemblies. On Group 1 assemblies the snaps are on the pack and the D-rings on the harness. On Group 2 assemblies the rings are on the pack and the snaps are on the harness.

Parachutes of Group 1 are not interchangeable with parachutes of Group 2.

The pilot is responsible for prevention of mismatching quick-attachable chutes in his airplane.

Before the airplane moves for takeoff, inspect *all* attachable parachutes to see that the pack fits the harness. Snap each pack to its harness to make certain it matches.

If you find any pack which does not fit the harness, change either pack or harness to get the correct assembly.

Each group is to be identified by a color. The same color must be on both pack and harness.

Red identifies Group 1.
Yellow identifies Group 2.

BE SURE ALL PACKS AND HARNESSES IN YOUR PLANE MATCH

RESTRICTED

See that an inspection check has been made within the last ten days and entered on the AAF Form 46 in the chute.

Check pack cover for oil, grease, dirt, and worn spots. Turn the chute in if you find any.

See that the opening elastics are tight, and that the corners of the pack are neatly stowed so that no silk is visible.

Open the flap.

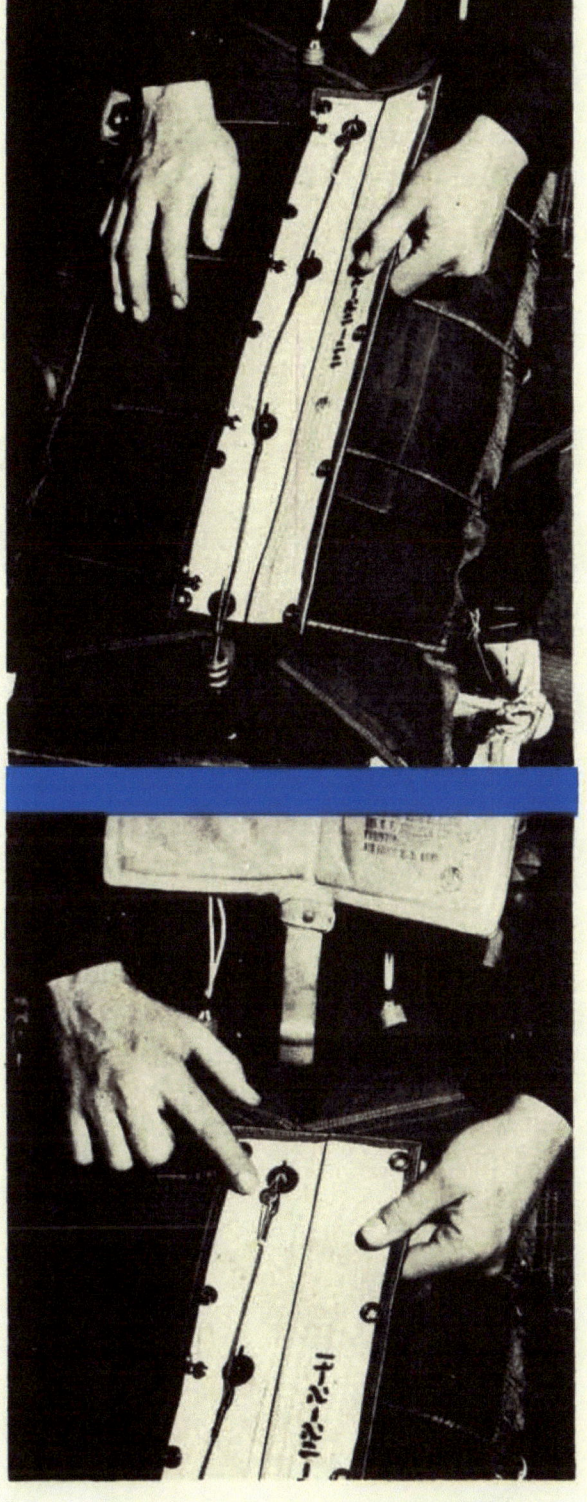

Make sure seal is not broken. See that the ripcord pins are not bent. A bent pin or jammed wire may make it impossible to pull the ripcord.

Carry chute by leg straps, like this.
Or slip harness over shoulders.

RESTRICTED

HIGH ALTITUDE JUMPS

Bailouts from high altitudes present special problems. The higher the altitude, the greater the dangers in bailing out. Stay with the airplane as long as you safely can; down to 15,000 feet if possible.

Except in extreme emergency, do not attempt a bailout without bailout oxygen equipment above 30,000 feet.

The chief hazards of high altitude jumping are:

1. Intense cold.
2. Lack of oxygen.
3. High G forces induced by the parachute opening at high altitudes.

If it is necessary to bail out at high altitude, you can reduce the hazard by making a long free fall to about 10,000 feet before pulling your ripcord. A free fall enables you to reach warmer regions more rapidly; it reduces the hazard of anoxia, and insures less shock when the parachute opens.

At high altitudes the opening shock of the parachute develops excessive G forces. The higher the altitude, the greater the shock.

Judging Altitude in Free Falls

Do not depend upon counting or timing to judge distance above the ground. In the excitement it is difficult if not impossible to judge time.

Look at the ground and judge your altitude. For instance, at 5000 feet the earth begins to look green, you can distinguish details, the horizon spreads, and the ground rushes up at you.

Changing Your Falling Attitude

If your falling attitude is such that you can't see the ground, you can alter your position by extending an arm and the resulting turr gives you a look at the ground. Then pull in your arm and legs and straighten out your knees to stop tumbling before you pull the ripcord.

Terminal Speed

Remember that in many emergency jumps you may leave the airplane at speeds so high that an immediate parachute opening would be dangerous. Hence, if you have sufficient altitude, you should wait 5 to 15 seconds to slow down before pulling the ripcord. This reduces the chance of injury to yourself or damage to your parachute. You actually slow down during the first few seconds in a free fall until you lose the momentum imparted by the speed of the airplane. The lower the altitude, the lower the terminal velocity. So in making a free fall you do not tend to drop faster the longer you fall. Your speed actually decreases the lower you get, because the air becomes denser. This is also true with your parachute open.

Notice: In all jumps from above 10,000 feet, fall free to 10,000 feet or less before pulling the ripcord if you can. This reduces your exposure to cold, anoxia, enemy action, and lessens the opening shock of the parachute. If you do not have bailout oxygen equipment, just hold your breath and dive out. Then continue to hold your breath as long as possible before pulling the ripcord.

CLEARING THE AIRPLANE

The most important step in the average parachute jump is to **clear the plane before you pull the ripcord.**

Keep your eyes open. Look around, and be sure that you are well away from the airplane before you open the chute. If you have enough altitude, wait at least five or ten seconds before pulling the ripcord.

PULLING THE RIPCORD

The ripcord stage of the parachute jump is fairly simple if you follow these directions:

1. Straighten your legs and put your feet together. This maneuver keeps you from spinning or somersaulting. It reduces the danger of tangling up in the harness when the chute opens, and eases the opening shock.

2. Use both hands to grasp the ripcord pocket. Look down at it; hold the harness strap out with one hand so that you can grab it with the other.

3. Grasp the ripcord handle with the right hand and yank! Keep your eyes open and look at the ripcord as you pull it.

THE DESCENT

About two seconds after you pull the ripcord you will feel a short, strong tug as the canopy opens.

Look up to see that the chute is fully open. If a suspension line is crossed over the canopy, or if the lines are twisted, manipulate them until they straighten out.

As you come down you will probably swing back and forth in the parachute. This oscillation of the chute is not dangerous. Don't attempt to check the swing or slip the parachute. Only experts know when and how to do that safely.

Your rate of descent will be approximately 1000 feet per minute.

Observe your drift by craning your neck forward and sighting the ground between your feet, keeping your feet parallel and using them as a driftmeter.

Face in the direction of your drift.

While you cannot steer your chute, you can turn your body in any desired direction. The **body turn** is the most useful maneuver you can learn. With the body turn you can make certain that you land facing in the direction of your drift, thus reducing materially the chance of injury on landing.

HOW TO MAKE BODY TURNS

TO TURN YOUR BODY TO THE RIGHT:

1. Reach up behind your head with your right hand and grasp the left risers.

2. Reach across in front of your head with your left hand and grasp the right risers. Your hands are now crossed, the right hand behind, and in each you have two risers.

3. Pull with both hands at the same time; this will cross the risers above your head and turn your body to the right. You can readily turn 45°, 90°, or 180° by varying the pull.

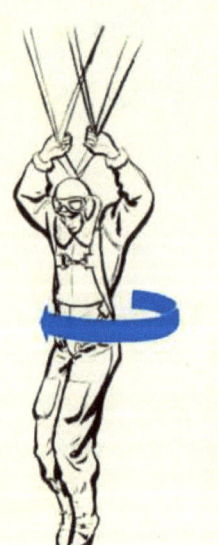

TO TURN TO THE LEFT, REVERSE THIS PROCEDURE

Study the pictures. Practice the body turn in a suspended harness if you get the chance.

The instructions for making the body turn may sound backward to you. Just remember this:

"To turn right, right hand behind my head."

"To turn left, left hand behind my head."

In the descent, start your body turn high enough to allow you to master it. Once you have made the turn, you will find that you can control your direction of drift perfectly. Hold the turn, or slowly ease up if necessary, to bring you in facing **downwind**. Continue to hold the risers, whether you have had to twist them to make a body turn or not, and ride on into the ground this way.

THE LANDING

1. NORMAL LANDINGS

Keep your hands above your head, grasping the risers.

Look at the ground at a 45-degree angle, not straight down. This procedure will aid you in judging your height above the ground more accurately.

Set yourself for the landing by placing your feet together and slightly bending your knees so that you will land on the balls of your feet.

Don't be limp; don't be rigid. Just partially relax, and ride on into the ground, drifting face forward.

As you hit the ground, fall forward or sideways in a tumbling roll to take up the shock.

2. HIGH WIND LANDINGS

When there is a high wind blowing across the ground carry out the procedures described for normal landings, including the body turn to face you in the direction of your drift.

Then, once you are down, roll over on your belly and haul in on the suspension lines nearest the ground. Keep on hauling until you grab silk. Then, drag in the skirt of the canopy to spill the air and collapse the chute.

If you can't manage this maneuver on your face, roll over on your back and do it.

3. TREE LANDINGS

Tree landings are usually the easiest of all.

If you see that you are going to come in on a tree, let go the risers, cross your arms in front of your head, and bury your face in the crook of an elbow.

Keep your feet and knees together.

If you get hung up in a high tree and you know that rescue is coming immediately, it's better to stay there and wait for help down. Otherwise, get out of the harness and cut lines and risers to make a rope for climbing down.

4. WATER LANDINGS

If you see that you are going to land in water, start getting ready early:

Follow the procedure outlined here for all types of parachutes except the QAC AN6513-1A (which has no risers on pack or harness) and the single-point quick-release, instructions for which are given separately.

1. Throw away what you won't need.
2. Pull yourself back into the sling as far as possible.
3. Undo your chest strap by hooking a thumb beneath one of the vertical lift webs, and pushing firmly across your chest to loosen the cross webbing so that you can undo the snap.
4. Free the leg straps by doubling up first one leg then the other, unsnapping the fasteners each time. Hang onto the risers and ride on into the water.
5. As you go into the water, but not before, throw your arms straight up and shrug your shoulders out of the harness, so that the canopy will blow clear.
6. Inflate the Mae West, **but never until your chest strap is unfastened.** If you find yourself in the water before freeing your leg straps, the Mae West will support you while you unfasten the straps or slide them off over your feet. Use a knife to cut yourself free of harness and suspension lines, if necessary.

Procedure for QAC AN6513-1A
(no risers on pack or harness)

Modify the standard procedure as follows:
1. Reach under the pack cover and unfasten the chest strap.
2. Pull yourself well back in the sling and undo the leg straps, if you have time.
3. As soon as you are in the water, release both sides of chest pack from harness and immediately swim upwind, away from the canopy and lines.
4. Inflate the Mae West, one-half at a time, but never until the chest strap is unfastened.
5. When clear of the canopy and shroud lines, you can slip out of your harness at leisure.

Procedure for Single-Point
Quick-Release Harness

Modify the standard procedure as follows:
1. Before reaching the water, turn the locking cap 90° to set the release mechanism for immediate operation.
2. As soon as you are in the water, but not before, pull the safety clip, and press hard on the cap to release the lock. The harness then slides off.
3. Inflate the Mae West, one-half at a time, but never until the harness has been released.
4. Stay clear of the parachute.

Caution

When you land in the water your parachute sometimes blows downwind away from you. Then when you collapse the chute by pulling on the bottom lines it stays put in the water. But as soon as you inflate your Mae West, you float, and tend to drift toward the collapsed chute. **Therefore, immediately work back and away from the collapsed chute so that you won't drift into it while inflating your raft or floating around waiting for rescue.**

To use your one-man life raft in the water, pull the cover off the pack and remove the raft, then pull out the locking pin from the carbon dioxide cylinder and open the valve. Enter the raft by grasping the hand straps and pulling it under you as it inflates. Once in the raft, tie down all the accessories to keep from losing them.

DITCHING EQUIPMENT

Twelve drift signals are stowed under the navigator's table and the drift signal chute is in the door just behind the navigator. Take the signals with you.

One hand axe is secured on the navigator's control stand next to the fire extinguisher and another on the aft compartment auxiliary panel. These axes may be useful in breaking out of the plane after ditching or crash landing.

There are two 6-man life rafts carried in the airplane, in the left and right raft compartments atop the fuselage. After landing, one crew member pulls both raft releases, located on each side of the tunnel opening in the forward pressurized compartment.

There are two raft release handles. Pull both handles to release and inflate both rafts.

Pulling the handles automatically releases the rafts from the compartments and inflates them. If the internal mechanism jams, you can open the compartments by external release levers on top of the fuselage next to the compartment doors.

If a third raft is carried inside the fuselage, it is thrown out of the rear hatch by crew members and inflated by pulling a ripcord on the CO_2 cylinders.

Don't jump from plane into rafts; you'll go right through. If a raft inflates inverted don't jump on it to right it. You'll only push out the air underneath and make it harder to turn the raft over. It may be possible for two or more men to right the raft from the wing. This may also be done by getting into the water, climb-

ing up on one side of the raft and pulling on the handline attached to the opposite side of the raft. Remember, however, that it is better to keep dry, if possible, when the weather is cold.

Fend the rafts off the wings of the plane while launching and boarding them. Wing flaps

are usually torn loose in ditching and jagged edges of flaps or wings can easily puncture rafts.

When all men are aboard, tie rafts together to keep them from drifting apart.

RESTRICTED

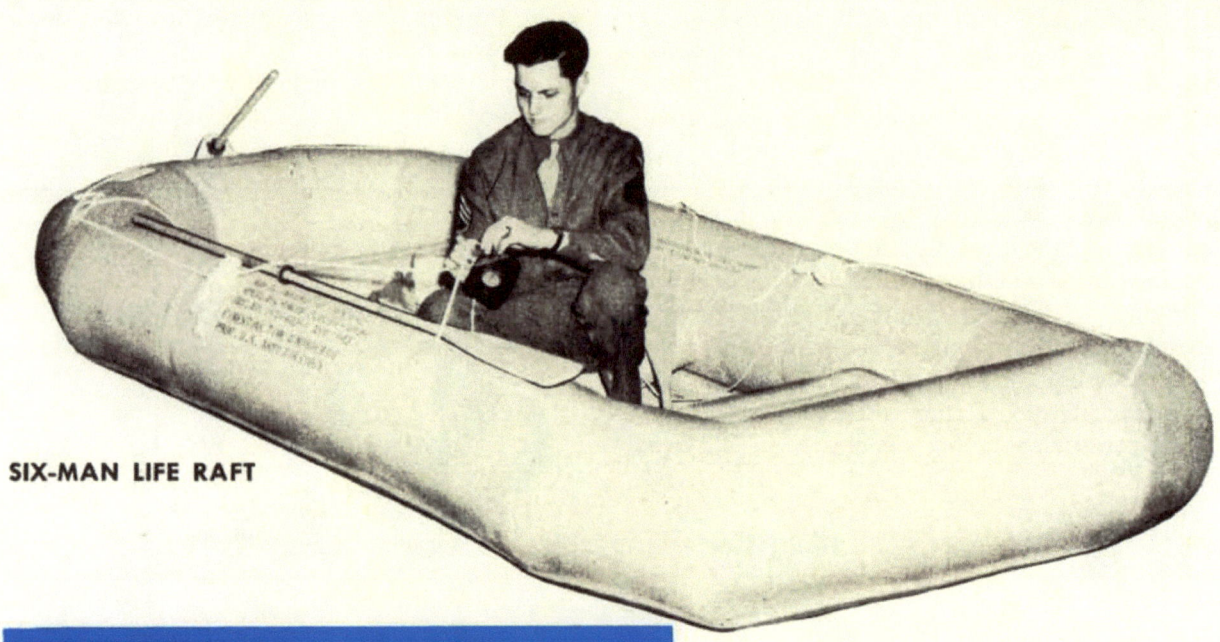

SIX-MAN LIFE RAFT

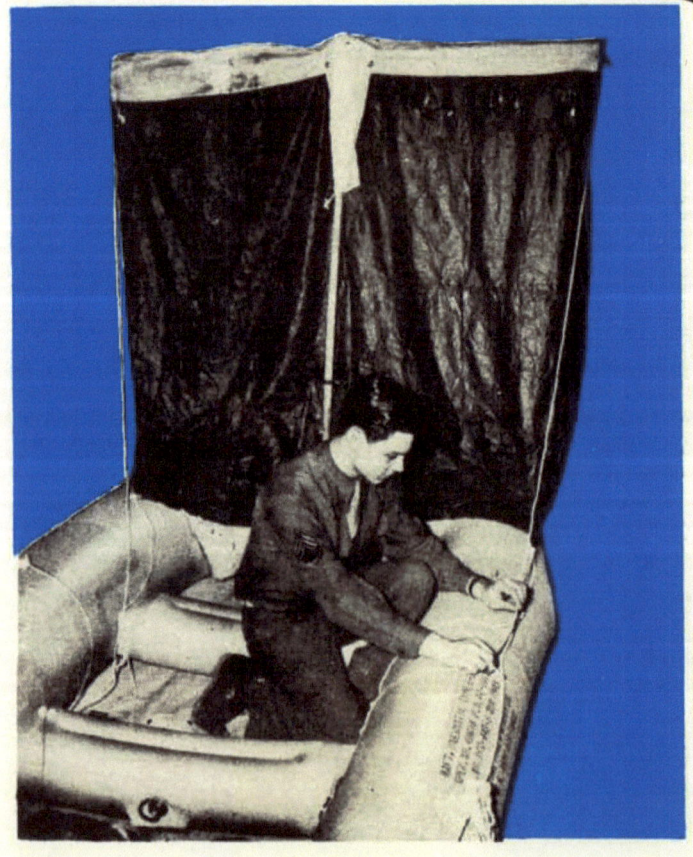

RIGGING THE RAFT SAIL

RESTRICTED

Raft Accessory Kits

An accessory kit is furnished with each raft. Kits are normally secured inside the raft case. Stowage difficulties sometimes make it necessary to keep the kits inside the fuselage, separate from the rafts. In that case, certain crew members must be designated to take the raft kits along when leaving the plane.

You may find sunburn ointment, religious booklets, and desalination kits—either sun still or chemical type—for making sea water drinkable in later raft accessory kits.

Keep the separate items of equipment securely in the kit or tie them to the handline of the raft so they won't be lost if the raft capsizes. It is important to keep signaling equipment accessible, because the opportunity to use this equipment is sudden and short.

Emergency Radio

Get the emergency radio set into operation as soon as weather permits. The kit is contained either in one case, or in two strapped together, which are brought out of the plane after the ditching by the radio operator.

Complete instructions for operating the radio are included in the kit. When you use the radio, try to keep the antenna out of the water, or your signals won't be heard. If possible, be sure to send during the 3-minute international silent periods, at 15 and 45 minutes past the hour.

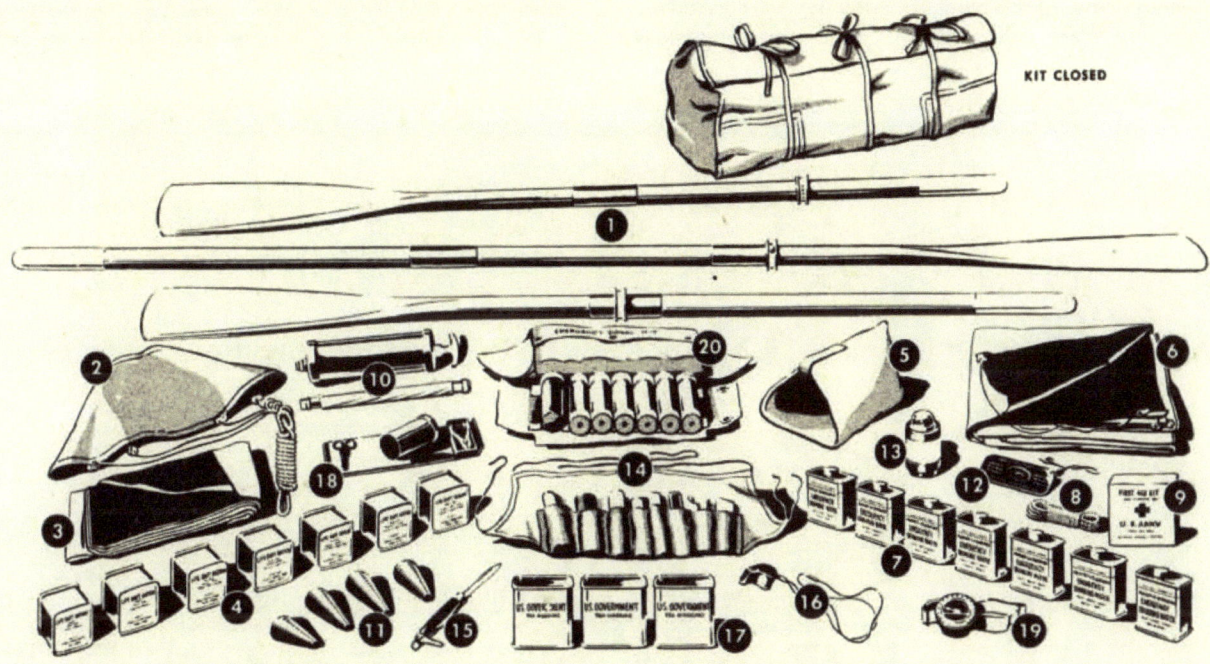

KIT CLOSED

ACCESSORY KIT CONTAINS:

1. Oars
2. Sea anchor
3. Sail
4. Rations
5. Bailing bucket
6. Shade and camouflage cloth
7. Drinking water
8. Line
9. First-aid kit
10. Inflating pump
11. Puncture plugs
12. Signal mirror
13. Flashlight
14. Fishing tackle
15. Jackknife
16. Whistle
17. Sea marker
18. Repair patch kit
19. Wrist compass
20. Signal kit

RESTRICTED

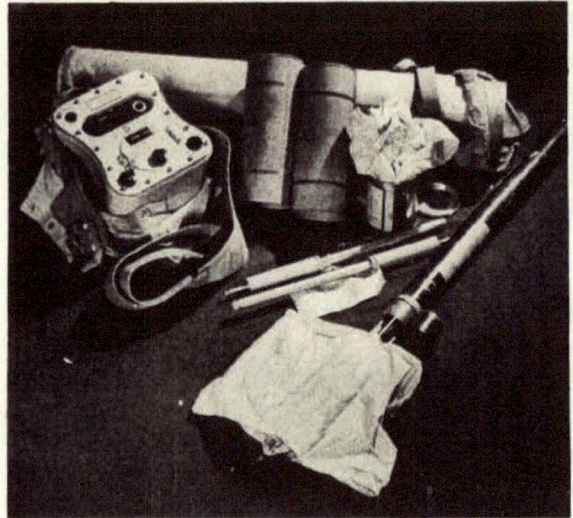

Emergency radio. Accessories include: balloon and kite for raising antenna, hydrogen generators for inflating balloon, signal lamp, extra roll of antenna wire, and an instruction book.

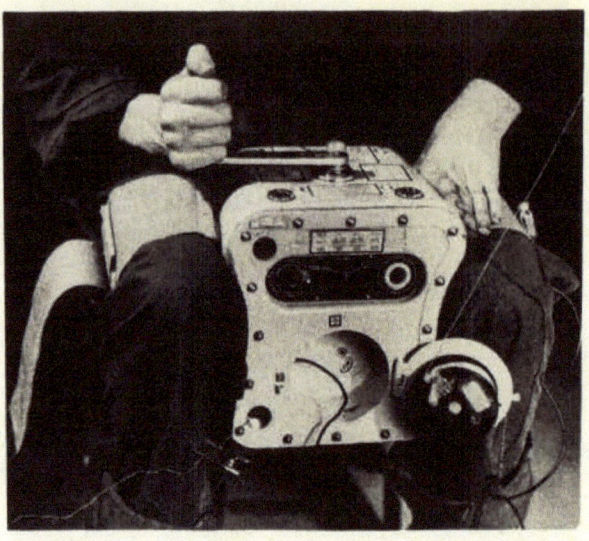

Current for operating the set is supplied by turning a hand crank. Don't lose the crank. There is only one and the radio won't work without it. Pack it in the receptacle after use so it won't be broken.

C-1 Vest Type Emergency Kit

An adjustable vest-type garment, fitted with pockets into which the items of the kit are conveniently stowed. Wear the vest under the life preserver vest and parachute harness.

THE FOLLOWING ITEMS OF EQUIPMENT ARE CARRIED IN THE POCKETS OF VEST:

- 1 hat (yellow on one side, OD on the other)
- 1 pair polaroid sun goggles
- 1 signal mirror, with lanyard
- 1 sharpening stone
- 1 fishing-sewing kit, in plastic container
- 1 collapsible spit and gaff
- 1 plastic water canteen (3-pint capacity)
- 1 Boy Scout knife
- 1 large knife (with 5-inch saw and blade)
- 1 package toilet tissue
- 10 yds. bandage (with sulfa powder)
- 1 waterproof match-box with compass
- 40 matches
- 11 fire starting tabs
- 1 signal whistle
- 1 oil container
- 1 waterproof cover for .45 cal. pistol
- 20 .45 cal. shot cartridges
- 1 first-aid kit
- 1 Survival manual
- 2 emergency parachute rations in tin containers
- 2 five-minute signal flares
- 1 mosquito headnet
- 1 pair woolen insert gloves
- 1 pair leather outer gloves
- 1 collapsible razor with 10 blades
- 1 can insect repellant

FIRE FIGHTING

Nacelle fires during flight are handled by the pilot and flight engineer by use of the automatic fixed carbon dioxide extinguishers.

Cabin fires must be controlled by use of the portable fire extinguishers.

Notify the pilot as soon as a fire is discovered. He pulls the pressure relief valve.

If it's an electrical fire the flight engineer cuts the proper electrical power switches at the direction of the pilot.

In the forward compartment the navigator operates the CO_2 extinguisher.

In the case of fires in the aft compartment the nearest men should grab the nearest extinguisher and use it. If possible, use the carbon tetrachloride extinguisher first, and then the CO_2 if necessary.

Keep all exit doors and windows closed unless you are ordered to bail out.

When the flight formation is under attack the inboard gunner (nearest to your formation) will switch control of his turrets to the outboard gunner and operate the extinguisher in the rear compartment. If the formation is not under attack either gunner can operate the extinguisher.

If the fire cannot be controlled the airplane commander will decide if and when you are to leave the airplane. Don't bail out until you are ordered to do so.

Warning

Carbon tetrachloride extinguishers produce a poisonous gas. When using that equipment stay as far away from the fire as you can. Wear your oxygen mask with Auto-Mix "OFF" ("100% OXYGEN"). Open the bomb bays for ventilation as soon as possible after use of either type of extinguisher.

CO_2 type extinguisher located on inboard side of flight engineer's control board.

CO_2 type extinguisher located in aft pressurized compartment, aft of auxiliary equipment panel.

Carbon Tetrachloride (Pyrene) type extinguisher located beside rear entrance door.

RESTRICTED

FLIGHT MESSING

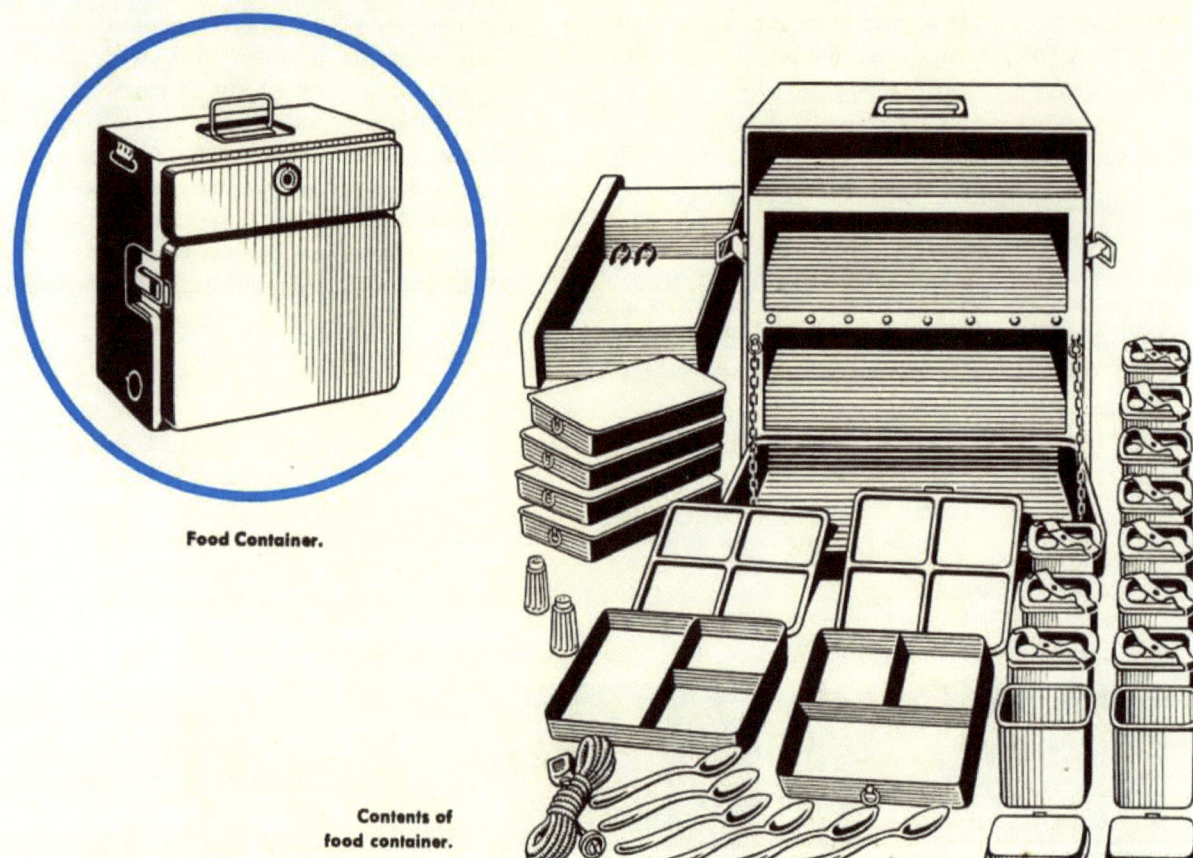

Food Container.

Contents of food container.

Your airplane carries two food containers for the serving of hot meals during flight. One is in the forward compartment and one in the aft compartment.

The insulated drawer in the top has space for utensils, salt and pepper shakers, and for bread, cake, cookies, sandwiches, and fruit.

The lower part of the cabinet has two sections. The upper one contains 12 covered metal beverage cups for soup and hot drinks. The lower section contains six food trays. Each tray carries one meal for one man.

The trays are individually marked so that a man can return part of his meal to the container and be sure of getting his own tray back later.

The containers are wired for either ground or airplane currents.

Attach the cord for the container to the right hand plug of any 24 volt electrical outlet on the plane. To heat up a meal, the container must be plugged into the current two to three hours before the meal is desired.

Follow this procedure before the flight:

Call the kitchen as early as possible before takeoff (at least 45 minutes) and tell them at what time you need the food container.

The mess crew handles the necessary cooking and packing of food, and will have the container ready for you when you call for it.

The crew then arranges for some member to pick up the apparatus at the appointed time, and to return it to the kitchen after the mission.

Check to be sure that food containers are on the plane before take-off.

INDEX

A

	Page
After landing check	86
Ailerons	72
Airplane commander's, amplified checklist	34
duties	6
instrument panel	16
control stand	15
Aisle stand	15
Amperage loads, table of	121
Anoxia, treatment of	200
Antennas	132, 133
Approaches	84, 160
Autopilot, operation	124

B

Bailout	153, 210
Before landing check	78
Bombardier—DR navigator, duties	9
Bomb bay door operation, emergency	107
Bomb release, emergency	107
Brakes, checking	37
emergency operation	37
hydraulic system	119
Broken bones, treatment of	198
Burns, treatment of	198

C

C-1 autopilot	124
Cabin, depressurizing	149
fires	112
pressurizing	149
Carbon dioxide extinguishers	111
Carburetor, ice	145
type	13
Center of gravity, allowable limits	23, 151
Central fire control specialist gunner, duties	9

	Page
Characteristics, dead engine	75
flight	71
stall	73
Chart, center of gravity limits	151
climb control	65
cruise control	67
detonation	70
engine operating limits	70
excessive fuel consumption	70
maximum range	69
oil dilution	143
oxygen duration	189
power-off stalling speeds	74
propeller windmilling speeds	98
takeoff control	58
Check, after landing	86
before landing	78
before takeoff	51
before taxiing	47
brake	37
clothing	22, 34
flaps	54
hydraulic pressure	37
magnetos	53
oxygen	43
parachutes	207
pre-starting	34
trim tabs	55
Checklist, airplane commander's amplified	34
bombardier	28
crew personal equipment	179
flight engineer	26
left or right gunner	32
navigator	29
pilot	24
radio operator	30
tail gunner	33
top gunner	31
Checks and inspection	17

	Page
Climb, control chart	65
procedure	64
Clothing check	22, 34
Cold weather, clothing	191
operation	138
starts	141
Command radio set	132
Communication equipment	131
Compass, flux gate	135
radio	132
Controls, general	13
Control stand, airplane commander's	15
copilot's	15
flight engineer's	14
Copilot, control stand	15
duties	8
instrument panel	16
Cowl flap openings	61
Crash landings	108, 109, 110, 154
Crew, discipline	10
duties	8
inspection	22, 89
personal equipment	177
training	8
Crosswind, landing	85
taxiing	50
Cruising	66
control chart	67
procedure	64
Cylinder head temperatures	61

D

	Page
Dead-engine characteristics	75
Depressurizing cabin	149
Detonation, chart	70
Dilution, oil	142
Ditching	155
equipment	215
Dives	75

E

	Page
Electrical, loads	121
systems	120
system, emergency	121
Elevators	71

	Page
Emergency, bomb bay door operation	107
bomb release	107
brake operation	37
electrical system	121
flap operation	101
kit, vest type	218
landing gear operation	103
landing gear operation, manual	105
landings	108, 109, 110, 154
power	123
radio	217
takeoff	62
Endurance, maximum	68
Engine, cold weather starts	141
failure on takeoff	62
fires	111, 112, 113
liquid lock	22
operating limits	70
run-up	52
starting	45, 161
type	13

F

	Page
Feathering propellers	98
Fire-fighting	219
equipment	111, 219
Fires, cabin	112
engine	112, 113
First aid	195
kits	201
Flak helmets and suits	194
Flaps, emergency operation	101
normal operation	54, 83, 84
Flight, formation	94
night	91
rules	11
Flight characteristics	71
Flight controls, checking	21, 38
Flight engineer, control stand	14
duties	9
Flight messing	220
Flux gate compass	135
Form 1 and 1A	23, 89
Form F	151
Frostbite, treatment of	200

	Page
Fuel, excessive consumption	70
system	115
transfer	116

G

Generators, location of	120
Go-around	90
Gunners, duties	9

H

High altitude bailout	210
High altitude operation	146
Hydraulic system	119

I

Ice prevention and elimination	145
IFF radio set	133
Instrument approach	160
Instrument panel, airplane commander's	16
copilot's	16
flight engineer's	14
Inspection and checks	17
Inspection, crew	22, 89
pre-flight	17
visual outside	17
Interphone	133

L

Landing, after, check	86
approach	84
before, check	78
crosswind	85
emergency	108, 109, 110, 154
night	93
procedure	84
roll	85
Landing gear, emergency operation	103
emergency operation, manual	105
normal operation	59, 81
Liaison radio set	132
Life preserver vest	193
Life raft	215
accessory kit	217
Liquid lock, engines, relieving	22
Loads	151

	Page

M

Magnetos, check	53
Maneuvers, restricted	77
Manifold pressure surge at high altitude	161
Marker beacon receiver	133
Maximum endurance	68
Maximum range	68
Morphine, use of	197

N

Navigational radio equipment	134
Navigator—radar, duties	9
Night, flying	91
landings	93
takeoff	92
taxiing	93

O

Oil, dilution	142
system	117
Oxygen, bailout cylinders	188
check	43
duration	188
duration chart	189
flow indicators	186
masks	182
panels	185
pressure gages	186
regulators	184
system	150, 180
walk-around equipment	187

P

Parachutes	207
check	208
jumps	210
Pattern, traffic	84
PDI, manually flying	130
Pitot tube, heater	145
Power, emergency	123
Power plants	13
Pre-starting check	34
Pressurizing cabin	149

	Page
Propeller, anti-icer	145
feathering	98
pulling through	22
runaway	63
type	13
unfeathering	100
windmilling speeds	98
Putt-putt	120

Q

	Page
Questionnaire, pilot's	162

R

	Page
Radio equipment	131
emergency	217
Radio operator, duties	9
Range, maximum	68
Restrictions, dives	75
maneuvers	77
Rudder	72
Run-up, engines	52
Runway, lining up with	59

S

	Page
Shock, treatment of	199
Signals, formation	95
Specialist gunners, duties	9
Stability	73
Stall characteristics	73
Stalls, power-off speeds	74
Standards, training	7
Starting don'ts	46
Starting engines	45
Step, getting on the	66

	Page
Superfortress, history	5
size comparison	12

T

	Page
Takeoff, before check	51
control chart	58
emergencies	62
instrument	160
night	92
procedure	59
Taxiing, before	47
crosswind	50
night	93
procedure	50
Temperatures, cylinder-head	63
Traffic pattern	84
Training accomplished, chart	6
Training, standards	7
Trim tabs, adjusting	55, 71, 83
Turbo-superchargers	122
control, electronic	123
high-altitude operation	123
runaway	63
type	13
Turns	74

V

	Page
Vacuum pumps, location	13
Vest, life preserver	193

W

	Page
Weather flying	160
Weights and balance	151
Wing, ice	145
Wounds, treatment of	196

©2014 Periscope Film LLC
All Rights Reserved
ISBN #978-1-940453-33-0
www.PeriscopeFilm.com

www.ingramcontent.com/pod-product-compliance
Lightning Source LLC
Chambersburg PA
CBHW042130010526
44111CB00031B/44